The Quintessential Quiz Book 2

The Quintessential Quiz Book 2

A Lighthearted Romp Through the Fields of Knowledge

Minnie & Norman Hickman

St. Martin's Press, New York

To Timothy Dickinson,
a curious figure in more ways than one,
who has been an ongoing sinister presence,
and for Mimi, Mary, and Rosie James

Copyright © 1981 by Norman G. Hickman and Minnie C. Hickman
For information write: St Martin's Press,
175 Fifth Avenue, New York, N.Y. 10010
Manufactured in the United States of America

Design by Mina Greenstein
10 9 8 7 6 5 4 3 2 1
First Edition

Library of Congress Cataloging in Publication Data

Hickman, Norman G.
  Quintessential quiz book II.

    1. Questions and answers. I. Hickman, Minne.
II. Title.
AG195.H524   031'.02   81-16604
ISBN 0-312-66121-5   AACR2

Acknowledgments

■ ■

We are grateful to those who read the typescript and made valuable suggestions—Judith Frank, Arthur Prager, and Professor Edgar Rosenberg—as well as to others of our friends and experts in various fields who helped with certain sections: James A. Ackerman, Cleveland Amory, Roy Bartolomei, Patricia Birch Becker, A. William J. Becker III, Anthony Montague Browne, David Brigstocke, Harry A. Brooks, William F. Buckley, Jr., Shirley Oakes Butler, Bruce Cummings, Andrew Carduner, Alexander Cassatt, Jr., Dudley F. Cates, Julia Child, Craig Claiborne, Ormonde de Kay, Vicomte Paul de Rosière, Hugh Downs, Peter Duchin, Isabel Eberstadt, Rear Admiral E.M.R. Eller, U.S.N. (Ret.), Willard R. Espy, Douglas Fairbanks, Jr., Penelope Forbes-Adam, Dr. Randolph Frank, Seth B. French, Jr., The Viscount Gage, Robert B. Gardner, Riley Miles Gilbert, Mike Gladstone, Mark Goodson, Professor David Gordon, Julie and George Gould, Phyllis Hall, Robert P. Hastings, Dr. Mason Hicks, Center Hitchcock, Chauncey Howell, George S. Johnston, Jr., Professor Alfred Kazin, Patricia Le Balme, John D. Le Vien, De Forest Manice, Aileen Mehle, Gwen Meyer, Bishop Paul Moore, Jr., Ted Morgan, Coleman W. Morton, Clyde M. Newhouse, Brenda T. Norris, Henry B. Platt, Dr. Edgar Alsop Riley, R. Stockton Rush, Richard L. Russell, Jerome E. Shaw, Glenvil Smith, J. Bogert Tailer, Hon. Benson E. L. Timmons III, John Train, Garry Trudeau, and the Rev. Walter D. Wagoner.

We also wish to acknowledge the assistance provided by the Academy of Motion Picture Arts and Sciences, American Museum of Natural History, H.B.M. Embassy, Washington, (Office of the Naval Attaché), Museum of Cartoon Art, New York Public Libraries Telephone Service, National Archives and Records Service, New York Zoological Society, Smithsonian Institution, U.S. Department of the Treasury, U.S. Military Academy, West Point (Office of Public Affairs), Greater London Council, H.M. Department of the Environment, Imperial War Museum, National Maritime Museum, and New Scotland Yard.

Finally, our thanks are due to the following who so capably coped with the typescript: Patricia Bloomer, Susan Davis, Margaret Leilich, Anne Morea, and Catherine Treat.

Permissions

■ ■

Grateful acknowledgment is made to the following for permission to reprint copyrighted material from the sources listed below.

A. D. Peters & Co., Ltd., London, for *Sonnets and Verse* by Hilaire Belloc, published by Gerald Duckworth & Co., Ltd.

Charles Scribner's Sons for *My Early Life* by Winston S. Churchill; *The Crack-Up* and *The Great Gatsby* by F. Scott Fitzgerald; *For Whom the Bell Tolls* by Ernest Hemingway; *Look Homeward, Angel* by Thomas Wolfe.

Contemporary Books for *Collected Poems of Edgar A. Guest*, © 1934.

Dodd, Mead & Co. for *The Collected Poems of Rupert Brooke*.

Doubleday & Co. for *The Naulahka* by Rudyard Kipling; *Private Lives* by Noël Coward; *archy and mehitabel* by Don Marquis © 1927; "Plain Geometry" by Emma Rounds from *Creative Youth* by Hugh Mearns, © 1925.

Elsvier-Dutton Publishing Co. for *Metropolitan Life* by Fran Lebowitz.

Faber and Faber Ltd. for *Collected Poems 1909–1962* and *Old Possum's Book of Practical Cats* by T. S. Eliot.

Hamlyn Publishing Group Ltd. for *My Early Life* by Winston S. Churchill.

Harcourt Brace Jovanovich, Inc. for *Collected Poems* by Carl Sandburg, © 1916 by Holt, Rinehart & Winston, © 1944 by Carl Sandburg; *Collected Poems 1909–1962* by T. S. Eliot; *Old Possum's Book of Practical Cats* by T. S. Eliot, © 1939, renewed 1967 by Esme Valerie Eliot.

Harper & Row for *Collected Poems*, © 1922, 1950 by Edna St. Vincent Millay; *Civilization* by Kenneth Clark; and *The Dictionary of Misinformation* and *More Misinformation* by Tom Burnam.

Harvard University Press and the Trustees of Amherst College for *The Poems of Emily Dickinson*, edited by T. H. Johnson, © 1951, 1955, 1959 by the President and Fellows of Harvard College.

Houghton Mifflin Co. and Cassell Ltd. for Volume 4 of *The Second World War, The Hinge of Fate*, by Winston S. Churchill.

Little, Brown & Co. for *Verses from 1929 On* by Ogden Nash, © 1931, 1935 by Ogden Nash, © 1939 by Curtis Publishing Co.

Contents

■ ■

Firsts, 1

American History, 3
American Literature, 5
Animals, 7
Architecture, 9
"As Time Goes By," 11
Automobiles, 13

Baseball and Football, 15
Bass Ackwards, 17
Bathrooms and Boudoirs, 19
Beauty and the Beast, 21
Below Stairs, 23
Bible, 25
Big and Little, 27
Bird Watching, 29
Bookworms, 31
British Royalty and Peerage, 33
Buildings, 35
Business and Finance, 37

Cap and Gown, 39
Capitals, 41
Cartoons and Comic Strips, 43
Cats, 45
Christmas, 47
Cities and Towns, 49
Clotheshorses, 51
Clubs and Societies, 53
Color Scheme, 55
Communications, 57
Connections, 59
Countries, 61
Crazy Quilt, 63
Criminal Proceedings, 65
Curious Derivations, 67

Dance, 69
Days and Dates, 71

De Mortuis, 73
Dining Out, 75
Dogs, 77
Drink, 79

Earth, 81
Energy, 83
English History, 85
English Literature, 87
Espionage, 89
Exit Lines, 91

Familiar Misquotations, 93
Farrago, 95
Fashion, 97
Fictional Characters, 99
Fire, Fire!, 101
Flights of Fancy, 103
Flowers, 105
Food, 107

Gallilmaufry, 109
Games and Pastimes, 111
Gemstones, 113
Golf and Tennis, 115
Government, 117
Graffiti, 119
Great Britain, 121

High and Low, 123
Hills and Mountains, 125
Hodge and Podge, 127
Horse Sense, 129
Hotels and Inns, 131
House and Home, 133
Hunting, Shooting, and
    Fishing, 135

Inner Space, 137
Inscrutable East, 139

Insects, 141
In Vino Veritas, 143
Island Hopping, 145

Jazz and Pop, 147
Journeys, 149

Kings and Queens, 151

Law and Order, 153
Literary Endings, 155
Long and Short of It, 157

Manners and Mores, 159
"Matters Mathematical," 161
Medicine, 163
Meetings, 165
Middle East, 167
Mixed Bag, 169
Money, 171
Movies, 173
"Murder Will Out," 175
Musical Interlude, 177

Naval and Nautical Lore, 179
North of the Border, 181

Olla Podrida, 183
Openers, 185
Opera, 187
Oscars, 189
"Out Where the West Begins,"
    191

Painting, 193
Pairing Off, 195
Phrase Origins, 197
Pick a Number, 199
Pirates, 201
Plants and Trees, 203
Political Leaders, 205
Potpourri, 207
Power of the Press, 209
Put-Downs, 211

Quartets, 213
Quiz for All Seasons, 215

Relatively Speaking, 217
Religion, 219
Reptiles and Amphibians, 221
Resorts, 223
R.I.P., 225

Salmagundi, 227
Science, 229
Sculpture, 231
Sea Creatures, 233
Seconds, 235
Sex, 237
Shakespeare, 239
Ships and Boats, 241
Sporting Life, 243
States of the Union, 245
Superlatives, 247
Superquiz, 249

Television, 251
Theater, 253
Three of a Kind, 255
Titles, 257
Transportation, 259

U.S. Presidency, 261

Variety Show, 263

"War is Hell," 265
"Water, Water, Every Where,"
    267
Weather, 269
Weights and Measures, 271
Women, 273
World Literature, 275
World War II, 277

X-rated, 279

Lasts, 281

The spring of action which, perhaps more than any other, characterized my life, was curiosity.

—*William Godwin*

■ ■

When you steal from one author, it's plagiarism; if you steal from many, it's research.

—*Wilson Mizner*

■ ■

Writing a book is an adventure. To begin with it is a toy and an amusement. Then it becomes a mistress, then it becomes a master, then it becomes a tyrant. The last phase is that just as you are about to be reconciled to your servitude, you kill the monster, and fling him about to the public.

—*Winston S. Churchill*

■ ■

In research the horizon recedes as we advance, and is no nearer at sixty than it was at twenty. As the power of endurance weakens with age, the urgency of the pursuit grows more intense . . . And research is always incomplete.

—*Mark Pattison*

Firsts

■■

1. Of which famous work is this the first line: "Idle reader you need no oath of mine to convince you that this book, the child of my brain, were the handsomest, the liveliest, and the wisest . . ."?

2. What was God's first command?

3. Who recaptured "the first fine careless rapture"?

4. State the first three words of the U.S. Constitution.

5. According to Greek mythology, who was the first mortal woman on earth?

6. For which distinctions is Elizabeth Ann Seton remembered?

7. On what occasion did who move the following resolution in Congress: "To the memory of the Man, first in war, first in peace, and first in the hearts of his countrymen."?

8. Who was the first President born in the United States?

9. Who heard "the first Noël"?

10. Upon the brilliant career of which benefactor of many students—the man who said: "Remember that you are an Englishman and have therefore won first prize in the lottery of life"—did Mark Twain reflect in *Following The Equator*: "I admire him, I frankly confess it; and when his time comes I shall buy a piece of the rope for a keepsake"?

Firsts

1. *Don Quixote*, by Miguel de Cervantes.
2. "Let there be light"—Genesis I:3.
3. The wise thrush, according to Robert Browning in his poem, "Home-Thoughts, from Abroad":
That's the wise thrush; he sings each song twice over,
Lest you should think he never could recapture
The first fine careless rapture!
4. "WE, THE PEOPLE . . ." (The only phrase in capitals in the whole document, to mark the solemn authority which ordains it.)
5. Pandora, who was endowed by the gods with every charm, together with curiosity and deceit. Disobeying Zeus, she opened a box he had given her and released all the evils that have since afflicted man, Hope alone remaining.
6. Not just for being a saint, but for being the first native-born American canonized by the Roman Catholic Church in 1974.
7. Henry Lee, "Light-Horse Harry" of the American Revolution and the father of Robert E. Lee, on the death of George Washington in 1799.
8. Martin Van Buren, the eighth President, who was born in 1782. His predecessors were all born when the Colonies were under British rule.
9. "Certain poor shepherds in the fields as they lay," in the words of the famous Christmas carol.
10. Cecil Rhodes, British imperialist and business magnate, who in 1888 secured a monopoly of South African diamond production by the creation of the De Beers Consolidated Mines, which reputedly had the largest capitalization of any limited company in the world. His agents conquered a large part of Central Africa; and Northern and Southern Rhodesia (now Zambia and Zimbabwe) bore his name. He is chiefly remembered for his two-year Rhodes Scholarships to Oxford, of which 75 are awarded annually, most going to the United States, followed by Canada and South Africa.

American History

■ ■

1. Albion is an ancient poetical name for Britain, perhaps derived from its white (Latin *albus*) cliffs, visible from the coast of Gaul. Which region of the present United States was once known as New Albion?

2. The word "CROATOAN" evokes what still-unsolved mystery?

3. Which document ensured effective self-government for New England's early settlers and represented the first formal contribution to democracy in the New World?

4. Complete this memorable sentence: "I know not what course others may take . . ."

5. Of George Washington, Thomas Jefferson, and Benjamin Franklin, who was the only one to sign both the Declaration of Independence and the Constitution?

6. Which President gave the longest inaugural address and as a result served the shortest term in office of any President?

7. Who wrote to whom the day after which ceremony, "I wish that I could flatter myself that I had come as near to the central idea of this occasion in two hours as you did in two minutes."?

8. Who was reputed to have said, "We stole it from them fair and square," and in which connection? What famous palindrome arose out of this?

9. How did tea and oil make an unsavory mixture in the 1920s?

10. What was Calvin Coolidge's reply to a young lady at a dinner party who turned to him and said she had made a bet that she could get more than two words out of him?

American History

1. Not New England, but the Northwest Pacific coast, starting at San Francisco. Sir Francis Drake gave it this name in 1579 during his circumnavigation of the world from 1577 to 1580 with the squadron of which the *Golden Hind* alone returned.

2. The disappearance of the Roanoke Island Colony off the North Carolina coast. When a later group arrived from England in 1591, they found the settlers gone and the word "CROATOAN" on the stockade, probably meaning that the colony had tried to escape to an island of that name. Virginia Dare, the first child born of English parentage in the New World, had been born there.

3. The Mayflower Compact, signed in 1620 when the ship was anchored off the shore where Provincetown now stands. The Pilgrims agreed to be governed by laws they themselves would make; among the signers were 41 of the *Mayflower*'s company, including not only the original proprietors, but also workingmen and servants.

4. ". . . but as for me, give me liberty, or give me death!" This was part of a speech made by Patrick Henry at the Virginia Convention held at Richmond in 1775.

5. Benjamin Franklin.

6. William Henry Harrison, the hero of the Battle of Tippecanoe, spoke for two hours coatless and bareheaded in the freezing rain, dying of pneumonia exactly a month later.

7. Edward Everett, the principal speaker at the dedication of the Civil War cemetery at Gettysburg in 1863, to Abraham Lincoln, whose brief but enduring address followed Everett's long speech, now forgotten.

8. Theodore Roosevelt, referring to the U.S.-sponsored insurrection which formed the Republic of Panama out of Colombia and ensured terms favorable to the United States for the Panama Canal. The palindrome is "A MAN A PLAN A CANAL PANAMA."

9. The Teapot Dome Scandal, when two large naval petroleum reserves were leased by Interior Secretary Albert B. Fall to the oil operators Harry F. Sinclair and Edward L. Doheny. The ensuing investigation embarrassed the already-corrupt Harding administration.

10. "You lose." He was not known as "Silent Cal" for nothing.

American Literature

■ ■

1. Who was the first American to earn his living by his pen?

2. Which novelist was named after a lawyer and poet who is most remembered for what he wrote as a particular noisy night in 1814 drew to its close?

3. Name a leading Transcendentalist who wrote these lines:

> By the rude bridge that arched the flood,
>   Their flag to April's breeze unfurl'd,
> Here once the embattled farmers stood,
>   And fired the shot heard round the world.

4. Who said, "The difference between the right word and the almost right word is like the difference between lightning and the lightning bug."?

5. Who was called "The most publicized unread author around"?

6. Who favored double-ended candles?

7. Identify "the Sage of Yoknapatawpha."

8. ". . . so potent a distillation of nectar and wormwood, of ambrosia and deadly nightshade, as might suggest to the rest of us that we write far too much." Who thus appraised whose work?

9. Leon Uris wrote *QB VII*, a novel about a British libel trial. What does QB VII denote?

10. Fill in the blank spaces with the name of the author whose self-description was: "Button-cute, rapier-keen, wafer-thin and pauper-poor is _____, whose tall, stooping figure is better known to the twilit half-world of five continents than to Publishers' Row. That he possesses the power to become invisible to finance companies; that his laboratory is tooled up to manufacture Frankenstein-type monsters on an incredible scale; and that he owns one of the rare mouths in which butter has never melted are legends treasured by every schoolboy. Retired today to peaceful Erwinna, Pennsylvania, _____ raises turkeys which he occasionally displays on Broadway, stirs little from his alembics and retorts. Those who know hint that the light burning late in his laboratory may result in a breathtaking electric bill. Queried, he shrugs with the fatalism of your true Oriental. '*Mektoub*,' he observes curtly. 'It is written.'"

American Literature

1. Washington Irving, whose most noted work, *The Sketch Book*, includes "Rip Van Winkle" and "The Legend of Sleepy Hollow."

2. F. Scott (Francis Scott Key) Fitzgerald, who was named after a kinsman who wrote the words of "The Star-Spangled Banner." The tune was taken from the popular English song "To Anacreon in Heaven." (Anacreon was a Greek lyric poet.)

3. "The Sage of Concord," Ralph Waldo Emerson. The passage is from a hymn sung at a ceremony held at the completion of the Concord Battle Monument in 1837.

4. Samuel Langhorne Clemens, otherwise known as Mark Twain, writing to William Dean Howells, the American novelist, critic, and editor.

5. Gertrude Stein, who ignored traditional plot structure and stressed the sounds and rhythms rather than the sense of words. During the 1920s in Paris she presided over a literary salon that influenced such authors as Hemingway, Anderson, and Fitzgerald. The phrase "lost generation," that she had heard used of the shaken postwar youth of France, was picked up by Ernest Hemingway and applied to the American expatriates of the twenties.

6. Edna St. Vincent Millay. In "First Fig" from *A Few Figs from Thistles* she wrote:
> My candle burns at both ends;
> It will not last the night;
> But, ah, my foes, and, oh, my friends—
> It gives a lovely light.

7. William Faulkner, whose novels transform his homeland around Oxford, Mississippi, into the haunting, Gothic landscape of "Yoknapatawpha County."

8. Alexander Woollcott on Dorothy Parker.

9. Queen's Bench No. 7, the court in which the trial takes place.

10. Who else but the master of phantasmagorical prose, S. J. Perelman, whose works include *Strictly from Hunger, Crazy Like a Fox, Acres and Pains*, and *Westward Ha!* among other classics.

Animals

■ ■

    1. Why is a type of African antelope, the wildebeest, a favorite of crossword-puzzle makers?

    2. Pigs are generally conceded to be among the more intelligent of animals. What was Winston Churchill's opinion of them?

    3. How did Ogden Nash succinctly sum up the cow?

    4. Explain the difference between a tiglon and a liger.

    5. What is the only animal to be hunted almost to extinction to satisfy man's desire for sexual potency?

    6. Who wrote, "All animals are equal but some animals are more equal than others"?

    7. What has been called "a horse put together by a committee"; and how many types of this animal are there?

    8. Name the mythical animal that uniquely supplies all man's needs: it lays bottled grade-A milk and packaged fresh eggs; when broiled, it tastes like sirloin steak, and when fried, like chicken.

    9. In Kenneth Grahame's *The Wind in the Willows*, which members of the genus *Mustela* had the effrontery to invade Toad Hall, Mr. Toad's riverside residence, and by whom were they ousted?

    10. Give the appropriate collective noun for the blanks below:

a) A _____ of lions	f) A _____ of hogs
b) A _____ of bears	g) A _____ of moles
c) A _____ of colts	h) A _____ of leopards
d) A _____ of cats	i) A _____ of foxes
e) A _____ of rhinoceroses	j) A _____ of apes

Animals

1. Because it is also a gnu.
2. "I like pigs," he said. "A dog looks up to you, a cat looks down on you, but a pig treats you like an equal."
3. In a verse in his book *Free Wheeling*, he wrote:

> The cow is of the bovine ilk;
> One end is moo, the other milk.

4. Both are crosses between a tiger and a lion. A tiglon has a tiger for a father; a liger is sired by a lion.
5. The rhinoceros, which has long been hunted for its horn, a compacted mass of hair and gelatine weighing about 4½ pounds. This is believed, over much of Asia, to have aphrodisiac qualities when powdered or mixed into a potion and has commanded very high prices for centuries.
6. The pig oligarchs in George Orwell's *Animal Farm* secretly substituted this for the Animal Ten Commandments.
7. A camel, of which there are two types. A Bactrian has two humps and is native to central and southwestern Asia, while a dromedary, with one hump, is domesticated and widely used as a beast of burden in northern Africa and Arabia. It is also called an Arabian camel.
8. Al Capp's lovable Shmoo, from his comic strip "L'il Abner."
9. A band of stoats and weasels who were routed by the Toad, Badger, Mole, and the Water Rat.
10.

a) pride	f) drift
b) sloth	g) labor
c) rag	h) leap
d) clowder	i) skulk
e) crash	j) shrewdness

Architecture

■ ■

1. Which great literary figure called architecture "frozen music"?

2. Gothic architecture first appeared in Paris around 1140 in the Île-de-France, the royal domain of the Capetian kings, and was the dominant style for about 400 years. What did the Goths have to do with it?

3. What is popularly considered to be the finest example of Moorish architecture in Spain?

4. The influence of which noted Italian architect can be seen in the manor houses of Southern estates, such as Thomas Jefferson's Monticello?

5. What name is given to the following type of verse and who invented it?

> Sir Christopher Wren
> Said, "I am going to dine with some men.
> If anybody calls
> Say I am designing St. Paul's."

6. How did the window get its name?

7. The epitaph for which dramatist and architect is found in this couplet?

> Lie heavy on him, Earth! for he
> Laid many heavy loads on thee!

8. Which noted architect designed buildings that have been called "the purple peopleseater" and "an upside-down toilet bowl"?

9. Three Europeans have been acknowledged as the pioneers of the modern movement in architecture. Can you name them?

10. Which foreign-born architect is responsible for such outstanding buildings as the East Wing of the National Gallery in Washington, D.C., the John F. Kennedy Library in Boston, Massachusetts, and the Atmospheric Research Center, in Boulder, Colorado?

Architecture

1. Johann Wolfgang von Goethe, in a letter to a friend.
2. Nothing at all. The term was first used in the Renaissance by painters and writers to whom such architecture seemed barbarous. (The Goths had been among the worst despoilers of ancient Rome.) Gothic architecture introduced the flying buttress and the pointed arch, which made it possible to build walls less thick than before.
3. Alhambra, on a hill overlooking the city of Granada. (Alhamrā means "the red" in Arabic.) It is the great citadel complex of the Moorish kings in Spain. The superb geometric ornamentation is executed in marble, alabaster, carved plaster, and glazed tile.
4. Andrea Palladio, whose books and buildings also had a profound effect on the work of such formal English architects as Inigo Jones and Sir Christopher Wren.
5. A clerihew, named for its inventor, the mystery writer Edmund Clerihew Bentley: a humorous quatrain about a person usually mentioned in the first line.
6. The word literally means "wind's eye" and derives from Old Norse *vindr*, wind, plus *auga*, eye.
7. Sir John Vanbrugh, a dramatist and architect, designed "the culmination of the English baroque"—Blenheim Palace—for the first Duke of Marlborough: a gift of a grateful nation for Marlborough's victories in the War of the Spanish Succession.
8. Frank Lloyd Wright. The buildings are a purple Performing Arts Hall in Sarasota, Florida, and New York's Solomon R. Guggenheim Museum, which features dynamic interior spaces with spiral ramps. He also built what is believed to be the first earthquake-proof building, the old Imperial Hotel in Tokyo, Japan.
9. Walter Gropius, Le Corbusier (pseudonym of Charles Édouard Jeanneret), and Ludwig Miës van der Rohe.
10. The Chinese-born I. M. Pei, whose work is characterized by crisp geometrical shapes. Called the master-builder of the seventies—and perhaps of the eighties—Pei also designed the new U.S. Embassy in Peking.

"As Time Goes By"

■ ■

1. What were Nürnberg eggs?

2. Who first advocated daylight saving time?

3. Which English author wrote, "The clock struck eleven with the respectful unobtrusiveness of one whose mission in life is to be ignored."?

4. Of whom was it said, "He's murdering time! Off with his head!"?

5. In what manner did Dr. Johnson compare dictionaries and watches?

6. Who said, "In the real dark night of the soul it is always three o'clock in the morning."?

7. Can you define a nanosecond and give its derivation?

8. Where did Andrew Marvell hear "Time's wingèd chariot"?

9. Who designed the first wristwatch and for whom?

10. Dorothy Parker was notoriously famous for her inability to have her work ready on time. What answer was she alleged to have given a messenger from the editor of *Vanity Fair* inquiring about the lateness of her copy?

"As Time Goes By"

1. They were the first widely used watches. Egg-shaped, they were invented in Nürnberg around 1500 by Peter Henlein.

2. Benjamin Franklin, when serving as U.S. Minister to France, recommended earlier opening and closing of shops to save the cost of lighting. During World War II daylight saving time was established by law in the United States (except Tennessee, which now observes it as well) on a year-round basis. A simple way to remember how to change the clock is "Spring forward, fall back."

3. H. H. Munro, who wrote his famous short stories under the pseudonym "Saki."

4. In Lewis Carroll's *Alice's Adventures in Wonderland*, the Queen of Hearts shouted this about the Mad Hatter who had been singing the following:

> Twinkle, twinkle, little bat!
> How I wonder what you're at!

5. According to Mrs. Piozzi in her *Anecdotes of Johnson*, he said, ". . . the worst is better than none, and the best cannot be expected to go quite true."

6. F. Scott Fitzgerald in *The Crack-up*, which was also the title of a collection of his essays edited by Edmund Wilson after Fitzgerald's death.

7. A nanosecond is one billionth (10^{-9}) of a second. It derives from the Greek *nanos*, dwarf, literally "little old man."

8. ". . . by the tide/Of Humber," the navigable estuary, near which Marvell was born, of the Rivers Trent and Ouse on the east coast of England. In the poem "To His Coy Mistress" he wrote:

> But at my back I always hear
> Time's wingèd chariot hurrying near;
> And yonder all before us lie
> Deserts of vast eternity.

9. Louis Cartier in 1904 for Alberto Santos-Dumont, the Brazilian aeronaut, who in France was a pioneer in the development of lighter-than-air craft and in 1901 won 100,000 francs for a round-trip flight between Saint-Cloud and the Eiffel Tower.

10. "Tell him I've been too fucking busy—or vice versa."

Automobiles

■ ■

1. In 1895 there were only two cars in the whole state of Ohio. What did they do?

2. How can you readily recognize a pre-1933 Rolls-Royce?

3. Name the car made by a) Horace and John, b) Gaston and Louis, c) August and Frederick.

4. FIAT is an acronym for what?

5. When did the rearview mirror originate?

6. Give the derivation of the word "jeep."

7. With which activity are these terms associated and what do they mean: a) skins, b) snowballs, c) raking, d) chopping, e) sparking?

8. In most of the world all cars crossing frontiers are required to display plaques showing the international registration letters. For example, France is F, Belgium is B, and the United Kingdom is GB. Where are cars bearing these plaques registered: IS, FL, GBZ, MC, and IL?

9. What are meant by ORVs?

10. The 1981 Bentley Mulsanne replaced the Bentley T2 series. Who or what is Mulsanne?

Automobiles

1. They collided with one another, according to John Train in *True Remarkable Occurrences*.

2. The color of the superimposed initials RR on the radiator badge was changed in the 1933 models from red to black as a sign of mourning for Sir Henry Royce, the surviving member of the original partnership, who died in April of that year. His partner, the Hon. Charles Rolls, a pioneer aviator as well as motorist, had in 1910 been the first Englishman killed in a flying accident.

3. Dodge, Chevrolet, Dusenberg.

4. *Fabrica Italiana di Automobili Torino*. It is also a pun: in Latin *fiat* means "let it be done."

5. In the early days of dirt-track or speedway racing, which started in Australia and was introduced to Britain in 1928.

6. It is popularly believed to come from the army nomenclature of World War II—General Purpose, or G.P., Vehicle. H. L. Mencken argues convincingly, however, that the name was borrowed from Eugene the Jeep, a character who appeared in 1936 in E. C. Segar's comic strip, "Popeye the Sailor," which also gave the language the word "goon."

7. Driving hot rods, which are cars rebuilt or remodeled for increased speed and acceleration. The terms mean: a) tires, b) whitewalls, c) lowering the front end, d) lowering the roof, e) cruising around aimlessly.

8. Iceland (*Island* to its people), Liechtenstein, Gibraltar, Monaco, and Israel.

9. Off-road vehicles, such as truck vans, campers, four-wheel-drive jeeps, dune buggies, and motorcycles.

10. It is the name of the extremely fast backstretch of the Le Mans automobile track; somewhat similarly, the Pontiac Bonneville is named after the Utah salt flats famous as the site of car speed records.

Baseball and Football

■ ■

1. How did the complexion of major-league baseball change markedly in 1947?

2. Which was the first college football team to win 700 games?

3. Name the only four baseball players to reach both the 3,000-hit and 400-homer plateaus.

4. What were the locations of these one-time odd-bowl football games: a) Flower Bowl, b) Turkey Bowl, c) Vulcan Bowl, d) Oil Bowl, e) Arab Bowl?

5. Who is the only player in baseball history—both before 1900 and since—to hit more than 300 career home runs while his home run-to-strikeout ratio was almost exactly 1–1?

6. What was remarkable about the record 63-yard field goal kicked by Tom Dempsey of the New Orleans Saints in the last play of their 19–17 victory over the Detroit Lions in 1970?

7. Baseball's 1971 World Series was won by the Pittsburgh Pirates as Willie Stargell scored the winning run in the seventh game, played in Baltimore on October 17. How did history literally repeat itself in 1979?

8. He was an All-American football player at the University of Colorado, where he was a member of Phi Beta Kappa. He went to Oxford as a Rhodes Scholar and later played professional football with the Detroit Lions while attending Yale Law School, where he graduated first in his class. Who was he and what happened to him?

9. Which short story by James Thurber ultimately led to a change in the rules of baseball?

10. Can you name the only team twice to win the NFL championship three years in a row?

Baseball and Football

1. In that year Jackie Robinson joined the Brooklyn Dodgers, becoming the first black to play in the major leagues. In the course of a ten-year career with the Dodgers he set many batting, fielding, and base-stealing records.

2. Yale, in 1979 with a 23–20 victory over Cornell.

3. Stan Musial, Willie Mays, Hank Aaron, and Carl Yastrzemski.

4. a) Jacksonville, Florida, b) Tokyo, Japan, c) Birmingham, Alabama, d) Houston, Texas, e) Oran, Algeria, during World War II.

5. Joe diMaggio, with 361 career home runs and 369 strikeouts. His record 56-game hitting streak in 1941 has not been seriously threatened in four decades. His active playing years were from 1936 to 1942 and 1946 to 1951.

6. He kicked it with his deformed right foot.

7. The 1979 World Series was won by the Pittsburgh Pirates as Willie Stargell scored the winning run in the seventh game, played in Baltimore on October 17.

8. Byron "Whizzer" White, who, in 1962, became an Associate Justice of the U.S. Supreme Court.

9. "You Could Look It Up," in which a midget is put in to bat, thus demoralizing the pitcher by presenting a minute strike zone. This led to Bill Veeck putting a midget up at bat for the St. Louis Browns and to the baseball commissioner forbidding any such action in the future.

10. The Green Bay Packers in 1929–31 and in 1965–67.

Bass Ackwards

■ ■

Can you supply the questions to which the following are the answers?

1. Chicken Teriyaki.

2. Washington, Irving.

3. "Ain't Misbehavin'."

4. I don't know, I've never kippled.

5. 9 W.

6. Immanuel Kant.

7. Yes, but I'd miss you.

8. Dr. Livingston I Presume.

9. Shoofly pie and apply pandowdy
   Make my eyes light up and my stomach say howdy.
   I just can't get enough,
   Of that wonderful, wonderful stuff.

10. There's nothing new under the sun and no reason why there should be. There's nothing new except each new man's slow, unwilling application to himself of the ancient and inexorable laws.

Bass Ackwards

1. Who is the longest-surviving kamikaze pilot?

2. Who was the first President of the United States, Morris?

3. How you doin', Fats?

4. Do you like Kiplng?

5. Do you spell your name with a V, Herr Wagner?

6. Can Manny do it?

7. Would you still love me if I lost all my money?

8. May we have your first name and middle initial, Dr. Presume?

9. *Et pour Monsieur?*

10. Hi, what's new?

Bathroom and Boudoir

■ ■

1. What curious ingredient causes the shine in expensive eye shadow?

2. Who said in which film, "Go, and never darken my towels again!"

3. What was the specialty of Lem Putt, the character created by Charles "Chic" Sale in his little classic, *The Specialist*?

4. In the slang of which country would you "point Percy at the porcelain"?

5. Who penned the following lament common to all mankind?

> Oh often have I washed and dressed
>   And what's to show for all my pain?
> Let me lie abed and rest;
>   Ten thousand times I've done my best
>   And all's to do again.

6. In Paris what traditional structures are slowly disappearing?

7. Which king offered this practical advice on getting through a public life: "Never stand when you can sit, and never sit when you can lie down, and take every opportunity to relieve yourself."?

8. Where would one have found this quaint sign: "Gentlemen will please adjust clothing before leaving."?

9. Which absurd and pretentious item of furniture is known as a *chaise percée*?

10. According to the teachings of Iran's Ayatollah Ruhollah Khomeini, what must Moslems be careful to do in the bathroom?

Bathroom and Boudoir

1. Fish scales.

2. Groucho Marx in the part of Rufus T. Firefly, the dictator of Freedonia, dismissing Louis Calhern in the film *Duck Soup*.

3. The building of privies, or outhouses. Lem Putt claimed to have made his reputation with "the average eight-family three-holer." Lem was particular about interior necessities, such as a hook or nail for the catalog, but the catalog had to be from a "reckonized house." *The Specialist* has been translated into ten languages and sold over a million copies.

4. Australia.

5. A. E. Housman in *Last Poems*.

6. The public *pissoirs* or *vespasiennes*—the green, partly-enclosed urinals for men—named after the Roman Emperor Vespasian who leased the public urinals to fullers to bleach fabrics. When his son, the future Emperor Titus, complained that this was undignified, Vespasian pulled out a coin: "Doesn't smell, does it? Came from the urinals." This became so proverbial as to be the most remembered act of the unfortunate Emperor. The new, fully-enclosed models of what were once called *chalets de necessité* will be for both men and women.

7. George V of England.

8. In the lavatories of British trains.

9. A type of chair, usually with a hinged wicker seat, designed to hide the toilet. *Chaise percée* means a chair with an opening.

10. In his own words: "When urinating or defecating, one must squat in such a way as not to be turning one's back on Mecca."

Beauty and the Beast

■ ■

1. Who wrote the famous fairy story, "The Sleeping Beauty"?

2. By what other names are the Yeti and Sasquatch known? Where might you expect to find them?

3. Whose beauty is "to me/ Like those Nicean barks of yore"?

4. Which legendary hero successfully fought the water-monster Grendel?

5. Give the line preceding, "Picks my ties out, eats my candy, drinks my brandy."

6. The giant in which fairy story roared as follows?

> Fe fi fo fum!
> I smell the blood of an Englishman;
> Be he alive or be he dead,
> I'll grind his bones to make my bread.

7. Whose face and body were so beautiful that she hid them with her hair to persuade her husband to do what?

8. What do the following have in common: the Lion, Griffin, Falcon, Black Bull, White Lion, Yale, Greyhound, Red Dragon, Unicorn, and White Horse?

9. Who or what said: "Beauty is truth, Truth beauty."

10. Which famous monster read Plutarch's *Lives* and Milton's *Paradise Lost*, was concerned about the American Indian, and spoke perfect French?

Beauty and the Beast

1. The French poet and critic Charles Perrault, in 1697. The tale was originally titled *La Belle au bois dormant*.

2. The Abominable Snowman and Big Foot. They have been reported seen in the Himalayas and the Pacific Northwest, respectively, but there has been no conclusive proof of their existence.

3. Helen of Troy. It is from Edgar Allan Poe's poem "To Helen," which contains the lines:

> To the glory that was Greece
> And the grandeur that was Rome.

4. Beowulf, the hero of England's oldest epic, which was derived principally from Scandinavian folk tales and mythology.

5. "The Most Beautiful Girl in the World," from the song of the same title by Richard Rodgers and Lorenz Hart.

6. "Jack and the Beanstalk."

7. Lady Godiva, who rode naked through the streets of Coventry at high noon with the understanding that if she did, her husband, the Earl of Mercia, would remit the heavy taxation on the people of the town. Peeping Tom had a good look, but it was his last; his eyes were put out.

8. They are the King's (now the Queen's) Beasts, the heraldic animals which support the British Royal Arms at Hampton Court, the palace of Henry VIII.

9. These words are imagined as being spoken by the urn in John Keats' "Ode on a Grecian Urn."

10. The monster in Mary Wollstonecraft Shelley's novel *Frankenstein,* subtitled *The Modern Prometheus* and published in 1818. It was only very much later that Hollywood created its own version of the monster as an entity with no more brainpower than a producer.

Below Stairs

■ ■

1. The paternal grandparents of which noted novelist were a butler and a maid?

2. What did the 9th Duke of Marlborough say when he was told that one of his servants was sick?

3. "No man is a hero to his valet" is a phrase attributed to which famous woman of letters?

4. Whose attempt to seduce an innocent serving man made a successful comic novel which was later made into a film?

5. Who ran the household of Loam House in London?

6. According to an unwritten law, what two things should never adorn a proper butler?

7. The wife of Noah Webster caught him kissing the maid and said, "I am surprised." How did the great lexicographer correct her?

8. In the words of W. Somerset Maugham, American women expect to find what in their husbands?

9. Name the manservant employed by a courtesy lord with three given names and a flair for detection.

10. Whose humorous writings contain this line: "The butler entered the room, a solemn procession of one."?

Below Stairs

1. Charles Dickens.
2. "Tell him that the lower orders are never ill."
3. Mme. de Sévigné, although the phrase rightly belongs to Mme. Cornuel. It is the cleaned-up version of an observation of Antigonus, one of the successors of Alexander, who when his court intellectual hailed him as "Son of the Sun," replied, "Check with the man who empties my chamber pot."
4. Lady Booby in Henry Fielding's first novel *Joseph Andrews*, which was a parody of Richardson's *Pamela*; the name Joseph recalls the chastity of the Biblical Joseph when approached by Potiphar's wife.
5. The Admirable Crichton, the butler in Sir James M. Barrie's play of the same name. Barrie borrowed his title from the epithet applied to James Crichton, a remarkable Scottish adventurer and scholar who could speak ten languages and displayed amazing erudition. The original Crichton was slain in a street brawl in Mantua at the age of 22.
6. Neither spectacles nor a mustache.
7. "My dear, *I* am surprised; *you* are astonished." ("Surprised" still had the primary meaning, in Webster's day, of "taken by surprise.")
8. "The perfection that Englishwomen only hope to find in their butlers."
9. Bunter, who used to be the batman, or soldier-servant, to Lord Peter Death Bredon Wimsey in the novels by Dorothy L. Sayers.
10. P. G. Wodehouse (Sir Pelham Grenville Wodehouse).

Bible

■ ■

1. Is the Lord's Prayer found in the Bible?

2. Who "went out of the presence of the Lord, and dwelt in the land of Nod"? Where is the land of Nod?

3. Give the Biblical derivation of the word "maudlin," meaning effusively sentimental.

4. Which one of the following countries is *not* referred to in the Bible: Armenia, Ethiopia, India, Italy, Libya, Malta, Spain, Tunisia?

5. What is the origin of the translated phrase *Noli me tangere*?

6. Who observes that "The Book of Life begins with a man and a woman in a garden"; and who responds that "It ends with Revelations."?

7. The Gileadites used the word "shibboleth" (meaning "an ear of corn" in Hebrew) as a password. Why was this word fatal to the Ephraimites?

8. Who were the only two angels mentioned in the Bible, and what third name is incorrectly added to them?

9. Which three Marys were present at Jesus' crucifixion?

10. Why did I Corinthians 14:34—"Let your women keep silent in the churches: for it is not permitted unto them to speak . . ."—cause thousands of people to be castrated?

Bible

1. Yes, twice: in Matthew 6:9–11 and, in a shorter form, in Luke 11:2–4.

2. Cain, after slaying his brother Abel. The land of Nod may be found "on the east of Eden"—Genesis 4:16. (Jonathan Swift, in *A Complete Collection of Polite and Ingenious Conversation*, makes one of his characters say that he was "going to the land of Nod"—that is, to sleep—a meaning the phrase has retained ever since.)

3. It comes from Mary Magdalene, commonly identified as the prostitute who anointed Jesus' feet (Luke 7:36–50 and 8:2). The name Magdalene has come to typify tearful repentance and has given the adjective "maudlin" to English.

4. Tunisia.

5. In John 20:17 the risen Christ says, "Touch me not, for I am not yet ascended to my Father." The phrase *Noli me tangere* is a warning against meddling or touching.

6. Lord Illingworth and Mrs. Allonby, in Oscar Wilde's *A Woman of No Importance*.

7. Because they could not pronounce the "sh" sound, they could not give the password correctly and hence were slain by the Gileadites (Judges 12:6). Shibboleth has come to mean a usage or custom that distinguishes one group or class from another.

8. Gabriel and Michael. But in Isaiah 14:12 the prophet denounces the doomed King of Babylon as the morning star fallen from the sky ("How art thou fallen from Heaven, Lucifer, son of the morning!"). Lucifer is only the Latin name for the morning star; but somehow the Latin fathers of the early Christian church came to believe that this was Satan's name before he was cast out of Heaven.

9. The Virgin Mary, Mary Magdalene, and Mary the mother of James.

10. St. Paul was clearly forbidding women preachers only; but in the 17th century, as the great age of sung church music began, his words were construed to forbid any raising of women's voices whatsoever. Since, however, the composers provided for soprano and alto parts, it was necessary to obtain high-voiced people from somewhere: with the result that for almost 300 years the cathedrals and opera houses had female parts sung by castrated men.

Big and Little

■■

1. What is the approximate density of population in America's largest city?

2. Where is Zug, and what is its chief distinction?

3. Which literary character was called Quinbus Flestrin, "the Great Man-Mountain," by his captors?

4. What has been sometimes cited as the smallest state in the world, with accredited representatives to foreign governments?

5. Which group of people is thought to be the tallest in the world?

6. Where would you find the largest enclosed park in Europe?

7. To which city was Carl Sandburg referring in the following?

Hog butcher for the world,
Tool maker, stacker of wheat,
Player with railroads and the nation's freight handler;
Stormy, husky, brawling,
City of the big shoulders.

8. Which is the world's largest airport?

9. Who, in 1938, had occasion to hire 124 midgets?

10. Name the largest Roman Catholic country in the world.

Big and Little

1. Less than 5 per square mile, which is reasonable when you consider that Juneau, the capital of Alaska, encompasses 3,108 square miles, or 2½ times the area of Rhode Island.

2. In Switzerland. It is the smallest of the country's twenty undivided cantons.

3. Lemuel Gulliver, by the Lilliputians, in Swift's *Gulliver's Travels*.

4. The Order of the Knights of Malta, whose Grand Master has occupied the three-acre Villa del Priorato in Rome since 1834.

5. The Tutsi, who are also known as Watutsi, Watusi, or Batutsi. They are herdsmen of Burundi and Rwanda in central Africa.

6. Phoenix Park, Dublin, where the residences of the Irish President, the Papal Nuncio, and the U.S. Ambassador are located, as well as the Zoological Gardens.

7. Chicago, in his poem of the same name.

8. The Hartsfield International Airport at Atlanta, the business center of the Southeast. The new jetport passenger complex sprawls over an area equivalent to 11½ football fields and is far larger than its nearest rival at Dallas/Fort Worth. It will eventually be able to handle 75 million passengers per year.

9. Mervin LeRoy, the producer of the film *The Wizard of Oz*. The midgets were needed to play the Munchkins, to whose land Dorothy Gale was blown by a cyclone from her Uncle Henry's farm in Kansas.

10. Brazil, with a population of 120 million. It is also the only nation whose people's complexion is growing on the average lighter because of an enormous influx of immigrants from northern Europe.

Bird Watching

■ ■

1. Do peacocks lay eggs?

2. What "puts all heaven in a rage"?

3. The secretary bird is a large African bird of prey. How did it come by its name?

4. Which was the first bird to leave Noah's Ark? The second bird?

5. Identify the author of the following:

That time of year thou mayst in me behold
When yellow leaves, or none, or few, do hang
Upon these boughs which shake against the cold,
Bare ruin'd choirs, where late the sweet birds sang.

6. What was Benjamin Franklin's opinion of the North American bald eagle as a symbol of the national emblem of the United States, and which bird would he have preferred?

7. Give another name for "Mother Carey's chickens" and the probable derivation of this term.

8. What were Joel Cairo and Kasper Gutman looking for?

9. Which large flightless bird from the island of Mauritius has been extinct since the late 17th century?

10. Which is the largest flying bird extant?

Bird Watching

1. No, but peahens do.

2. "A robin redbreast in a cage"—"Auguries of Innocence," by William Blake.

3. Its crest of black feathers suggested the quill pens behind the ear of an 18th-century male secretary.

4. A raven "which went forth to and fro, until the waters were dried up from off the earth" (Genesis 8:7). Later, a dove brought back an olive leaf. This told Noah that "the waters were abated from off the earth," and that the anger of the Lord was appeased. Hence, the dove and olive branch are symbols of peace.

5. William Shakespeare, "Sonnet LXXIII."

6. Not much. He wrote: "I wish the bald eagle had not been chosen as the representative of our country; he is a bird of bad moral character; like those among men who live by sharping and robbing, he is generally poor, and often very lousy. The turkey is a much more respectable bird, and withal a true original bird of America." (The bald eagle is not bald; its head is covered with slicked-down white feathers.)

7. Any of the petrels, especially the stormy petrel, probably because the Virgin Mary, patroness of seamen, is invoked as *Mater Cara*, dear mother. Petrel is a contraction of *petrillo*, little Peter, because by flying so close to the waves with legs extended it seems to be walking on water, as the Apostle Peter is said to have done at the instigation of Christ.

8. The Maltese Falcon, in the novel of the same name by Dashiell Hammett, and later a movie starring Humphrey Bogart. In the film the part of Joel Cairo was played by Peter Lorre, and Kasper Gutman (the Fat Man) by Sidney Greenstreet.

9. The clumsy dodo, whose name means "simpleton" in Portuguese.

10. The condor, a vulture of the Andes and the high mountains of California, with a 9–10 foot wingspan. The gold coins of several South American countries bear its likeness.

Bookworms

■ ■

1. Can you define "incunabula," and say where the largest collection of them is to be found?

2. What was the first book to be printed in what is now the United States?

3. Which eminent author wrote: "I would sooner read a timetable or a catalogue than nothing at all. They are much more entertaining than half the novels that are written."?

4. In novel writing, what is meant by O.S.S., and who coined it?

5. Who said, "If you want to get rich, write the sort of thing that's read by persons who move their lips when they're reading to themselves."?

6. In book printing, what distinguishes a folio from a quarto?

7. Whose unwritten *Guide to Good Writing* confides: "Before I start to write, I always treat myself to a nice dry Martini. Just one, to give me the courage to get started. After that I am on my own."?

8. Which statesman and popular novelist wrote: "Books are fatal: they are the curse of the human race. Nine-tenths of existing books are nonsense, and the clever books are the refutation of that nonsense. The greatest misfortune that ever befell man was the invention of printing."?

9. Winston S. Churchill once tangled with a persnickety editor who amended all his copy that ended with a preposition. How did Churchill cut the editor down to size?

10. What chilling thought is awakened when we look at a book published today?

Bookworms

1. Incunabula, or "cradle books"—*cunae* means cradle in Latin—are books printed from movable type before 1501. The world's largest collection of incunabula is in the Huntington Library in San Marino, California.

2. The Bay Psalm Book, which was printed in Boston, Massachusetts, in 1640.

3. W. Somerset Maugham in his autobiographical work *The Summing Up*. About his own place in English literature Maugham was quite candid: "I know just where I stand. In the very first row of the second-raters."

4. Obligatory Sex Scene, a phrase circulated by the polysyllabic William F. Buckley, Jr., which he borrowed from Vladimir Nabokov.

5. Don Marquis, the American author who invented the characters of "archy the cockroach" and "mehitabel the cat" and set forth their story in *archy and mehitabel*.

6. A folio is a large sheet of paper, folded over to make two leaves or four pages of a book or manuscript; also a large book of such pages, about 15 inches tall. A quarto (4to or 4°) is a whole sheet folded into four leaves, or a book with such pages.

7. That witty and sardonic observer of contemporary American society, E. B. White, for many years a member of *The New Yorker* staff, and adapter of William Strunk, Jr.'s admirable little book *The Elements of Style*.

8. Benjamin Disraeli, British prime minister, political biographer, and prolific novelist.

9. "This is the sort of English up with which I will not put."

10. Unless it is printed on acid-proof stock, the book will disintegrate within about 50 years because of the sulphite content of the paper.

British Royalty and Peerage

■ ■

1. Which English king, who was born and died in France, could speak only a form of French?

2. Of the 26 surviving nonroyal dukedoms, name the only two created for military achievement.

3. In whose play does this line appear: "You should study the peerage, Gerald . . . it is the best thing in fiction the English have ever done"?

4. If he wished to travel incognito, who could call himself the Earl of Merioneth or Baron Greenwich?

5. To what event was the poet Andrew Marvell referring in these lines?

> He nothing common did or mean
> Upon that memorable scene.

6. With the coming of the Industrial Revolution, so many brewers were elevated to the peerage that they became known as what?

7. The phrase, "A king's ransom," is associated with whom?

8. Who was the first native-born American to be ennobled in England since the founding of the republic?

9. Which princess was engaged to two royal dukes?

10. Which pink-cheeked, sleek-haired future statesman was reputed to dine at Blenheim Palace, the seat of the Marlboroughs, once a week?

British Royalty and Peerage

1. William I, "The Conqueror," King of England from 1066 to 1087, spoke Norman French.

2. Marlborough in 1703 and Wellington in 1814.

3. Oscar Wilde's *A Woman of No Importance*.

4. H. R. H. The Prince Philip, Duke of Edinburgh.

5. The beheading of Charles I in 1649 in London, outside Whitehall Palace's Banqueting Hall, which alone survives of that edifice. The King's dignified bearing was remarked upon by all.

6. The Beerage. As A. E. Housman wrote in poem LXII from *A Shropshire Lad*:

> Oh many a peer of England brews
> Livelier liquor than the Muse,
> And malt does more than Milton can
> To justify God's ways to man.

7. Richard I Lion-Heart (Richard Cœur de Lion), returning from the Third Crusade, was taken by Leopold V of Austria and handed over to the Emperor Henry VI. His ministers promised the huge ransom of 150,000 gold marks (£100,000) and used this as an excuse for unprecedented taxation, but it was never fully paid.

8. The press lord William Waldorf Astor, who was made a baron in 1916 and a viscount in 1917.

9. Princess "May" of Teck, who was engaged to the Duke of Clarence, son of the future Edward VII and, after Clarence's death, to his brother the Duke of York. He later became George V and she Queen Mary.

10. George Curzon, later 1st Marquess Curzon of Kedleston, who served as Viceroy of India and Foreign Secretary, attracted many sardonic comments: the first couplet below was written when he first went up to Oxford, the second years later, after he was a conspicuously well-established careerist.

> My name is George Nathaniel Curzon,
> I am a most superior person.
> My face is pink, my hair is sleek,
> I dine at Blenheim once a week.

Buildings
■ ■

1. Name the largest building complex in the world owned entirely by women.

2. Which famous monument is known derisively as "the wedding cake"?

3. The centerpiece attraction at Disneyland in California is the Sleeping Beauty Castle, and at Walt Disney World in Florida it is Cinderella's Castle. The inspiration for these comes from which well-known structure?

4. Following their term of office, which U.S. Presidents retired to a) Montpelier, near Charlottesville, Virginia, b) The Hermitage, near Nashville, Tennessee, c) the Waldorf-Astoria Towers in New York City?

5. Who is the author of the following lines?

I will arise and go now, and go to Innisfree,
And a small cabin build there, of clay and wattles made.

6. After whom was the Parthenon, the most glorious of all the Greek temples, named? Where is there an almost perfect reproduction of it?

7. Describe a gazebo and give a probable derivation of the word.

8. Lying in central Spain near Madrid, this ancient palace of Spanish sovereigns contains a church, a monastery, a mausoleum, a college, and a library. Do you know its name?

9. The ruins of which famous slave-built fortress dominate a mountaintop in Haiti?

10. What has been called "the greatest compliment ever paid to a woman"?

Buildings

1. The headquarters of the Daughters of the American Revolution at 1776 D Street, in Washington, D.C., which includes Constitution Hall. Eleanor Roosevelt resigned her membership after the D.A.R. refused to let Marian Anderson, the great black contralto, sing there.

2. The massive and fussily ornate edifice which dominates the Piazza de Venezia in Rome. It is a monument to Victor Emmanuel II, the first king of a united Italy.

3. The fairylike castle of Neuschwanstein built by the demented "Dream King" Ludwig of Bavaria. (His successor, Otto, was also mad.)

4. a) James Madison, b) Andrew Jackson, c) Herbert C. Hoover.

5. William Butler Yeats, who was much influenced by Henry David Thoreau, in the poem "The Lake Isle of Innisfree."

6. Athena Parthenos—Athena the Virgin—the wisest of the Greek deities. A replica of the Parthenon stands in a city that calls itself "The Athens of the South"—Nashville, Tennessee.

7. A gazebo, also called a belvedere, is a small, open structure, usually sited so as to command a good view of its surroundings in a park or landscape. The name is probably a pseudo-Latin formation of the English word gaze plus a Latin future suffix -ebo as in *videbo*, meaning "I shall see." Alternatively, it has been suggested that gazebo is a play on the French *Que c'est beau!* (How beautiful it is!)

8. The Escorial. Its art collection includes works by El Greco, Tintoretto, and Velásquez.

9. The citadel of La Ferrière, a formidable mountaintop fortress in Haiti, built by the tyrannical Henri Christophe. A freed black slave, he called himself Henri I and created an autocracy patterned after the royal courts of Europe. Eugene O'Neill based the main character in his play *The Emperor Jones* on Christophe.

10. The Taj Mahal, built in India in the 17th century by the bereaved Mogul Emperor Shah Jehan as a tomb for his beloved wife, Mumtaz Mahal ("Chosen of the Palace"). Shah Jehan is also buried in this most beautiful and extravagant mausoleum in the world.

Business and Finance

■ ■

1. What did Ben Stolberg, the labor historian, say about Judge Elbert T. Gary, who ran U.S. Steel from his New York office?

2. In Arthur Miller's play, *Death of a Salesman,* the protagonist got by "on a smile and a shoeshine." Who was he and what was he selling?

3. Give the meaning of the acronym GIGO as it is used by people who work with computers.

4. In *Gone With the Wind* Rhett Butler persuades Scarlett to call her store "Caveat Emptorium." She did not realize this derived from what?

5. Which well-known commentator is responsible for this sound tip on how to get rich in the stock market: "Take all your savings and buy some good stock and hold it till it goes up. If it don't go up, don't buy it"?

6. Whatever became of the Computer, Tabulating, and Recording Company?

7. Scripophily is a new hobby for collectors. What does it mean?

8. Who or what would benefit from buying "flower bonds"?

9. Handling other people's money has for centuries been the province of bankers and lawyers, but the first so-called investment-counseling firm started in Boston, probably because Yankee entrepreneurs with large fortunes did not want their children squandering the money. What was the name of this firm?

10. Who said, "The business of America is business"?

Business and Finance

1. "Judge Gary never saw a blast furnace until after he was dead."

2. Willy Loman, who says, "A salesman is got to dream, boy. It comes with the territory." His "line" was ladies' hosiery.

3. "(Put) Garbage In, (Get) Garbage Out."

4. In Latin *caveat emptor* means "let the buyer beware."

5. Will Rogers in October 1929, the month of the great crash on Wall Street.

6. It became IBM (International Business Machines), the largest company in the United States in terms of market value, exceeding such giants as A.T.& T., Exxon, and General Motors.

7. Collecting share certificates of companies—generally banks, mines, and railroads—that no longer exist and bonds that were never redeemed. Particularly prized are Chinese Imperial Bonds, which are outstanding both in size and decorative artistry.

8. The estate of one who is about to die. "Flower" or "tombstone" bonds are U.S. Treasuries which sell for sums substantially below face value because of their low interest rates. They are, however, redeemable at the holder's death at face value for payment of Federal taxes. (The Treasury stopped issuing these bonds in 1971, but there are still at least $1 billion worth outstanding.)

9. Scudder, Stevens, and Clark, founded in 1919, which is still a leader in its field today. Theodore T. Scudder originated the term "investment counseling."

10. President Calvin Coolidge in a 1925 speech.

Cap and Gown

■ ■

1. What is the literal meaning of *alma mater*?

2. Which American university stretches over four time zones?

3. Name the scathing satirist who coined the acronym SWINE for "Students Wildly Indignant about Nearly Everything."

4. What is the C.I.A. doing in Hyde Park, New York?

5. Who denigrated a university figure in the following terms?

> Remote and ineffectual Don
> That dared attack my Chesterton,
> With that poor weapon half impelled,
> Unlearnt, unsteady, hardly held,
> Unworthy for a tilt with men—

6. Which play by whom contains this famous line, "He who can, does; he who cannot, teaches"?

7. Identify the noted educator who said that "we have not the three R's in America; we have the six: remedial readin', remedial 'ritin', and remedial 'rithmetic."

8. Which college song contains a sentiment that has been cynically termed "one of the great anticlimactic sentences of all time"?

9. What villainous old Etonian is eaten by a crocodile?

10. The extension program of which great university once offered a course entitled "Introduction to Sandcastle Building"?

Cap and Gown

1. In Latin it means "fostering mother," a Roman title for the earth mother and grain goddess, later transferred by the English to schools and universities.

2. The University of Alaska, which extends from a college in Kitchikan in southeastern Alaska to a "learning facility" in remote Adak in the Aleutians.

3. The cartoonist Al Capp, creator of "L'il Abner." Capp's later work and speeches reflected his extremely subjective political views.

4. The Culinary Institute of America at Hyde Park offers a twenty-month course to persons wishing to become professional cooks.

5. Hilaire Belloc, in "Lines to a Don," defending his friend and fellow author, Gilbert Keith Chesterton. Belloc was a versatile English writer of essays, novels, verse, travel books, history, biography, and criticism.

6. *Man and Superman*, by George Bernard Shaw. And, as Anthony Montague Browne observed, "Those who cannot teach, teach teachers. If this fails, they become consultants."

7. Robert M. Hutchins, once chancellor of the University of Chicago, where, because the school was founded primarily by gifts of Rockefeller money, the students used to intone, "Praise God from whom oil blessings flow."

8. Yale's anthem "Bright College Years" which concludes:

> Then let us pray that ever we
> May let these words our watchwords be,
> Where'er upon life's sea we sail:
> For God, for country and for Yale.

9. Captain James Hook in Sir James M. Barrie's play *Peter Pan*. He goes to his death with the words *"Floreat Etona"* on his lips.

10. The University of California. According to the catalog, "the course will explore the medium and dynamics of beach sand as a building material and emphasize design, technique, and aesthetics in the building process."

Capitals

■■

1. Give the simple derivation of the word "capital," whether used in a geographic, financial, or architectural sense.

2. Of which town is Phil a prominent character?

3. Which European capital started as two cities divided by a river?

4. Who asserted that, "When a man is tired of London, he is tired of life; for there is in London all that life can afford."?

5. What do Nellie Forbush of *South Pacific* and Lorelei Lee of *Gentlemen Prefer Blondes* have in common, besides being musical comedy heroines?

6. According to a World Bank study, which capital city will be the largest in the world by the end of the 20th century, and, as a consequence, what other unenviable distinction does it already possess?

7. The capitals of Corinthian columns are decorated with the leaves of which plant?

8. What has been called the Paris of the Pacific?

9. To which capital was Byron referring in "Childe Harold's Pilgrimage" when he wrote: ". . . my country! city of the soul!"?

10. What extremes connect Reykjavik and Wellington?

Capitals

1. It is from the Latin *caput*, meaning head.

2. Punxsutawney in western Pennsylvania, which is considered the groundhog capital of the United States. Punxsutawney Phil is said to leave his warren there at Gobbler's Knob on February 2, Groundhog Day, only to return underground for six weeks if he sees his shadow. Thus a sunny February 2 supposedly means six more weeks of winter.

3. Budapest, the capital of Hungary. Buda lies on the right bank and Pest on the left bank of the Danube. Buda, situated among a series of hills, was traditionally the center of government buildings, palaces, and villas belonging to the landed gentry. Pest, a flat area, has long been a commercial and industrial center.

4. Dr. Samuel Johnson, in Boswell's *Life of Johnson* (20 September 1777).

5. They are both "little girls from Little Rock," the capital of Arkansas.

6. Mexico City, with a population anticipated to exceed 30 million. Its exploding population has drawn so heavily upon its water table that it is the world's fastest-subsiding city—downtown, around the Presidential Palace, is already 35 feet below its level of a hundred years ago.

7. The acanthus, and occasionally laurel and olive. The leaves of tobacco, corn, and cotton plants have been substituted in the capitals of the U.S. Capitol.

8. Nouméa, the capital of New Caledonia, an overseas territory of France. Saigon was once called the Paris of the Orient; that was, of course, before it was given its present name of Ho Chi Minh City.

9. Rome, after a three-week visit there in 1818.

10. They are, respectively, the most northerly and southerly national capitals—Iceland's and New Zealand's respectively. Reykjavik is probably the cleanest capital in the world, as the whole city is heated by underground springs. The city's name refers to these hot springs and means "smoking bay" in Old Norse. Also, dogs are not permitted within the city limits.

Cartoons and Comic Strips
■ ■

1. Whose cartoons, in which magazine in the 1870s, played an important part in breaking the power of Tammany Hall and in putting Boss Tweed behind bars?

2. The first color comic strip was "The Yellow Kid," published in 1895 in the New York *World*, a Pulitzer paper. Hearst countered two years later with "The Katzenjammer Kids." What does "Katzenjammer" mean in German slang?

3. The anniversary issue of which weekly magazine has a cover depicting its imaginary arbiter of taste, Eustace Tilley, dressed as a Regency buck and peering at a butterfly through a quizzing-glass?

4. Food is a recurring theme in comic strips. Name four characters who were partial to, respectively: a) corned beef and cabbage, b) hamburgers, c) sundaes, and d) triple-decker sandwiches.

5. During World War II Bill Mauldin achieved fame for his sardonic sketches of the life of the enlisted man, titled "Up Front," which were published in *The Stars and Stripes* and elsewhere. What were the names of the two unshaven, unkempt GIs that Mauldin created?

6. Whose characters rode the West Po'k Chop Railroad, built by Stubborn P. Tolliver, which goes up the Onnecessary Mountain but never reaches the other side, and drank Kickapoo Joy Juice, brewed in Big Barnswell's Skonk Works, the fumes of which have been known to be lethal?

7. Who drew an unsettling cartoon showing a skier whose individual ski tracks appear on either side of a tree?

8. Can you name the offspring of that gruesome twosome, Gravel Gertie and B. O. Plenty?

9. Which master of the gag cartoon, embodying the *New Yorker* style, satirized the mores of the times with the insight of a Daumier and the playfulness of a Rowlandson?

10. Whose prize-winning comic strip focuses on what is current in the cultural and political scene on and off campus?

Cartoons and Comic Strips

1. Thomas Nast, whose work appeared in *Harper's Weekly*.

2. A hangover—literally, "the yowling of cats." "The Katzenjammer Kids" is the oldest continuous comic strip still in existence.

3. *The New Yorker*. The drawing by Rea Irvin appeared on the cover of the first issue in February 1925 and is repeated on every anniversary.

4. a) Jiggs ("bringing up Father"), b) Wimpy ("Popeye"), c) Harold Teen ("Harold Teen"), and d) Dagwood Bumstead ("Blondie").

5. Willie and Joe. A memorable cartoon shows one of them with a medic (medical corpsman) who is handing out Purple Heart medals to those wounded in action. The caption reads: "Just gimme a coupla aspirin. I already got a Purple Heart."

6. Al Capp, in "L'il Abner," who also conceived Lower Slobbovia, ruled by King Nogoodnick, whose subjects are eternally adrift in snow up to their necks. John Steinbeck, who called Capp the best satirist since Laurence Sterne, wrote: "Capp has taken our customs, our dreams, our habits and thoughts, our social structure, our economics, and examined them gently like amusing bugs."

7. Charles Addams, in *The New Yorker*.

8. Sparkle Plenty, in Chester Gould's strip "Dick Tracy."

9. Peter Arno, whose real name was Curtis Arnoux Peters, Jr. His satirical cartoon world was peopled with breezy, busty chorines; randy aristocrats; bejeweled matrons; and prehistoric-minded clubmen.

10. Garry Trudeau's "Doonesbury," which first appeared in *The Yale Daily News* in 1968. Trudeau became the first comic-strip artist to win a Pulitzer Prize, in 1975.

Cats

■ ■

1. Which variety of cat is small, muscular, roundheaded, and has a satin-textured coat of deep sable brown?

2. Who wondered at a cat's symmetry?

3. Give a synonym for a dupe, or a person who is easily deceived or used.

4. What, specifically, are Turkish, Smoke, Birman, Color-point, and Blue Cream?

5. Who chronicled the activities of "Bustopher Jones: The Cat about Town" in a poem which begins:

> Bustopher Jones is *not* skin and bones—
> In fact, he's remarkably fat.
> He doesn't haunt pubs—he has eight or nine clubs,
> For he is the St. James's Street Cat!

6. Which American humorist defined a cat as "a pygmy lion who loves mice, hates dogs, and patronizes human beings"?

7. Who "vanished quite slowly, beginning with the end of the tail, and ending with the grin, which remained some time after the rest of it had gone"?

8. What literary fellow typed the following to his friend, who happened to be a cat?

> oh i should worry and fret
> death and i will coquette
> there s a dance in the old dame yet
> toujours gai toujours gai

9. In the field of aviation what does the acronym CAT stand for?

10. What does an underground burial chamber have in common with a raised platform for a coffin during a state funeral?

Cats

1. A Burmese.
2. William Blake in his poem "The Tyger":

> Tyger! Tyger! burning bright
> In the forests of the night,
> What immortal hand or eye
> Could frame thy fearful symmetry?

3. A cat's-paw, which dates back to the fables of Aesop and La Fontaine. Apparently a monkey persuaded a rather gullible cat to pull some nuts out of the fire for him. The monkey got the nuts and the cat got a singed paw.
4. Varieties of long-haired cats.
5. T. S. Eliot, in *Old Possum's Book of Practical Cats*, which ends:

> But he's so well preserved because he's observed
> All his life a routine, so he'll say.
> Or, to put it in rhyme: "I shall last out my time"
> Is the word of this stoutest of Cats.
> It must and it shall be Spring in Pall Mall
> While Bustopher Jones wears white spats!

6. Oliver Herford.
7. The Cheshire Cat in Lewis Carroll's *Alice's Adventures in Wonderland*.
8. Archy, the literary cockroach, to his friend Mehitabel, the cat, whose motto is "toujours gai." (Archy writes in modern free verse because he is unable to use the typewriter shift key for capitals and punctuation, according to Don Marquis, the author of *archy and mehitabel*.)
9. Clear Air Turbulence, which can be extremely violent and cannot be detected by ordinary aircraft or airport radar.
10. They both begin with cat: catacomb and catafalque.

Christmas

■ ■

1. What kind of animals carried the Wise Men on their journey from the East to Nazareth? Their gifts to the newborn Child were gold for a king, frankincense for His anointing, and myrrh for His burial. What do the latter two consist of?

2. What memorable presents did Charlemagne and William the Conqueror receive on Christmas Day?

3. Who is generally given credit for bringing the Christmas tree to England?

4. Give the derivation of the word "yule."

5. Which famous Christmas story begins with the line, "One dollar and eighty-seven cents"?

6. The name of the seventh tiny reindeer mentioned in Clement Moore's famous poem "A Visit from St. Nicholas," which begins "'Twas the night before Christmas," is variously spelled "Donner" and "Donder." Which is correct?

7. Which master of light humorous verse observed that "Roses are things that Christmas is not a bed of them"?

8. Who are the Whos?

9. Which part of Africa got its name because it was first sighted on Christmas Day?

10. Who, at Christmas dinner, "beat with the handle of his knife upon the table and feebly cried, 'Hurrah'"?

Christmas

1. No one knows how they traveled. The Bible simply says ". . . there came wise men . . ." (*Matthew* 2:1). Frankincense and myrrh are aromatic gum resins used for incense, embalming, and perfumes.

2. Crowns. Charlemagne was crowned first Carolingian Emperor of the Roman Empire by Pope Leo III in Rome in the year 800, and William the Conqueror was crowned King of England in Westminster Abbey in 1066.

3. Prince Albert, the Consort of Queen Victoria, who popularized the Christmas tree, although it was first introduced into Britain in 1800 by Queen Charlotte, the wife of George III.

4. It comes from the Old Norse *jol*, a pagan feast which occurred during the time of the winter solstice. From this we get the word "jolly."

5. "The Gift of the Magi," by O. Henry. With Christmas fast approaching, Jim Young had only that amount with which to buy a present for his wife Delia. (O. Henry was the pen name used by William Sydney Porter.)

6. Donder. The original manuscript is lost, but a holograph, written by Moore many years later, is exhibited by the New York Historical Society at Christmas and clearly says Donder—Thunder in Dutch—just as Santa Claus is a contraction of the Dutch Sint Nicolaes, the patron saint of children. Donner means thunder in German.

7. Ogden Nash in "April Yule, Daddy!" from his book *Good Intentions*.

8. In Dr. Seuss' holiday story "How the Grinch Stole Christmas," the Whos are whimsical creatures who dearly loved Christmas. North of Whoville lives the Grinch, with a heart two sizes too small—and an evil plan to steal Christmas.

9. Natal, now a province of the Republic of South Africa. It was originally named *Terra Natalis*, Land of [Christ's] Birth, by Vasco da Gama.

10. Tiny Tim in Charles Dickens' *A Christmas Carol*.

Cities and Towns
■ ■

1. Explain the origin of the phrase "jerkwater town."

2. What is the only major city to be located on two continents, and what were its former names?

3. Who compared London and Paris as follows?

Oh, London is a man's town, there's power in the air;
And Paris is a woman's town, with flowers in her hair.

4. Where do St. James, the Angels, and St. Francis lie in a line?

5. By what names are the following better known: Karlovy Vary, Brugge, and Baile Atha Cliath?

6. Who said, "When I am dead and opened, you shall find 'Calais' lying in my heart."?

7. It has been said that in the United States there are only three cities—New York, New Orleans, and San Francisco. What are "all the others" according to Heywood Broun?

8. In which cities would you find a Soho and a SoHo?

9. What is "the typical American city" according to two classic books, *Middletown* (1929) and *Middletown in Transition* (1937), written by Robert S. Lynd and his wife Helen?

10. Who spoke of Marrakech to whom in the following terms, and on what occasion?

My description of Marrakech was "the Paris of the Sahara," where all the caravans had come from Central Africa for centuries to be heavily taxed *en route* by the tribes in the mountains and afterwards swindled in the Marrakech markets, receiving the return, which they greatly valued, of the gay life of the city, including fortune-tellers, snake-charmers, masses of food and drink, and on the whole the largest and most elaborately organized brothels on the African continent. All these institutions were of long and ancient repute.

Cities and Towns

1. It is an early railroad expression for a remote town where the water for the engine's boiler had to be "jerked"—that is, not drawn from a special overhead pipe, but pumped from a well and carried to the locomotive.

2. Istanbul, Turkey, which is located on both sides of the Bosporus at its entrance into the Sea of Marmara, thus lying in both Europe and Asia. Originally Byzantium, the city was the capital of the Byzantine Empire, the eastern part of the later Roman Empire. It became Constantinople in A.D. 330 in honor of the Emperor Constantine, and Istanbul in 1930.

3. Henry Van Dyke, in the poem "America for Me."

4. In California. They are the largest cities on the coast: San Diego, Los Angeles, and San Francisco. (The original name of Los Angeles was *El Pueblo de Nuestra Señora la Reina de Los Angeles*.)

5. Carlsbad, Czechoslovakia; Bruges, Belgium; Dublin, Republic of Ireland.

6. Queen Mary I (Mary Tudor), referring to the loss of Calais by the English in 1558 during the war between France and Spain.

7. Bridgeport.

8. Soho, a section of London noted for its foreign restaurants and night life, derives its name from an old hunting cry. New York's SoHo, a center for arts and crafts in a renovated loft area, lies *So*uth of *Ho*uston Street.

9. Muncie, Indiana. A new team of sociologists, updating the previous work with a study titled *Middletown III*, have found that the Munconians still hold to the homespun values of 19th-century rural America.

10. Prime Minister Churchill to President Roosevelt, following the Casablanca Conference in January 1943, as they drove to Marrakech where Churchill painted the only picture he attempted during the war, *The Tower of Katoubia Mosque*, with the snows of the Atlas Mountains in the background lit by the setting sun. He sent this painting to Roosevelt as a memento of their visit.

Clotheshorses

■ ■

1. What were codpieces and when were they fashionable?
2. How did the word "cravat" come into the English language?
3. Explain the basic difference between a tartan and a plaid.
4. Who advised whom to dress in this fashion?

> Costly thy habit as thy purse can buy,
> But not express'd in fancy; rich not gaudy;
> For the apparel oft proclaims the man.

5. What is the basic difference between British and American striped ties?
6. How did "hunting pinks," the scarlet jackets worn by fox hunters, come into fashion?
7. Which war was unique in that it gave the English language the names of three articles of clothing?
8. Whose quaint attire, described below, was much admired according to whom?

> His queer long coat from heel to head
> Was half of yellow and half of red.

9. The stiff felt hat with a round crown and a narrow, curved brim is known as a derby in America and a bowler or billycock hat in England. Where did these terms originate?
10. Which distinctive cloth is called by a corruption of the Persian phrase *shir-o-shakar*, which translates as "milk and sugar"? And which by that of an American-Spanish word meaning "toasted"?

Clotheshorses

1. Codpieces were pouches worn at the crotch by men in the 15th and 16th centuries. The word derives from the Middle English *cod*, meaning bag or scrotum.

2. It was originally a neckband worn by Croatian mercenaries in the service of France during the 17th century. The soldiers called themselves Hrvati, and when the scarf style was picked up by smart Parisians, it became known as a *cravate*.

3. A tartan is a pattern of various widths and colors crossed at right angles against a solid background, every Scottish clan now claiming a distinctive design. A plaid properly refers to the rectangular woolen tartan scarf worn over one shoulder by Scottish Highlanders, and originally used as both blanket and kilt.

4. Polonius to his son, Laertes, in Shakespeare's *Hamlet*.

5. The diagonals are reversed: as one looks at them, the stripes on British ties slope downward from right to left, while those on American ties slope from left to right.

6. They were originally the faded red coats worn by former British army officers when they took up the sport. They were not first made by a tailor named Pinks nor introduced by a gentleman called Pincus.

7. The Crimean War. From it came the raglan overcoat, the cardigan sweater, and the Balaclava helmet. Lord Raglan was commander of the British forces, while the Earl of Cardigan led the disastrous cavalry charge which Tennyson immortalized in "The Charge of the Light Brigade." Balaclava, the British supply base outside Sevastopol, was the site of a famous allied victory.

8. The Pied Piper of Hamelin in Robert Browning's poem.

9. Because his tall hat was frequently swept off by overhanging branches, the Norfolk landowner Thomas William Coke, later 1st Earl of Leicester, asked Lock the hatters to design a lower-crowned hat. This was made by one John Bowler and is also called a billycock hat after Coke (pronounced "cook" or "cock"). The derby is named after the 12th Earl of Derby who in 1780 was one of the founders of the race known as the Derby (pronounced Dár-bie), the first such event run as a sweepstake. To the Derby he usually wore a bowler, which crossed the Atlantic to become the derby.

10. Seersucker and chinos.

Clubs and Societies

■ ■

1. What is the oldest club in the United States still in existence?

2. Who was always to be found at the Diogenes Club in London from a quarter to five till twenty to eight?

3. Which famous club evolved from a chocolate house founded by the Italian Francesco Bianco?

4. What is the proper and resplendent name of the organization to which the Shriners belong?

5. After World War II the state of the British economy forced the Bath and Conservative Clubs in London to merge. What nickname was given to the newly united institution?

6. Which club has as its motto "Weaving spiders come not here," and where does the line originate?

7. The name of what notorious secret organization is taken from the Greek word for circle?

8. Which men's club maintains the largest library devoted solely to sporting subjects?

9. Which caterpillars were commemorated by the Caterpillar Club?

10. P. G. Wodehouse's immortal Bertie Wooster naturally was a member of The Drones, but to which appropriately named club did his imperturbable manservant Jeeves belong?

Clubs and Societies

1. Philadelphia's State in Schuylkill, which was founded in 1732. More commonly known as "The Fish House," its Fish House Punch is justly famous.

2. Mycroft Holmes, the portly, older, more brilliant, but lazier brother of Sherlock Holmes.

3. White's on London's St. James Street. The oldest club in the world, it was founded in 1693—just one year earlier than the Bank of England—as White's Chocolate House, by Francis White, who had anglicized his name.

4. The Ancient Arabic Order of Nobles of the Mystic Shrine, North and South America, World Jurisdiction, Inc.

5. The Lava-Tory.

6. The Bohemian Club in San Francisco. Its summer encampment at Bohemian Grove attracts prominent men from all over the world. The Bohemian Club's motto alludes to the rule that discussion of business and worldly careers is frowned upon, and comes from Shakespeare's *A Midsummer Night's Dream*. Supposedly, only the arts, literature, and other pleasures are to be discussed within the gates of the Grove. But, as Shakespeare put it in *Hamlet*, "the rule is more honour'd in the breach than the observance."

7. The Knights of the Ku Klux Klan, from the Greek *kuklos*, circle. Organized in the South after the Civil War, its object was to reassert white, and especially ex-Confederate white, supremacy with terrorist methods.

8. The Racquet and Tennis Club in New York City. In particular its collection of books on court games—court tennis (also called Royal or real tennis), lawn tennis, racquets, and squash—is outstanding.

9. The silkworms that made the silk for parachutes which saved the lives of club members, airmen who had been forced to bail out.

10. The Junior Ganymede. Ganymede was a Trojan boy of great beauty whom Zeus carried away to be cupbearer to the gods and from whose name derives the English word catamite, a homosexual boyfriend (though Jeeves would have been shocked).

Color Scheme

■ ■

1. Which widely divergent groups are known as the Blue People?

2. How did General John J. Pershing, commander in chief of the American Expeditionary Force in the First World War, get his nickname "Black Jack"?

3. Name the author of the following:

It were a vain endeavor that I should gaze forever
At that green light that lingers in the west
I may not hope from outward forms to win
The spirit and the passion whose fountains lie within.

4. Which legendary movie queen said, "I used to be Snow White, but I drifted"?

5. In F. Scott Fitzgerald's novel *The Great Gatsby*, what did the green light at the end of the dock symbolize?

6. Who suffered from "The Mean Reds," "Black Dog," and the "Yellowstain Blues"?

7. Who wrote: "The Moon rides like a Girl—Through a Topaz Town"?

8. White, blue, brown, and black are ascending orders of what?

9. What had who just done to prompt this lament?

Will all great Neptune's ocean wash this blood
Clean from my hand? No, this my hand will rather
The multitudinous seas incarnadine,
Making the green one red.

10. Give the title of Huw Morgan's reminiscences of life in the Glamorganshire valleys.

Color Scheme

1. The Picts—that is, the "tattooed ones"—of Scotland; and the Tuareg, the Berbers of the Sahara, whose men wear blue veils which stain their skin.

2. It arose from his several years of service with a predominantly black regiment, the Tenth U.S. Cavalry. He was first called Nigger Jack, but this was later softened to Black Jack.

3. Samuel Taylor Coleridge in "Dejection: An Ode."

4. Mae West. Among her many memorable lines is: "When I'm good, I'm very, very good, but when I'm bad, I'm better."

5. The goal—unobtainable by Jay Gatsby—of being accepted into the social milieu of Daisy Buchanan.

6. Holly Golightly in Truman Capote's *Breakfast at Tiffany's*, and Winston S. Churchill, referring to their depressions; and the wardroom of the U.S.S. *Caine* in Herman Wouk's *The Caine Mutiny*, alluding to Captain Queeg's apparent cowardice under fire.

7. Emily Dickinson in an 1862 letter to Samuel Bowles, editor of the Springfield *Republican*.

8. Proficiency in judo, karate, and aikido—the Japanese systems of unarmed-self defense. The colors refer to the belts the participants are entitled to wear.

9. Lady Macbeth, who with her husband had just murdered King Duncan in Shakespeare's *Macbeth*.

10. *How Green Was My Valley*, the novel by Richard Llewellyn. (Lord Louis Mountbatten, later 1st Earl Mountbatten of Burma, when Supreme Commander in Southeast Asia during World War II, observed drily of the American units under him, "How green was my ally.")

Communications

■ ■

1. What did Rowland Hill advocate in 1839 that expedited communication throughout the world?

2. How did this familiar nursery rhyme by Sarah Josepha Hale assist in spreading other words and music?

> Mary had a little lamb,
> Its fleece was white as snow . . .

3. In 1843 Sir Charles Napier was said to have sent the most laconic dispatch ever issued—*"Peccavi"*—to Lord Ellenborough, the Governor General of India. What did this signify?

4. During the administration of President Theodore Roosevelt, Secretary of State John Hay sent this cable to Sultan Abd al-Aziz IV of Morocco: "This government wants Perdicaris alive or Raisuli dead." Explain the circumstances for sending what John Hay called the "concise impropriety" and state what principle was at stake.

5. During World War I who, reporting back to headquarters that his right flank had been shot away, his left hand crumbled, and his rear had deserted, was supposed to have ended the communiqué with the words, *"Situation excellente; j'attaque"*?

6. Why is a "Penny Black" unique, and by what omission can its successors be identified?

7. What did the Metropolitan Opera's presentation of Mozart's *The Marriage of Figaro* mark in the history of mass media?

8. How did Senator Stephen R. Young of Ohio reply to offensive messages in the mail?

9. What is the only post office in the United States that does not have a zip code?

10. Who, on his first visit to Venice, sent this urgent cable home: "Streets flooded. Please advise"?

Communications

1. The use of prepaid adhesive postage stamps, which began in England in 1840 and rapidly spread throughout the world.

2. These were the first words recorded by Thomas Alva Edison in 1877 on his newly invented phonograph.

3. Napier's orders were to conquer the Amirs of Sindh, a sovereign state in what is now Pakistan, and he accomplished this in 1843. The Latin word *Peccavi* means simply, "I have sinned."

4. Ion Perdicaris, an allegedly American businessman in Morocco, was kidnapped by the Berber bandit and tribal chieftain, Raisuli. The principle involved was the nation's obligation to protect its citizens abroad. After Perdicaris was released, it was discovered that he had given up his American citizenship when he moved away to avoid the Civil War draft 40 years earlier.

5. General Ferdinand Foch, who later became Commander in Chief of the Allied Armies in the West.

6. It is the world's first postage stamp and bears a portrait of the young Queen Victoria. In honor of Britain's originating the modern postal system, British stamps need not carry the country's name if the sovereign's head appears on them.

7. In 1940 Texaco began radio broadcasting the longest-running commercial presentation of the same type of program, opera, by the same sponsor.

8. "Dear Sir: I just think you ought to know that some nut has got hold of your name and address and is signing it to letters."

9. The B. Free Franklin Post Office in Franklin Court at 316 Market Street in Philadelphia. Bejamin Franklin, who had franking privileges as the nation's first Postmaster General, used "B. Free Franklin" as a political slogan.

10. Robert Benchley, American humorist.

Connections

■ ■

What do the following have in common?

1. Besides being literary figures: Thomas Browne, A. Conan Doyle, Anton Chekhov, A. J. Cronin, Oliver Wendell Holmes, Sr., Robert Bridges, and W. Somerset Maugham.

2. River Avon, the hoi polloi, Mount Fujiyama, and pizza pie.

3. The Singular Affair of the Aluminium Crutch; the Repulsive Story of the Red Leech; the Singular Adventures of the Grice Patersons in the Island of Uffa; the case of Wilson, the Notorious Canary Trainer; and the Adventure of Ricoletti of the Club Foot and His Abominable Wife.

4. Brooklyn in New York City and Martha's Vineyard.

5. The 1910 Harvard football team and the Kremlin wall.

6. Pognotrophy and the harbor of Cádiz.

7. *Friendship, Aurora, Sigma,* and *Faith*.

8. Elizabeth I, Thomas Jefferson, George Bernard Shaw, Winston S. Churchill, Sinclair Lewis, and Moira Shearer.

9. George Gordon, Lord Byron, with computers and with the United Nations.

10. Ming-Toy Epstein, Marmalade P. Vestibule, Solomon Gemorah, Mary Maloof Teabaggy, T. Fud Pucker Tucker, and Suparporn Poopattana.

Connections

1. They were all medical doctors.

2. These are three examples of pleonasm or redundancy: *Avon* means river, *hoi* means the, *yama* means mountain, and *pizza* means pie.

3. Exploits of Sherlock Holmes mentioned but not recorded by Dr. Watson, along with the Shocking Affair of the Dutch steamship *Friesland*, "which nearly cost us both our lives," and the Story of the Giant Rat of Sumatra, "for which the world is not prepared." There are about as many unrecorded cases in the Sherlock Holmes canon as recorded ones.

4. Brooklyn is Kings County in New York City and State, and Martha's Vineyard is Duke's County in Massachusetts because they were named at the same time in honor of Charles II and his brother James, Duke of York.

5. The body of the team's cheerleader John Reed—American journalist, communist, and author of the best eyewitness account of the Russian Revolution, *Ten Days That Shook the World*—is immured in the Kremlin.

6. Pognotrophy is the cultivation of beards; when Drake burned the Spanish ships in Cádiz harbor in 1587, he termed the enterprise "The singeing of the King of Spain's Beard."

7. These were the names of the first manned American spacecraft.

8. They were all redheaded.

9. Byron's daughter, Lady Lovelace, invented the technique now called computer programming. At a conference at the White House in 1941, Churchill persuaded Roosevelt to substitute the term "United Nations" for "Associated Powers" in the pact which the two leaders were urging the anti-Axis nations to sign, by quoting from Byron's *Childe Harold's Pilgrimage*:

> "Here, where the sword united nations drew,
> Our countrymen were warring on that day!"
> And this is much, and all which will not pass away.

10. They are names of people compiled by John Train in two delightful books, *Remarkable Names of Real People* and *Even More Remarkable Names*.

Countries

■ ■

1. Who observed that Great Britain and the United States are two countries separated by a common language?

2. Which country maintains a nationwide grid of bomb and radiation-proof underground installations believed to be unmatched in the world?

3. Why, according to Noël Coward, is the country air in France so fresh and sparkling?

4. What is the smallest nation in Asia?

5. Which country consists of ten federated provinces and two territories? Can you name them?

6. How did Winston Churchill neatly sum up Russia during World War II?

7. Besides all being in Europe, what fact of capital importance do these have in common: Belgium, Hungary, Northern Ireland, Rumania, Switzerland, West Germany, and Yugoslavia?

8. Which countries are connected by a) the Mont Cenis Tunnel, b) the Simplon Tunnel, c) the Brenner Pass, d) the St. Gotthard Tunnel, which with a length of 10 miles is the world's longest road tunnel and was completed in 1980?

9. Name the nation bordering, in part, on Mali, Niger, and Mauretania.

10. Which island nation takes its name from the bearded fig trees that abounded there?

Countries

1. George Bernard Shaw.
2. Switzerland.
3. Because the natives sleep with their windows shut.
4. The Republic of Maldives, consisting of 1,196 islands (203 inhabited) scattered over 50,000 square miles of the Indian Ocean, to the southwest of the southern tip of India. There are 17 resort islands that lie within a few miles of the capital island of Malé.
5. Canada, which is made up of Alberta, British Columbia, Manitoba, New Brunswick, Newfoundland, Nova Scotia, Ontario, Prince Edward Island, Québec, Saskatchewan, Yukon Territory, and the partially subdivided Northwest Territories.
6. In the course of a broadcast in October 1939, Churchill said, "I cannot forecast to you the action of Russia. It is a riddle wrapped in a mystery inside an enigma . . ."
7. Their respective capitals all begin with the same letter: Brussels, Budapest, Belfast, Bucharest, Berne, Bonn, and Belgrade.
8. a) France and Italy, b) Switzerland and Italy, c) Austria and Italy, d) Switzerland and Italy.
9. Algeria, which also touches Morocco, Tunisia, and Libya.
10. Barbados, which was probably discovered by the Portuguese and called Los Barbados.

Crazy Quilt

■ ■

1. When a passing ship was asked, "What ship?" by the Gibraltar signal station, how did it reply?

2. In bullfighting, what is the name of the maneuver in which the matador stands immobile and passes the cape slowly before the charging bull?

3. Why did three superimposed American flags cost $1 million in 1980?

4. Name the components of grog as served in the Royal Navy, and give the derivation of the word. And how does Mount Vernon enter the picture?

5. What would happen if you ran away from a mob of boomers, flyers, and joeys?

6. The term "male chauvinist pig" is commonly bandied about. What precisely does chauvinist mean, and whence is it derived?

7. After one of Dorothy Parker's repeated attempts at suicide, what did Robert Benchley say to her?

8. What is the U.S. Department of the Treasury's official explanation of the origin of the dollar sign—$?

9. The world's greatest collection of chastity belts, devices supposed to have been forced upon medieval women by husbands, before they embarked on journeys, to prevent sexual intercourse, is reputed to be in the Musée de Cluny in Paris. Why are they never on exhibition?

10. Who said he always kept some whiskey handy in case he saw a snake, which he also kept handy?

Crazy Quilt

1. "What rock?"

2. A veronica.

3. Why indeed, you may well ask. The Whitney Museum of American Art paid that price for a painting titled *Three Flags* by Jasper Johns which sold for $900 in 1959. The $1 million was at the time the highest price ever paid for the work of a living artist. Johns himself was quoted by *The New Yorker* as saying, "It has a rather neat sound, but it has nothing to do with painting."

4. Grog was a British sailor's tot of rum diluted with water, for which a ration of beer has now been substituted. It was named after Vice Admiral Edward Vernon who, in 1740, ordered the mixture served instead of neat spirits. He was nicknamed "Old Grog" because of his grogram (from *gros grain*, rough cloth) cloak. As he was a friend of George Washington's brother, Mount Vernon was named for him.

5. They would catch up with you, as they are male, female, and baby kangaroos respectively.

6. Chauvinism is militant and boastful devotion to and glorification of one's group—originally one's country—in short, truculent attachment to some collective. This word derives from Nicholas Chauvin, a legendary French soldier extremely devoted to Napoleon. (*Chauvin* literally means Baldy.)

7. "Dotty, if you don't stop this kind of thing, you'll make yourself sick."

8. The sign for the U.S. dollar—a currency authorized in 1785 but not actually issued until 1795—has nothing to do with the letters US. It seems to have evolved from two symbols, the figure 8 on the so-called Spanish dollar or "piece of 8" (the 8-real piece) and the abbreviation PS (for pesos) written with the "P" superimposed on the "S". Such coins were current throughout the Americas, not just in the Spanish colonies.

9. They have all been established as reproductions, and now there is considerable doubt if chastity belts in fact were ever worn at all.

10. Who else but Claude William Dukenfield, otherwise known as W. C. Fields.

Criminal Proceedings

■ ■

1. Which knavish fellow had the effrontery to try to steal the English Crown Jewels from the Tower of London?

2. Who was supposed to be able to open safes after sandpapering his finger tips?

3. What did the son of a woodwind player steal?

4. Underworld figures of America's gangster era had colorful nicknames. What were the sobriquets of: a) Charles Floyd, b) George Nelson, c) Vincent Coll, d) Jack Diamond, e) Arthur Flegenheimer?

5. What sublime object did the Mikado in the Gilbert and Sullivan light opera hope to achieve?

6. If a young horse could help an American crook, how would a clerical hat be of use to an Italian hoodlum, or a mouse catcher to a German criminal?

7. What is the proper name for Macbeth's crime?

8. Who has been described as follows: "He is the organizer of half that is evil and of nearly all that is undetected in this great city . . . He sits motionless, like a spider in the center of his web, but that web has a thousand radiations and he knows well every quiver of each of them."?

9. What are the only two crimes specified in the U.S. Constitution?

10. Name the authors who created the following fictional detectives:

a) Sergeant Cuff
b) Inspector Adam Dalgleish
c) Lew Archer
d) Arsène Lupin
e) Dr. Gideon Fell

f) Inspector Bucket
g) Peter McGarr
h) Hercule Poirot
i) Travis McGee
j) Superintendent Roderick Alleyn

Criminal Proceedings

1. Colonel Thomas Blood in 1671. Charles II pardoned him because he was so taken with the audacity of his enterprise and rewarded him with an estate in Ireland.

2. Jimmy Valentine in O. Henry's story "A Retrieved Reformation" in the book *Roads of Destiny*. This was later made into a popular play, *Alias Jimmy Valentine*.

3. The answer is found in the old nursery rhyme:

> Tom, Tom, the piper's son
> Stole a pig and away he run.

4. a) Pretty Boy, b) Baby Face, c) Mad Dog, d) Legs, e) Dutch Schultz.

5. In Gilbert and Sullivan's light opera *The Mikado*, he says:

> My object all sublime
> I shall achieve in time—
> To let the punishment fit the crime—
> The punishment fit the crime.

6. Because they are all types of handguns—Colt, Beretta, and Mauser.

7. Regicide, because he murdered King Duncan.

8. "The Napoleon of crime," Professor Moriarty, according to A. Conan Doyle in the Sherlock Holmes story, "The Final Problem."

9. Treason and bribery. The Constitution also refers to "other high crimes and misdemeanors": treason is the definitive high crime; and high misdemeanors, reckoned in the law books as "crimes next to treason," would seem to embrace such grave violations of the public trust as bribery.

10.
a) Wilkie Collins
b) P. D. James
c) Ross MacDonald
d) Maurice Leblanc
e) John Dickson Carr
f) Charles Dickens
g) Bartholomew Gill
h) Agatha Christie
i) John D. MacDonald
j) Ngaio Marsh

Curious Derivations

■ ■

Give the derivations of the following words:

1. Quiz

2. Curfew

3. Honeymoon

4. Pedigree

5. Boycott

6. Foible

7. Disaster

8. Mumbo jumbo

9. Company

10. Diplomat

Curious Derivations

1. Quiz is supposed to have originated in 18th-century Dublin, when a theatrical manager called Daly won a bet that he could force a meaningless word into the language by painting it all over town. The word may, however, have been derived from "inquisition," but this has never been proven.

2. In the Middle Ages, when the danger of fire was always present, a signal was rung for people to get off the streets and put out their home fires. The word derives from the Old French *cuevrefeu*, a covering of the fire.

3. From the practice of ancient Germanic peoples of drinking honey wine (hydromel or mead) for thirty days after a marriage. Attila the Hun indulged so freely in hydromel at his wedding feast that he died.

4. From Middle French *"pied de grue,"* crane's foot: a clawlike symbol used by medieval genealogists to mean "succeeded to."

5. The Earl of Erne's Irish land agent, Captain Boycott, was so rigorous that the tenant farmers destroyed his property, blocked his mail and food supplies, and eventually drove him from the country.

6. Foible is a fencing term and refers to the "feeble" part of the foil, from the middle to the tip. The strong part, the *forte*, is from the middle to the hilt.

7. Literally, an ill-starred venture or occurrence, from the Latin *dis*, badly, and *astrato*, starred.

8. In the language of the Mandingo of the southern Sudan, a standard formula employed when beset by family spirits. Literally, it means "Away, troubling grandmother!"

9. Company originally was one who breaks bread with you and derives from the Latin *cum*, with, and *panis*, bread. In a business company the "bread" you hopefully break with each other has a greenish color.

10. The Greek prefix *diplo-* means "folded twice," which anyone entrusted with sensitive documents, such as a diplomat, should take care to do.

Dance

■■

1. Which ruler was charmed by the dancing of Salome?

2. What was the first successful dance team to catch the mood of the years immediately preceding the Jazz Age?

3. Whose screen test is reputed to have received the comment: "Can't act. Can't sing. Balding. Can dance a little."?

4. What was the Australian dancer and choreographer Sir Robert Helpmann's view of nude dancing?

5. Who described what dance in the following lines?

> They are waiting on the shingle—
>   will you come and join the dance?
> Will you, won't you, will you, won't you,
>   will you join the dance?
> Will you, won't you, will you, won't you,
>   won't you join the dance?

6. What is labanotation?

7. To whose music is the ballet *Les Sylphides* set? What was it originally called?

8. "Break a leg!" is traditionally the actor's phrase for "Good luck!" on the stage. As this is hardly appropriate for dancers, who are naturally sensitive about their limbs, what monosyllabic French expletive have they adopted?

9. What does a famous dancer and choreographer have in common with the 1970 winner of the English Derby?

10. Name the occupation of the man who gave his name to the close-fitting one-piece garment worn by dancers and acrobats.

Dance

1. Herod Antipas, who executed John the Baptist and ruled Galilee at the time of Jesus' death.

2. Irene and Vernon Castle. The team originated the "Castle" walk, the one-step, and the "hesitation" waltz. Irene Castle introduced bobbed hair and the slim, boyish woman's figure to the ballroom and the world of fashion. Vernon Castle was a pilot who served with the Royal Flying Corps in France in World War I and was killed in 1918 while training aviation cadets in Fort Worth, Texas.

3. Fred Astaire. This has become a cherished Hollywood legend.

4. "The trouble with nude dancing is that not everything stops when the music stops."

5. The Mock Turtle singing about the Lobster Quadrille in Lewis Carroll's *Alice's Adventures in Wonderland*.

6. A system of diagraming the various movements and positions of a dance, similar to the score used in music. It was named after its creator, Rudolf Laban.

7. Chopin. The ballet, choreographed by Michel Fokine, was originally named *Chopiniana*. When the entrepreneur Sergei Diaghilev first presented it to a Parisian audience in 1909, he changed the title to *Les Sylphides*. The ballet was orchestrated by Igor Stravinsky.

8. *"Merde!"* ("Shit!")

9. They share the name Nijinsky.

10. He was the trapeze artist, Jules Léotard, who was the original "daring young man on the flying trapeze"; indeed, its inventor.

Days and Dates

■■

    1. In which year is it now generally agreed that Christ was born?

    2. Twelfth Night marks the end of the Christmas season. When does it fall?

    3. On which day do you never get jam, according to the White Queen in Lewis Carroll's *Through the Looking-Glass*?

    4. What happened on July 2, 1776?

    5. Who speaks the following lines?

> To-morrow, and to-morrow, and to-morrow
> Creeps in this petty pace from day to day,
> To the last syllable of recorded time;
> And all our yesterdays have lighted fools
> The way to dusty death.

    6. Mardi Gras, or "fat Tuesday," marks the last day before Lent, and in most Roman Catholic communities is celebrated by a carnival, which means literally what?

    7. From a Roman point of view what is unique about the year 1666?

    8. Queen Victoria reigned so long that she celebrated her Silver, Golden, and Diamond Jubilees. Which was celebrated in 1887?

    9. In the annals of organized crime, why is the date February 14, 1929, memorable?

    10. 1961 reads the same upside down. What is the next year that this will occur?

Days and Dates

1. 6 B.C. In that year three planets—Mars, Jupiter, and Saturn—were in such proximity as to account for the Star of Bethlehem which the Wise Men followed.

2. The evening of January 5, or the twelfth night from Christmas, counting Christmas as the first. It is also the eve of Epiphany, a celebration of the manifestation of the divine nature of Christ to the Gentiles as represented by the Magi.

3. Today. "The rule is jam tomorrow, and jam yesterday—but never jam today."

4. The Continental Congress resolved that the United States were and ought to be independent. On July 4, it approved a formal announcement justifying this, which simply expanded the resolution of two days earlier.

5. Macbeth, near the end of Shakespeare's great tragedy, when he hears of the death of Lady Macbeth.

6. Farewell to meat, from the Old Italian *carnelevare*, "the removing of flesh."

7. It is the only date, or number, where all the Roman numerals appear in proper descending order—MDCLXVI.

8. Her Golden Jubilee. Her Diamond Jubilee was celebrated ten years later.

9. That was the date of the St. Valentine's Day Massacre in Chicago, when seven members of the George "Bugs" Moran gang were gunned down in a Chicago garage at 2122 North Clark Street. The police believed the Purple Gang of Detroit was responsible, but Moran, who narrowly escaped by being late for the meeting, blamed Al Capone.

10. 6009.

De Mortuis

■ ■

1. How is the Greek tragedian Aeschylus said to have died?

2. Who said that "in this world nothing is certain but death and taxes"?

3. When he was told that his greatest enemy had died, George IV exclaimed, *"Has* she, by God!" Who had actually died, and of whom was the king thinking?

4. Which son of a famous schoolmaster wrote these lines?

> Her cabin'd ample Spirit,
> It flutter'd and fail'd for breath.
> To-night it doth inherit
> The vasty hall of death.

5. Since 1840 what has happened to every U.S. President elected in a year ending in zero?

6. Who wrote a poem that begins, "Because I could not stop for Death . . ."?

7. Why did Henry E. Huntington, founder of the Huntington Library and Art Gallery in San Marino, California, invite Dr. A. S. W. Rosenbach, the rare-book seller, and Joseph (later Lord) Duveen, the art dealer, to come to California in 1927 and sit on either side of his deathbed?

8. From which poetical work, celebrating a great event of Roman history, is the following passage taken?

> "To every man upon this earth
> Death cometh soon or late;
> And how can man die better
> Than facing fearful odds,
> For the ashes of his fathers,
> And the temples of his Gods?"

9. How did Ambrose Bierce define a mausoleum in *The Devil's Dictionary*?

10. Who were the first U.S. civilians to suffer the death penalty after an espionage trial?

De Mortuis

1. A soaring eagle, in an effort to smash the shell of a turtle held in its beak, is supposed to have dropped it on Aeschylus, whose bald head it had mistaken for a rock.

2. Benjamin Franklin, in a letter to a French friend. Today he might have amended it to: ". . . but death and tax evasion."

3. Napoleon had died. George IV thought the news referred to his long-estranged wife Caroline, who had been planning to force her way into his coronation.

4. The lines are from "Requiescat" by Matthew Arnold, the son of Thomas Arnold, headmaster of Rugby School from 1828 to 1842.

5. They all died in office: William Henry Harrison, (elected in 1840), Abraham Lincoln (first elected 1860), James A. Garfield (elected 1880), William McKinley (re-elected 1900), Warren G. Harding (elected 1920), Franklin D. Roosevelt (re-elected 1940), and John F. Kennedy (elected 1960).

6. Emily Dickinson, "The Belle of Amherst," in poem Number 712 from *The Complete Poems*:

> Because I could not stop for Death—
> He kindly stopped for me—
> The Carriage held but just Ourselves—
> And Immortality.

7. So that, as he is reputed to have explained, he could die like Christ, between two thieves.

8. "Horatius" in *Lays of Ancient Rome*, by Thomas Babington Macaulay. The speaker is Horatius, the Captain of the City Gate.

9. "The final and funniest folly of the rich."

10. Julius and Ethel Rosenberg in 1953, for their part in transmitting top-secret data on nuclear weapons to the Soviet Union. They were also the first married couple ever to be executed in the United States.

Dining Out

■ ■

1. A reasonably sound test of a fine French restaurant, such as Russell Baker's La Grande Addition, is how the name of the traditional first course is spelled. Which is correct: *hors d'oeuvres* or *hors d'oeuvre*?

2. What is the origin of the name "finnan haddie," the great British breakfast specialty?

3. The proprietor of which world-famous restaurant said, "Ghosts are our greatest invisible assets"?

4. According to a gourmet poll, what is Mexico's greatest contribution to the culinary art?

5. Should you encounter smoked salmon named Novy, Novie, or Nova on the menu, you can be sure it came from which ocean?

6. "Greasy spoons" throughout the country have a language of their own, known as hash-house Greek. Translate the following orders as transmitted verbally to the chef: a) Whiskey down, smeared; b) Bucket of mud; c) Stretch one, let it bleed; d) Radio; e) On wheels.

7. Name the three leading restaurant guidebooks of France. By which symbols are the top establishments indicated in these three guides?

8. Billi-Bi is a superb cream of mussel soup. Where was it first made, and for whom was it named?

9. To which city would you have to go to get an authentic *Sacher torte,* a rich chocolate cake filled with cream or jam and topped with chocolate icing?

10. In England savouries are generally served after the dessert, to clear the palate for such after-dinner wines as port or Madeira. Can you describe two typical savouries: Angels on Horseback and Scotch Woodcock?

Dining Out

1. *Hors d'oeuvre*. No matter how many are served, it is always spelled without the final "s." The term means "outside the work."

2. Finnan haddie is Scottish slang for smoked fillets of haddock which were originally prepared in Findhorn, a fishing port in Morayshire.

3. Louis Vaudable, proprietor of Maxim's at 3 rue Royale in Paris, which has figured in two ballets, three plays, more than a dozen movies, and a score of novels. Franz Lehàr set the entire third act of *The Merry Widow* in the Grande Salle, although he was too poor ever to have dined there.

4. The Caesar salad, which was first served at Caesar's Restaurant in Tijuana in 1920—the year the 18th Amendment drove drinkers into countries where liquor was legally served.

5. The Pacific, where the salmon are more abundant, more coarsely grained, and cheaper. Pacific salmon are also used to make lox, salmon first cured in a highly saturated salt brine. The far more delicate salmon from Nova Scotia is always labeled "Nova Scotia salmon." To be served correctly, smoked salmon should be cut so thinly that one can almost see through it, and one slice should cover the entire plate.

6. a) Rye toast, buttered; b) Chocolate ice cream; c) Cherry Coke; d) Tuna sandwich on toast (derives from "tune 'er down"); e) To go.

7. *Guide Michelin* and *Guide Kléber*, both published by tire companies; and *Gault-Millau Guide France*, the newest guide, written by two French journalists and gastronomes who popularized the *nouvelle cuisine*. The top restaurants are indicated as follows: *Michelin*, stars and crossed forks and spoons; *Kléber*, crowns, roasters, and marmites; *Gault-Millau*, *toques* (chefs' hats).

8. It was first prepared at Maxim's and named after the American tinplate heir and playboy William B. ("Billy B.") Leeds.

9. Vienna, where the Hotel Sacher is located.

10. Angels on Horseback are shucked oysters, wrapped in bacon, skewered and broiled; Scotch Woodcock consists of scrambled eggs on anchovy toast, topped with two flat fillets of anchovy.

Dogs

■■

1. How does the terrier come by its name?

2. Who observed that "The hounds of spring are on winter's traces"?

3. Can you name the owners of: a) Daisy, b) Bullseye, c) Argos, d) Nipper?

4. What enormous dog was shot seven times in the wilds of Dartmoor in England?

5. How did the Anglo-American novelist and essayist Aldous Huxley explain the constant popularity of dogs?

6. From what was the writer fleeing in the following lines?

> I fled Him, down the nights and down the days;
>   I fled Him, down the arches of the years;
> I fled Him down the labyrinthine ways
>   Of my own mind; and in the mist of tears
> I hid from Him, and under running laughter.

7. For which sport were bulldogs originally bred?

8. Who is generally regarded as the daydreamer *sans pareil*, the canine Walter Mitty?

9. What is peculiar about the graceful and gentle Cavalier King Charles spaniel, and how would a picky person introduce it?

10. The basenji is a small dog of a breed originally from Africa, having a short, smooth coat. In which respect may it be considered unique?

Dogs

1. Originally bred for hunting animals that live in burrows, the terrier's name derives from the French *terre*, earth.

2. Algernon Charles Swinburne in "Atalanta in Calydon."

3. a) Blondie and Dagwood Bumstead in the comic strip "Blondie," b) Bill Sikes in Dickens' *Oliver Twist*, c) Odysseus or Ulysses (his Latin name) in Homer's *Odyssey*, d) The Radio Corporation of America. (Nipper listening to an early phonograph—"His Master's Voice"—is an RCA trademark.)

4. The dog in *The Hound of the Baskervilles*, by Arthur Conan Doyle. A terrifying aspect of the hound was that its muzzle, hackles, and dewlap were anointed with phosphorus to make them glow like flame in the dark, to make it appear supernatural.

5. "To his dog, every man is Napoleon."

6. The Hound of Heaven, in the poem of that name by Francis Thompson.

7. The medieval sport of bullbaiting, for which the dog was trained to fasten onto the bull's snout and not let go. As Winston Churchill, who epitomized the bulldog spirit, once explained, "The nose of the bulldog is slanted backwards so that he can breathe without letting go." This cruel sport was not outlawed by Parliament until 1835.

8. Snoopy, in Charles Schulz's comic strip "Peanuts." Among his various incarnations, Snoopy is Joe Cool, a big man on campus, casually ogling the chicks around the student union, or else a World War I ace dogfighting with the Red Baron in his Sopwith Camel.

9. This distinctive breed is still not recognized by the American Kennel Club, and a picky person would naturally say, "This is my pet Peeve."

10. It cannot utter the barking sound characteristic of most dogs.

Drink

■■

1. For whom is the ubiquitous bloody mary named?

2. Why, until the reign of Edward VII, did no Hanoverian ruler of Britain have fingerbowls at the dinner table?

3. Which country created the margarita, a concoction of tequila, Triple Sec (orange liqueur), and lime juice, served with salt encrusted on the rim of the glass? From what is tequila distilled?

4. Who first noted that "absinthe makes the heart grow fonder"?

5. Who is the author of the following lines?

> There is something about a Martini,
> A tingle remarkably pleasant;
> A yellow, a mellow Martini;
> I wish that I had one at present.
> There is something about a Martini,
> Ere the dining and dancing begin,
> And to tell the truth,
> It is not the vermouth—
> I think that perhaps it's the gin.

6. Which is the only completely natural green liqueur in existence?

7. From which city is gin said to derive its name?

8. Punch was first made on which continent?

9. What do the following have in common: Badoit, Bru, Fachigen, Mattoni, and Ramlösa?

10. The *ne plus ultra* of concocted potables may be the layered after-dinner drink known as a *pousse-café*, or "coffee-pusher." Care must be taken to see that the lighter liqueur or cordial floats on the denser. With this caveat in mind, name the ingredients for the classic *Arc-en-ciel*, the famous Rainbow, which approximates the seven colors of the spectrum.

Drink

1. Mary I (Mary Tudor), daughter of Henry VIII and Katharine of Aragón. Because of the persecution of Protestants throughout her reign, she was posthumously abused as "Bloody Mary."

2. Because secretly Jacobite guests would drink the loyal toast holding their glasses over the bowls, thus making a gesture to the exiled Stuart "King over the Water."

3. It was first made in Los Angeles, although derived from the traditional Mexican way of drinking tequila: toss salt into your mouth, down a shot of tequila, and bite into a slice of lime. In Spanish, *margarita* means pearl or daisy. Tequila is made not from the cactus, but the Central American century plant, as are mescal and pulque.

4. Addison Mizner, American architect and bon vivant.

5. Ogden Nash in "A Drink with Something in It" from *Many Long Years Ago*.

6. Chartreuse, the color of which is imparted solely by aromatic herbs. It was first made by the Carthusian Fathers at their monastery, La Grande Chartreuse, near Grenoble. (Green crème de menthe is artificially colored.)

7. No city, and certainly not Geneva. The word Genever, used on some Dutch gin labels, is simply a corruption of the Old French *genièvre*, juniper, whose berries give gin its unique flavor. Gin originated in Holland and was once called "Hollands."

8. Asia. The name derives from the Hindustani word *panch*, meaning five, for its five original ingredients: arrack (an Indonesian liquor made from rice), tea, lemon, sugar, and water.

9. They are famous brands of European mineral waters from France, Belgium, West Germany, Italy, and Sweden respectively.

10. Starting at the bottom, spoon in one-seventh each of the following: crème de violette, crème de cassis, maraschino, green crème de menthe, yellow chartreuse, curaçao, and cherry liqueur. This concoction is not known as the bartenders' delight.

Earth

■ ■

1. Who is reputed to have said, referring to the use of the lever, "Give me somewhere to stand, and I will move the earth"?

2. Distinguish between a stalagmite and a stalactite.

3. Who has been closest to the center of the earth?

4. Which literary hero "felt the earth move out and away from under them"?

5. What is meant by continental drift?

6. The Richter scale is a measure of ground motion from 1 to 10 as recorded on seismographs. What is the difference between an earthquake registering 5.5 and one registering 4.5?

7. Who wrote: "Touch the earth, love the earth, honor the earth, her plains, her valleys, and her seas; rest your spirit in her solitary places"?

8. Describe a continental divide.

9. What did the Yugoslav geologist Andrija Mohorovičić establish in 1909?

10. Which poet and theologian wrote: "No man is an *Iland*, intire of it selfe; every man is a peece of the *Continent*, a part of the *maine*; if a *Clod* bee washed away by the *Sea*, *Europe* is the lesse, as well as if a *Promontorie* were, as well as if a *Mannor* of thy *friends* or of *thine owne* were; any man's *death* diminishes *me*, because I am involved in *Mankinde* . . ."?

Earth

1. Archimedes, the Greek mathematician, physicist, and inventor.

2. A stalagmite rises from the floor of a cave, whereas a stalactite hangs down from the roof. (A simple way of remembering the difference is: stalagmite, ground; stalactite, ceiling; or, the mites go up and the tights go down.) They are usually cylindrical or conical deposits of calcite formed by the dripping of mineral-rich water.

3. The atomic submarine crews who have passed under the North Polar ice. (The flattening of the earth caused by rotation makes its surface 10 miles closer to the center at the poles than it is at the equator.)

4. Robert Jordan, hero of Ernest Hemingway's *For Whom the Bell Tolls*, when he was making love to Maria.

5. The slow shifting of the continents believed continuously to be taking place because of weakness in the suboceanic crust. According to this tectonic plate theory, South America was once joined to Africa.

6. It is ten times stronger; every increase in the integer means a tenfold increase in the magnitude of the earthquake.

7. Henry Beston, in *The Outermost House*, the enduring classic about a solitary life in a small cottage on the Great Beach of Cape Cod. The book tells of the ceaseless rhythms of wind, sand, and ocean, the migration of birds—the events of a passing year.

8. A stretch of high ground from either side of which the river systems flow in opposite directions into different seas or oceans. In North America the crests of the Rocky Mountains mark the Continental Divide, which is also called The Great Divide.

9. The Mohorovičić discontinuity, known as the Moho, which is the boundary between the earth's relatively thin crust and subadjacent mantle rock. The third or inner part of the earth is a molten core.

10. John Donne. This line from his "Devotions" ends: "And therefore never send to know for whom the *bell* tolls; It tolls for *thee*." Hemingway took the title of his novel of the Spanish Civil War from this passage.

Energy

■ ■

1. Who drilled the first successful well specifically sunk to find oil, and for what purpose was the oil used?

2. The British and the French in a limited way have experimented with what unusual source of water power?

3. What originally religious motif is the symbol of a great oil corporation?

4. What is the difference between insulation and insolation?

5. Name the "Seven Sisters" of world oil.

6. Which country is the world's largest oil producer and the second largest oil exporter?

7. It is believed that biomass may help tide the world over an energy famine which threatens the coming decades. What is biomass?

8. What name is given to the energy process that powers the sun?

9. What is "yellowcake," and for which energy purpose is it used?

10. Sunny, talkative California and bleak, dour Iceland have both found a use for wet hot air. What is it?

Energy

1. Edwin L. Drake, who in 1859 hit oil at 69 feet on Oil Creek, Pennsylvania, at a place later named Titusville. Kerosene, used for lamps, was the chief finished product.

2. Tidal energy.

3. Shell Oil, whose emblem, the scallop shell, derives from the company's founder, Marcus Samuel, having been a dealer in ornamental seashells. In the Middle Ages pilgrims to the third shrine of Christendom, Santiago de Compostela (St. James of the Field of Stars) in northwestern Spain, wore a scallop shell in their hats on their return journey. Thus the scallop shell became a badge of pilgrimage and Christian knighthood.

4. Insulation is material used to minimize heat losses; insolation is the amount of solar radiation reaching the earth's surface.

5. Exxon, Royal Dutch/Shell, Mobil, British Petroleum, Texaco, Standard Oil of California, and Gulf, ranked in order of sales.

6. The Soviet Union, with reserves roughly one-third greater than those of Saudi Arabia.

7. All solid matter of animal or vegetable origin from which energy may be extracted through heat, fermentation, or chemical reaction with other materials.

8. Nuclear fusion, in which nuclei combine to form more massive nuclei with the simultaneous release of energy.

9. "Yellowcake" is a concentrate of oxidized uranium extracted from uranium ore to produce fuel for nuclear reactors.

10. They can both tap great resources of geothermal steam: Iceland to heat Reykjavik, and the Pacific Gas and Electric Company, for example, to draw on the Geysers area of northern California to supply the equivalent of all the electricity needs of the city of San Francisco. These sources, being heated by the earth itself, have a long life expectancy and provide clean, non-polluting, and safe energy. Magma Power, traded over the counter, is the only "pure play" in the field.

English History
■■

1. Why was Ethelred the Unready not ready?

2. In 1066 William the Conqueror defeated Harold at the battle of Hastings. From what battle had Harold just come?

3. Which princely houses were involved in the Wars of the Roses?

4. Robert Wilmot, the 2nd Earl of Rochester—courtier, rake, wit, and poet—wrote the following on the bedchamber door of which ruler?

> Here lies a great and mighty king
> Whose promise none relies on;
> He never said a foolish thing,
> Nor ever did a wise one.

What was the king's amiable response to this attack?

5. What is missing from the following list: Blenheim, Oudenarde, Malplaquet?

6. What was brought both by a statesman who was a dandy and a statesman who was prepared for rain; and what were their exact words?

7. The initials G.O.M. and M.O.G. were both applied to Gladstone. What do they mean?

8. During World War I why was there an improvement for the British forces on the Western Front when they switched from vermouth to whisky?

9. What was Winston Churchill's rejoinder when, having dined extremely well at the House of Commons, he was confronted in the Smoking Room by the formidable Labour M.P. Bessie Braddock: "Winston, you're drunk. You're abominably, disgracefully drunk. What do you have to say for yourself?"?

10. Who is known as "The Iron Maiden," "Attila the Hen," or "The Leaderine"?

English History

1. On the contrary, he was all too ready to act impulsively. The epithet does not mean "unprepared" but derives from the Old English *unraed*, meaning "without counsel." Ethelred the Unready was so called because he refused to take advice.

2. From the battle of Stamford Bridge, where he had routed the forces of Harold III of Norway. His defeat at Hastings has been attributed in part to the general exhaustion of his troops after the long march south.

3. The House of York, whose badge was a white rose, won the throne from its cousins of the House of Lancaster, which later was associated by poets and chroniclers with the red rose, and was in turn overthrown by its more distant kinsmen of the House of Tudor. The Wars of the Roses lasted from 1455 to 1485.

4. Charles II, who replied: "This is very true, for my words are my own, and my actions are my ministers'."

5. Ramillies. These are the four great victories credited to the Duke of Marlborough in the War of the Spanish Succession.

6. Benjamin Disraeli in 1879: "Lord Salisbury and myself have brought you back peace—but a peace I hope with honour." Neville Chamberlain in 1938: "I believe it is peace for our time . . . peace with honour."

7. "Grand Old Man" and "Murderer of Gordon." General Charles "Chinese" Gordon, ordered to evacuate the Egyptian garrisons from the Sudan during a rebellion, instead saw fit to organize resistance from Khartoum. An expedition was sent to relieve him but arrived two days too late. The Gladstone government may not have acted decisively, but it was far from wholly to blame for the consequences of Gordon's heroic but reckless disobedience.

8. Because General Sir Douglas Haig replaced Field Marshal Sir John French as Commander in Chief, British Expeditionary Force, in 1915. (Douglas Haig was a cousin of the grandfather of the U.S. Secretary of State, Alexander Haig.)

9. Churchill, feeling no pain, beamed: "Bessie, you're fat. You're abominably, disgracefully fat. And tomorrow, Bessie, I shall be sober."

10. Prime Minister Margaret Thatcher, Britain's first female prime minister.

English Literature
■ ■

1. Name the author of *The Faerie Queene*. Whom did Gloriana represent?

2. A famous novel ends, at the guillotine in Paris during the Terror, with this stirring affirmation: "It is a far, far better thing that I do, than I have ever done; it is a far, far better rest that I go to than I have ever known." Who gives utterance to these words?

3. What sober mathematics don of Christ Church, Oxford, had a penchant for having small girls pose for the camera "mother-naked," as he put it?

4. Who prophetically wrote the following?

When I have fears that I may cease to be
Before my pen has glean'd my teeming brain,
Before high pilèd books in charactery
Hold like rich garners the full-ripened grain . . .

5. In W. Somerset Maugham's *Cakes and Ale* the Grand Old Man of English letters is Edward Driffield, and the ambitious but untalented biographer is Alroy Kear. Although at the time Maugham denied any connection, which writers are believed to have been satirized in this *roman à clef*?

6. Who was called Tusitala, "The Teller of Tales," by 19th-century Polynesians?

7. How did Arthur Conan Doyle and Ian Fleming exercise the divine prerogative?

8. Which famous poem did Hugh Kingsmill parody in this verse?

What, still alive at twenty-two,
A clean upstanding chap like you?
Sure, if your throat 'tis hard to slit,
Slit your girl's, and swing for it.

9. Who wrote the satirical romance the title of which is an anagram of "nowhere"?

10. Name the street near Moorfields, London, that Samuel Johnson in his famous *Dictionary* describes as being "much inhabited by writers of small histories, dictionaries, and temporary poems."

English Literature

1. Edmund Spenser, who gave one of the several characters representing Queen Elizabeth the name of Gloriana.

2. No one, not even Sidney Carton, the hero about to sacrifice his life for another's in Charles Dickens' *A Tale of Two Cities*. Dickens, careful not to give the rather understated and apologetic Carton an uncharacteristically grand closing speech, overcomes the problem of providing an appropriately noble and eloquent finale by saying that *had* Carton uttered the prophetic thoughts that occupied him, they would have been these.

3. Charles Lutwidge Dodgson, who transposed, respectively, the Latinate and Old English forms of his first two names to form his pen name Lewis Carroll.

4. John Keats, who wrote these lines two years before his death in Rome in 1821 at the age of 25.

5. Thomas Hardy and Hugh Walpole. Years later, in an introduction to a new edition of *Cakes and Ale*, Maugham repudiated his earlier denial that there was any connection between Alroy Kear and Hugh Walpole.

6. Robert Louis Stevenson, who died in 1894 at his house "Vailima" in Samoa.

7. They brought back to life characters they had invented—namely, Sherlock Holmes and James Bond—and then killed off.

8. Poem XIII from A. E. Housman's *A Shropshire Lad*, which begins:

> When I was one-and-twenty
> I heard a wise man say,
> "Give crowns and pounds and guineas
> But not your heart away . . ."

9. Samuel Butler, author of *Erewhon*, who is most remembered for his autobiographical novel *The Way of All Flesh*.

10. Grub Street (called Milton Street or Cripplegate since 1830), which has become a synecdoche for work turned out by literary hacks. In his *Dictionary* Dr. Johnson defined a lexicographer as "a writer of dictionaries, a harmless drudge."

Espionage
■ ■

1. Yale's Nathan Hale, before he was hanged as a spy by the British, is famous for saying, "I only regret that I have but one life to lose for my country," a line similar to one in Joseph Addison's play *Cato*: "What a pity is it that we can die but once to serve our country!" According to the diary of a British officer who was there, what did Nathan Hale really say?

2. In espionage a "pianist" is jargon for what?

3. Name the predecessor to the Central Intelligence Agency, whose distinctly elitist recruiting policies won it the nickname of "Oh So Social."

4. What was the strange last mission of Major William Martin, Royal Marines, "The Man Who Never Was," during World War II?

5. *A Man Called Intrepid*, by William Stevenson, is a chronicle of the world's first integrated intelligence operation. Who was Intrepid, and which organization did he head?

6. Which term is used for an agent clandestinely placed within another power's intelligence apparatus?

7. Name the high-flying American spy who was shot down by the Russians in 1960. Which summit conference did his capture disrupt?

8. Can you explain the abbreviation K.G.B.?

9. Who was the most famous employee of Universal Export Ltd., and what was its chief competitor?

10. Graham Greene wrote the underworld thriller *The Third Man*. In Britain's infamous spy ring, who turned out to be the Fourth Man, and who were the first three?

Espionage

1. More prosaically, "It is the duty of every good officer to obey any orders given him by his commander in chief."

2. A radio-telegraphy operator.

3. The Office of Strategic Services (O.S.S.), which was formed in 1942 under General William J. Donovan as the first modern U.S. espionage agency.

4. This name was simply that assigned to a corpse in uniform, the apparent victim of a plane crash, which was floated ashore on the Spanish coast near Gibraltar from a British submarine. "Major Martin" was carrying spurious top-secret documents designed to mislead the Germans about Allied invasion plans. The operation was named Mincemeat.

5. Sir William Stephenson, a Canadian who headed the innocuous-sounding British Security Coordination in Rockefeller Center, New York. He was charged with maintaining the closest possible communication between Roosevelt and Churchill.

6. Readers of the excellent spy novels of John le Carré (David John Moore Cornwell) think of him as a "mole" quietly burrowing away beneath the surface, but intelligence professionals usually call him a "sleeper."

7. Francis Gary Powers, who was flying a U-2 reconnaissance mission over the Soviet Union. At a Paris summit conference that year, Khrushchev denounced Eisenhower for permitting such flights. The exchange of Powers for the Russian spy "Rudolf Abel" implied the legitimacy of espionage as a branch of foreign policy.

8. Literally, it is the Commission of State Security *(Komitĕt Gosudarstvĕnnoi Bezopasnost'i)*. In reality, it is the Russian secret police and espionage organization.

9. Commander James Bond, 007, worked for Universal Export, a cover name for the British counter-espionage organization in conflict with SMERSH, *Smiert Shpyonam* (the Russian for "death to spies"), and later with SPECTRE, the Special Executive for Counter-Terrorism, Revenge, and Extortion.

10. The Fourth Man was Sir Anthony Blunt, Surveyor of the Queen's Pictures. The first three, all of whom defected to the Soviet Union, were Guy F. Burgess, Donald D. Maclean, and Harold (Kim) Philby. After disclosure of his name in 1979, Blunt was stripped of his knighthood.

Exit Lines

■ ■

Who uttered the following famous last words?

1. *"Qualis artifex pereo!"* (What an artist dies with me!)

2. "We are as neere to Heaven by sea as by land!"

3. After he was assured he was going to die, he confessed, "All right then. I'll say it. Dante makes me sick."

4. "Let not poor Nelly starve."

5. "God will forgive me—that's His profession."

6. Pointing to his heart, he remarked, "Congestion." Then, feeling his pulse, he said, "Stopped."

7. "Let the tent be struck."

8. When asked whether he had made his peace with God, he replied, "I was not aware that we had quarrelled."

9. "Get my swan costume ready!"

10. "Die, my dear doctor?—That is the last thing I shall do."

Exit Lines

1. Nero, the last Roman emperor of the family of Julius Caesar.

2. Sir Humphrey Gilbert, English soldier, navigator, and explorer, who was the older half-brother of Sir Walter Raleigh. Returning in 1583 from Newfoundland, where he founded England's first colony outside Europe that marked the start of the British Empire, Gilbert and his little ship *Squirrel* went down in a gale off the Azores, but not before calling out these last words to the larger vessel accompanying him. They are remarkably close to a saying of Sir Thomas More's before his beheading. Gilbert had been reading from More's *Utopia* as the storm rose.

3. Félix Lope de Vega, prolific 16th- and 17th-century playwright and founder of the Spanish drama.

4. King Charles II, referring to his mistress Nell Gwyn.

5. Heinrich Heine, one of the greatest of German lyric poets.

6. Joseph Henry Green, English surgeon and metaphysician.

7. General Robert E. Lee, general in chief of the Confederate Army in the Civil War.

8. Henry David Thoreau, American essayist and author of *Walden*.

9. Anna Pavlova, the greatest Russian ballerina of her time, whose most famous role was in *The Dying Swan*, choreographed for her by Michel Fokine.

10. Viscount Palmerston, Whig Prime Minister under Queen Victoria.

Familiar Misquotations

■ ■

Complete these popular quotes correctly.

1. Variety's the _____ of life.

2. A penny for your _____.

3. How doth the _____ bee improve each shining hour.

4. Ask me no questions, and I'll tell you _____.

5. _____ oaks from little acorns grow.

6. Give him an inch, he'll take _____.

7. Pride goeth before _____.

8. Tomorrow to fresh _____ and pastures new.

9. Power _____ and absolute power corrupts absolutely.

10. Home is the sailor, home from _____,
    And the hunter home from the hill.

Familiar Misquotations

1. very spice (William Cowper, *The Task*)

2. thought (John Heywood, *Proverbs*)

3. little busy (Isaac Watts, *Divine Songs*)

4. no fibs (Oliver Goldsmith, *She Stoops to Conquer*)

5. Tall (David Everett, "For a School Declamation," imitating an anonymous Latin original.)

6. an ell (John Ray, *English Proverbs*)

7. destruction (*Proverbs* 16:18)

8. woods (John Milton, "Lycidas")

9. tends to corrupt, (Lord Acton in a letter to Bishop Creighton)

10. sea (Robert Louis Stevenson, *Underwoods*, "Requiem")

Farrago
■ ■

1. At one time he was hailed as "the world's greatest actor," yet, when he went to Hollywood, he failed even to be nominated for an Academy Award. Who was he?

2. What causes the celestial fireworks known as the Northern Lights or Aurora Borealis?

3. Name the first black man to be pictured on a U.S. postage stamp.

4. It is well known that lions roar, geese honk, dolphins whistle, whales sing, but what about gibbons and tigers?

5. In his celebrated poem "Invictus," William Ernest Henley wrote:

> Out of the night that covers me,
> Black as the Pit from pole to pole,
> I thank whatever Gods may be
> For my unconquerable soul.

In the next stanza, "under the bludgeonings of chance," what was the state of his head?

6. Why did the U.S. Navy have to requisition 60 saddles from the U.S. Cavalry during World War II?

7. Which lion-hearted world leader dropped one of his names, which means brave as a lion?

8. What is the world's oldest continuously offered sporting trophy?

9. Where are the Antipodes specifically, and to what is the name generally applied?

10. What is the only new art form in history that insisted from the beginning as being known as an industry?

Farrago

1. John Barrymore, whose 1922 portrayal of Hamlet electrified the public. In Hollywood his career went into a general decline, and in 1939 he made his last stage appearance in *My Dear Children*, a pathetic burlesque of his bizarre private life.
2. The injection of charged particles, especially of solar origin, into the polar regions by the earth's magnetic field.
3. Booker T. Washington, American educator and founder of Tuskegee Institute in Alabama.
4. Gibbons whoop and tigers chuffle, according to the New York Zoological Society.
5. Bloody, but unbowed:

> In the fell clutch of circumstance,
> I have not winced nor cried aloud:
> Under the bludgeonings of chance
> My head is bloody, but unbowed.

6. The saddles were needed as gifts for the Mongol tribesmen in the Gobi Desert where U.S. Navy meteorologists were operating a string of weather stations in Inner Mongolia. The tribesmen thus equipped were unofficially known as the 1st U.S. Mongolian Cavalry.
7. Winston (Leonard) Spencer Churchill.
8. The America's Cup, named for the yacht *America* that won it in 1851, off the Isle of Wight in England. Originally called the Royal Yacht Squadron's Hundred Guineas Cup, it has since been in the possession of the New York Yacht Club. The races, held at least every three years between a selected challenger and a selected American yacht, are an expensive event that generates neither gate receipts nor television revenues, and whose participants receive no compensation.
9. They are a group of rocky, uninhabited islands southeast of New Zealand to which they belong. The name is generally applied to Australia and New Zealand as a whole, and of course is the term designating the opposite point on the globe to any given position.
10. Motion pictures.

Fashion

■ ■

1. Who dressed the Empress Eugénie of France and was the first of the great couturiers?

2. Which designer, influenced by art nouveau and Oriental designs, staged the first theatrical fashion shows?

3. Not content with creating a classic in the fashion world with her suits, who branched out successfully into perfume?

4. Which famous English poet found a lack of sartorial neatness sexy?

5. For what principal innovations is Christian Dior remembered, and who succeeded him as head of the House of Dior?

6. The work of which former torpedo-bomber pilot is instantly recognized by its multicolored printed fabric with geometric or organic patterns?

7. Mary Quant originated a new "look" in the 1960s. What was it called?

8. Which manufacturer started the initials craze?

9. Clothes, particularly T-shirts, with writing and/or pictures on them seem to be a continuing and depressing fad. Which acute observer wrote: "If people don't want to listen to *you*, what makes you think they want to hear from your sweater?"

10. W, the biweekly fashion magazine in newspaper form, labels the overdressed woman as "FV," which stands for what?

Fashion

1. Charles Frederick Worth, founder of Maison Worth in Paris and London, who also dressed the Empress Elizabeth of Austria. The House of Worth still does business in London.

2. Paul Poiret, who dominated French fashions between 1909 and 1914. He was noted for his culottes and made boyishness the vogue. Edward Steichen and Man Ray, a founder of the Dada movement, took their first fashion photographs in his salon.

3. Gabrielle "Coco" Chanel. A noted designer in the mid-1920s, she bounced back in 1954. The Chanel suit was widely imitated, as was her entry into the perfume field with her Chanel No. 5 and later Chanel No. 19 scents.

4. Robert Herrick in "Delight in Disorder" from *Hesperides*:

> A sweet disorder in the dress
> Kindles in clothes a wantonness.

5. The "New Look," which featured narrow shoulders, cinched waist, and a long, wide skirt; and the A-line dress which hid many a flawed figure. Yves Saint-Laurent succeeded him at the age of 21.

6. The Marchese Emilio Pucci, whose outfits invariably bear the signature "Emilio."

7. The mod or Chelsea look which made London the new center of fashion and tied in with the notion of "swinging London."

8. Louis Vuitton, who in 1854 "personalized" his fine luggage with the initials LV intertwined as part of the overall motif of his suitcases, trunks, and other items. The various bags are called "elvees" by the cognoscenti.

9. Fran Lebowitz in *Metropolitan Life*.

10. Fashion Victim, *W*'s tag for a woman who dresses with naïve showiness uncomplicated by good taste.

Fictional Characters

■ ■

1. Who had "a lean and hungry look," according to whom?

2. By which name is Jack Dawkins better known?

3. Who described his heroes as having "guts"—that is, showing "grace under pressure"—and who publicized this phrase that English teachers have since used to summarize the essential message of the author's work?

4. Rudolph Rassendyl, an English gentleman, and the villainous Rupert of Hentzau carried on their adventures in which country?

5. He was a prominent citizen of the midwestern city of Zenith and a vice-president of the Boosters' Club. What was his name?

6. Name the man whose spirit is broken when he reads these lines from Scott's "Lay of the Last Minstrel":

> Breathes there the man, with soul so dead,
> Who never to himself hath said,
> This is my own, my native land!

7. Who packed a Walther PPK in a Berne-Martin holster and smoked Morland cigarettes?

8. Whose mother persisted in preparing her daughter for hypothetical secretarial work and for nonexistent "gentlemen callers"?

9. Who "glittered when he walked" and was further described as follows?

> And who was rich—yes, richer than a king—
> And admirably schooled in every grace:
> In fine we thought that he was everything
> To make us wish that we were in his place.

10. Whose world was peopled with characters such as Sir James Beanquist, Blanche and Hortensia Bavvel, Mrs. Vulpy, Comus Bassington, Waldo Plubley, Mrs. Quarbarl, Ada Spelvexit, Mrs. Thropplestance, and Clovis Sangrail, the Playboy of the Weekend World?

Fictional Characters

1. Cassius in Shakespeare's *Julius Caesar*. Early in the play Caesar expresses his concern:

> Let me have men about me that are fat;
> Sleek-headed men, and such as sleep o'nights;
> Yond' Cassius has a lean and hungry look;
> He thinks too much: such men are dangerous.

2. The Artful Dodger, the impudent young pickpocket in Charles Dickens' *Oliver Twist*.

3. Ernest Hemingway so characterized his heroes to Dorothy Parker in her adoring profile of the author, which appeared in *The New Yorker* in 1929.

4. Ruritania, in Anthony Hope's *The Prisoner of Zenda* and its sequel, *Rupert of Hentzau*.

5. George F. Babbitt in Sinclair Lewis' novel *Babbitt*, a scathing satire of the American Businessman.

6. Philip Nolan, who, in Edward Everett Hale's *The Man Without a Country*, cries out, "Damn the United States. I wish I may never hear of the United States again." For this he is condemned to a life at sea where he is denied any news of his country. He shows gallantry in the War of 1812 and dies during the Civil War after being told on his deathbed of his country's growth to greatness.

7. James Bond, 007, in Ian Fleming's stories.

8. Laura Wingfield, in Tennessee Williams' play *The Glass Menagerie*.

9. Richard Cory, in the poem of the same name by Edward Arlington Robinson, which concludes as follows:

> So on we worked, and waited for the light,
> And went without the meat, and cursed the bread;
> And Richard Cory, one calm summer night,
> Went home and put a bullet through his head.

10. Saki, the pseudonym of Hector Hugh Munro, who was killed in action on the Western Front in 1916.

Fire, Fire!
■ ■

1. When did the superstition about "three on a match" being unlucky arise?

2. What is referred to as "Vulcan's chimney"?

3. Can you describe *ignis fatuus*?

4. Name the author of these lines:

When you are old and grey and full of sleep,
And nodding by the fire, take down this book.

Whom was he imitating, and who in due course imitated him?

5. What is the simple derivation of the word "bonfire"?

6. Where is the "Ring of Fire" to be found?

7. When Ixion, a king of the Lapithae, attempted to seduce Hera and was discovered he said, "Adventures are to the adventurous." What unique punishment did Zeus, Hera's husband, devise for Ixion?

8. Who wrote the following?

Some say the world will end in fire,
Some say in ice.
From what I've tasted of desire
I hold with those who favor fire.
But if I had to perish twice,
I think I know enough of hate
To say that for destruction ice
Is also great
And would suffice.

9. How are Mauna Loa and Moana Kea alike, and how do they differ?

10. What did Richard Brinsley Sheridan say when he ordered a drink as he watched himself being ruined by the burning of his Drury Lane Theatre?

Fire, Fire!

1. During the Boer War. British soldiers believed that lighting three cigarettes on one match would give the enemy snipers ample time to take aim.

2. Mt. Etna on the east coast of Sicily. It is the highest (10,700 feet) active volcano in Europe.

3. *Ignis fatuus* is the phosphorescent light that hovers over swampy ground at night. It is caused by the spontaneous combustion of gases from rotting organic matter and is called "will-o'-the-wisp." It has come to mean something that deludes, a deception.

4. William Butler Yeats, Irish poet and playwright, in "When You Are Old." Yeats was imitating Pierre de Ronsard's *Sonnets pour Hélène*, and then Siegfried Sassoon imitated Yeats in "Base Details."

5. It is from the Middle English *banefyre*, bone-fire, a fire in which heretics were burned at the stake; the bodies of those slain in battle and the ordinary dead were cremated.

6. It is a volcanic belt surrounding the Pacific Ocean where 60 percent of the world's active volcanoes are to be found.

7. Ixion was strapped to a flaming wheel from one of Apollo's sun chariots and flung off by the gods to spin forever in Tartarus, the lowest region of the underworld. As the gods sped him on his way, he cried out, "Adventures are to the adventurous." (During World War II the officers of the British submarine H.M.S. *Upstart* adopted Ixion for their patron as the most brazen of upstarts and most adventurous of the heroes.)

8. Robert Frost, "Fire and Ice."

9. They are both volcanoes on the island of Hawaii. Moana Kea is extinct, Mauna Loa active.

10. "A man may surely be allowed to take a glass of wine by his own fireside."

Flights of Fancy

■■

1. What was the great distinction of Sir George Cayley's coachman?

2. Who missed their landfall at Howland Island in the course of a flight around the world?

3. Which "knife maker" developed what for World War II?

4. Peter Arno once drew a cartoon for *The New Yorker* of an engineer, with his blueprints under his arm and a crazed smile on his face, rubbing his hands and marching away from the scene of a plane crash toward which everyone was running. How did he caption it?

5. In a rare reference to aviation, Shakespeare wrote:

Why, what a peevish fool was that of Crete,
That taught his son the office of a fowl!
And yet, for all his wings, the fool was drowned.

Who uttered these lines, and who was the "peevish fool of Crete"?

6. How does the French aircraft designer Marcel Dassault come by his name?

7. Three men and a bag made aeronautical history in 1978. What did they do?

8. The collaboration of an Armenian and a Jewish engineer produced which aircraft?

9. What of aeronautical interest would you find in the Château de Balleroy, owned by the publisher and sportsman Malcolm Forbes, in Calvados, France?

10. Cole Porter's "A trip to the moon on gossamer wings" was not "just one of those things" for Bryan Allan. But what was *his* thing?

Flights of Fancy

1. In 1853 he made the first manned flight in a fixed-wing glider which was built by his employer, Sir George Cayley, who is recognized as the founder of aerodynamics on the basis of his pioneering experiments and studies of the principles of flight.

2. Amelia Earhart and her navigator, Frederick J. Noonan. Her plane, a Lockheed Electra, was lost in 1937 on a flight from New Guinea to Howland Island, and her fate remains a mystery.

3. The famous fighter designed by Willy Messerschmitt. In German, *Messer* means knife, and *Schmitt* is an old form of *Schmidt*, meaning smith or maker.

4. "Well, back to the old drawing board."

5. In *King Henry VI, Part III*, Richard, Duke of Gloucester, who will become Richard III, speaks sharply of Daedalus who taught his son to fly from Crete on artificial wings when they were detained by King Minos. Icarus did not survive to tell of his first solo.

6. While waiting to be murdered in a German concentration camp, he was rescued by American tanks—*chars d'assault* in French—and later, out of gratitude, he changed his name from Allatini-Bloch to Dassault.

7. Three Americans—Ben Abruzzo, Maxie Anderson, and Larry Newman—became the first to traverse the Atlantic in a balloon, the *Double Eagle II*, now on exhibition at the Smithsonian's National Air and Space Museum in Washington, D.C.

8. The Russian MiG fighters, which were designed by Mikoyan and Gurevich.

9. The most comprehensive collection of ballooning memorabilia from the Montgolfiers until today. Each June the International Invitational Balloon Meet sponsored by *Forbes* magazine is held there.

10. In 1979, he pedaled a flying machine in the first crossing of the English Channel by a man-powered plane. The *Gossamer Albatross*, a 75-pound triumph of technology and engineering with a 96-foot wingspread, made a crossing from Folkestone to Cap Gris-Nez in 2 hours and 49 minutes. It can be seen at The American Museum of Natural History in New York City.

Flowers

■■

1. A Latin word, borrowed from the Greek for star, will give you the name of which flower with white, pink, and purple blossoms?

2. What did the Fylemans find at the bottom of their garden?

3. Who makes "The Run for the Roses"?

4. Which British poet saw the following?

> A violet by a mossy stone
> Half hidden from the eye!

5. What did Lancelot Brown and André Le Nôtre have in common?

6. It was Dorothy Parker's luck to receive what?

7. The name of the lovely cowslip, a primrose or marsh marigold with fragrant yellow flowers, has what rather down-to-earth derivation?

8. Where were tulips first cultivated, and what does the word mean?

9. In which play, and later a motion picture, did this line become famous: "The calla lilies are in bloom again—such a strange flower, suitable to any occasion"?

10. What is the floral emblem of the imperial family of Japan?

Flowers

1. Aster.
2. "There are fairies at the bottom of our garden," wrote Rose Fyleman in her poem "The Fairies."
3. The horses in the Kentucky Derby, held each May at Churchill Downs, Kentucky.
4. William Wordsworth in "Lucy: She Dwelt Among the Untrodden Ways."
5. They were both distinguished landscape architects. Lancelot Brown laid out the grounds of Blenheim Palace, and André Le Nôtre created the gardens at Versailles. The former was called Capability Brown because he was reputed to say, when consulted on the landscaping of an estate, that it "had capabilities."
6. One perfect rose. As she put it in her poem of the same name:

> Why is it no one ever sent me yet
> One perfect limousine, do you suppose?
> Ah no, it's always just my luck to get
> One perfect rose.

7. It comes from the Old English *cuslyppe,* meaning "cow dung," or "meadow muffin," near which the cowslip flourishes.
8. Turkey, whence they were introduced to Holland. In the 17th century wild speculation on tulip bulbs was called "tulipomania." The name derives from the Turkish *tūlibend,* turban, for the plant's turban-shaped flower.
9. *Stage Door,* by Edna Ferber and George S. Kaufman.
10. The chrysanthemum. According to legend, a Japanese girl was told her future husband would live as many years as a flower has petals. Dividing each petal of a carnation into many sections, she produced the chrysanthemum. The word derives from the Greek *chrysos,* gold, and *anthemon,* flower.

Food

■■

1. What have been called "the grey diamonds of Pie-monte"?

2. Hushpuppies are fried cornmeal fritters commonly eaten in the South. How did the name arise?

3. What do biscuits and zwieback have in common?

4. With which historic event are croissants associated?

5. One recipe for which superb soup starts with the injunction: "First, you take a leek."?

6. Is it true that Charles II, in a festive mood while enjoying a great roast at Christmas dinner, knighted the loin of beef and titled it Sir Loin?

7. Who is the author of the following lines?

> . . . he from forth the closet brought a heap
> Of candied apple, quince, and plum, and gourd,
> With jellies smoother than the creamy curd,
> And lucent syrops, tinct with cinnamon;
> Manna and dates, in argosy transferr'd
> From Fez; and spiced dainties, every one
> From silken Samarcand to cedar'd Lebanon.

8. What is the origin of the term *macédoine*, referring to fruits or vegetables that have been cut into small pieces and served as an appetizer, salad, or dessert?

9. Name the only fictional detective to have a cookbook written in his name.

10. Which robber baron was responsible for potato chips?

Food

1. White truffles, which have been found nowhere else in the world except in this northwestern region of Italy, where they are located with the aid of truffle hounds.

2. Because at outdoor fish fries they were thrown to silence the whining and barking dogs, and the cook shouted, "Hush puppies!"

3. They are both twice cooked. The prefixes *bis* and *zwie* mean twice in French and German. The practice arose during the sailing era when fresh breads would rapidly go bad.

4. In 1683, some Viennese bakers working through the night heard the Turks, who were besieging the city, tunneling underground. The Austrian guards were alerted and the Turks repulsed. For this the Holy Roman Emperor Leopold I rewarded the bakers by giving them the privilege of making rolls in the shape of a crescent, the symbol on the Ottoman flag.

5. Vichyssoise, a leek and potato soup served chilled and topped with chopped chives. This soup is not French; it was first prepared in 1917 by Louis Diat, chef at the old Ritz-Carlton Hotel in New York, to reduce a surplus stock of potatoes, for which the Allier valley around Vichy is famous. (During the days of the German-controlled Vichy government, some restaurants changed this soup's name to DeGaulloise.)

6. No, this tale is of doubtful authenticity. The word derives from Old English surlonge: *sur*, above, plus *longe*, low.

7. John Keats in "The Eve of St. Agnes."

8. It is a French word suggesting Macedonia's mixture of nationalities, chopped up by a long history of border realignment.

9. Nero Wolfe. The description of the dishes he enjoyed so intrigued readers that his creator Rex Stout was persuaded to write a cookbook for them.

10. Commodore Cornelius Vanderbilt. In 1853, when he was dining at Moon's Lake House Restaurant in Saratoga Springs, New York, he complained about the thickness of the fried potatoes. The chef, George Crum, obliged by cutting them paper-thin, and potato chips were born. They were originally called Saratoga chips.

Gallimaufry

■ ■

1. Harold Ross, founder and editor of *The New Yorker*, kept the faintest off-color references out of the magazine. But he did allow one exception, a cartoon innocently titled "News." What was the subject?

2. What is the most popular given name in the world?

3. For two decades following Caesar's assassination, his great-nephew and adopted son Octavian was a dominant figure in Roman politics until in 27 B.C. Augustus was acclaimed unquestioned first citizen of the Roman state. What relation was Octavian to Augustus?

4. What did Finn McCool, the legendary Irish hero, allegedly build so that he could fight his Scottish foes, and where is it? What is it actually?

5. The morning star is a planet, most usually Venus, visible in the east just before sunrise. What else is called a morning star?

6. Which future Poet Laureate evoked the days of ancient commerce in these lines?

> Quinquireme of Nineveh, from distant Ophir
> Rowing home to haven in sunny Palestine,
> With a cargo of ivory,
> And apes and peacocks,
> Sandalwood, cedarwood, and sweet white wine.

7. The French laugh at Ouagadougou but solemnly bow to Pompidou. Who or what is Ouagadougou?

8. Define an oxymoron, and give an example of one.

9. Which American Indian succeeded in toppling an empire?

10. On seeing the Great White Way of Broadway for the first time, in 1921, who said, "What a glorious garden of wonders this would be to anyone who was lucky enough not to be able to read."?

Gallimaufry

1. A dog being sprayed by a defective fire hydrant.
2. Mohammed.
3. They were the same person. In 27 B.C. Octavian was given the title Augustus by which he was known thereafter.
4. The Giant's Causeway, which is located on the northern coast of County Antrim in Northern Ireland. It is a natural formation consisting of thousands of basaltic columns of volcanic origin.
5. In medieval warfare it was a spiked iron ball on the end of a chain used in hand-to-hand combat.
6. John Masefield in his poem "Cargoes," the last verse of which is in startling contrast to the first:

> Dirty British coaster with a salt-caked smokestack,
> Butting through the Channel in the mad March days,
> With a cargo of Tyne coal,
> Road-rail, pig-lead,
> Firewood, iron-ware, and cheap tin trays.

7. It is the capital of Upper Volta, a former French colony in West Africa.
8. Taken from a Greek word meaning "pointedly foolish," an oxymoron is a figure of speech in which an epigrammatic effect is created by the conjunction of incongruous or contradictory terms—for example, "a mournful optimist" or "a dashing Swiss officer."
9. Benito Juárez, first Indian President of Mexico, who was driven from Mexico City by a French army which installed the Austrian Emperor Franz Josef's brother Maximilian as Emperor of Mexico. Juárez, however, maintained a determined resistance with U.S. support, and Maximilian was overthrown and executed. (The Italian fascist dictator Benito Mussolini was named after Juárez.)
10. Gilbert Keith Chesterton, the English author, who has been called "the prince of paradox."

Games and Pastimes
■ ■

1. In which game do you "squidge" and "squop"?
2. What is the meaning of the term *manque* in roulette?
3. Who first said that the game was afoot?
4. Why is the nine of diamonds referred to as "the curse of Scotland"?
5. The word "checkmate" as used in chess seems to make little sense, but in its Arabic original, it makes a lot. What are the Arabic words?
6. To what art in which game does "the beaver" add a refinement?
7. Who attributed to another poker player "the calm confidence of a Christian holding four aces"?
8. Which pie company was responsible for a national craze?
9. What is the most popular pastime among adult males in Japan, and what is its American counterpart?
10. What apposite comment did the widely syndicated columnist Suzy Knickerbocker make about backgammon?

Games and Pastimes

1. Tiddlywinks, in which the players try to snap small disks into a cup with a larger disk.

2. *Manque* is any number between one and eighteen. (*Passe* is between nineteen and thirty-six.)

3. Not Sherlock Holmes but Shakespeare, who uses it in both *King Henry IV, Part I* and in *King Henry V*, where Harry makes it famous:

> The game's afoot:
> Follow your spirit; and, upon this charge
> Cry "God for Harry! England and St. George!"

4. This phrase originated in Scotland in 1746, when the English under the Duke of Cumberland defeated the Jacobite forces under Prince Charles Edward Stuart, who was popularly known as Bonnie Prince Charlie. According to legend, the duke wrote the order for the massacre of prisoners and wounded on the back of a nine of diamonds.

5. *Shàh màt*, which means "the king is dead." The word *shah* was indeed borrowed from the Persian, but the phrase itself is Arabic.

6. The art of doubling in backgammon. When you are doubled, the beaver rule enables you to redouble before your opponent rolls and still keep the doubling cube on your side. The beaver works to your advantage when you have been doubled in what you think is an even match or one where you have the edge.

7. Mark Twain.

8. The Frisbie Pie Company of Bridgeport, Connecticut, which went out of business in 1957. Their pie tins were first used by Yale students for playing catch in the 1950s. (The name of the skimmer was deliberately altered to Frisbee for trademark reasons.)

9. *Pachinko*, the American equivalent of which is the pinball machine.

10. "It's a great game, but all the wrong people are playing it."

Gemstones

■■

1. What are the only two distinct precious stones to have an identical chemical composition?

2. Name the four Cs which determine the value of diamonds.

3. The name for what gemstone originates from an ancient Spanish belief that it could exercise miraculous curative powers on kidney or urinary disorders?

4. Describe the principle behind the making of cultured pearls. What proportion of the total pearl trade do they account for?

5. Which famous gem, supposed to bring tragedy to the lives of those who owned or wore it, inspired this description: "A tiny fragment of midnight sky, fallen to earth and still aglow with star-gleam . . ."?

6. Do you know the name of the stone that is generally red inside, has a green "skin," and is sometimes called "watermelon"?

7. In her first movie, *Night After Night*, when Mae West walks into George Raft's fashionable clip joint, the checkroom girl takes one look at all the jewels she is wearing and exclaims, "Goodness, what beautiful diamonds!" What is Mae West's response?

8. Who named and popularized the gemstone known as tanzanite?

9. In which country are the world's finest emeralds found? What is the name for the blue-green semiprecious variety of the same mineral that forms emerald?

10. Where would you have to go to see the largest cut diamond in the world?

Gemstones

1. Rubies and sapphires. They are both forms of corundum, which is an aluminum oxide $(Al_2 O_3)$.

2. Carat weight, cut, clarity, and color.

3. Jade, which was originally called *piedra de ijada*, or "stone of the loins."

4. The pearl is produced by inserting a precut bead into the mollusk. Cultured pearls, which must always be labeled as such, account for 90 per cent of the trade.

5. The Hope Diamond, a 45½-carat stone of deep blue, one of the rarest of diamond colors and once described as "indignant indigo." In 1958 it was given by the noted New York jeweler Harry Winston to the Smithsonian's National Museum of Natural History, where it can be seen in the Hall of Gems.

6. Tourmaline.

7. "Goodness had nothing to do with it, dearie." She later used the line as the title of her autobiography.

8. Henry B. Platt, vice-chairman of Tiffany and Company, who called it after the then newly named country of Tanzania, a union of Tanganyika (where the stones are found) and Zanzibar. Tanzanite has an unusual amethyst-violet to sapphire-blue color and is actually a hydrated variety of zoisite.

9. Colombia in South America. The aquamarine, which is a transparent beryl.

10. To the Jewel House in the Tower of London, where the Crown Jewels of England are displayed in all their majesty and splendor. There in the royal sceptre is the pear-shaped brilliant known as the Star of Africa, of 530 carats, which was split from the famed Cullinan stone weighing an unbelievable 3,106 carats. This was discovered in South Africa and presented to King Edward VII on his birthday in 1907 by the Transvaal Government as a gesture of reconciliation; the Transvaal had been conquered only five years before. The second star of Africa, also cut from the Cullinan and weighing 317 carats, may be seen in the Imperial State Crown, which the Sovereign wears on leaving Westminster Abbey after the coronation ceremony and on all subsequent state occasions. (The St. Edward's Crown is worn by the Sovereign only once, at the moment of coronation.)

Golf and Tennis

■ ■

1. The *tuitje* played an important part in the beginnings of which game?

2. The numerical scoring in tennis proceeds 15, 30, 40. Why were these numbers first established?

3. Why did James II of Scotland attempt to delay the development of golf?

4. What is the origin of the tennis term "deuce"?

5. The Grand Slam of golf today involves winning the U.S. Open, the Masters, the P.G.A. Championships, and the British Open in a single year—a feat no golfer has ever accomplished. Four players, however, have captured the four titles in different years. Who are they?

6. What was the famed Impressionist museum of Paris, *Le Jeu de Paume*, originally used for?

7. Who was the first player to win two Masters in consecutive years and then fail to make the cut in the following year?

8. Which tournaments constitute the Grand Slam of tennis?

9. What is perhaps the most famous shot ever made at the Masters Tournament, which is held during the first full week in April at the Augusta National Golf Club in Georgia?

10. What feat did "tall trees by still waters" repeat in 1980?

Golf and Tennis

1. Golf. *Tuitje* (pronounced "toy*tee*") was the Dutch word for the small mound on which the ball was placed for driving. In those days the game was called *Het Kolven* and the hole a *put*.

2. The original scoring was based on a familiar number system that had a base of 60—for example, 60 seconds in a minute and 60 minutes in an hour. A game went to 60 points and was divided in four parts—15, 30, 45, 60. Today's 40 is simply an abbreviation of the original 45, and 60 has become "game."

3. Alarmed at the neglect of archery which he deemed necessary for defense, James II in 1457 issued a decree that "golfe be utterly cryed down and not be used."

4. It is a corruption of the French *à deux*, which meant that a player tied with his opponent at 45 had to win two consecutive points for the game.

5. Gene Sarazen, Ben Hogan, Gary Player, and Jack Nicklaus. In 1953 Hogan won three, being unable to enter the P.G.A. because its timing conflicted with that of the British Open, and is the one golfer to manage even that.

6. It was a tennis court. The early game was played without racquets; *jeu de paume* means simply "hand game."

7. Jack Nicklaus, who won it in 1965 and 1966. After failing to make the cut in 1967, he won it again in 1972. Nicklaus is the only player to have won five Masters.

8. Wimbledon, and the U.S., French, and Australian Opens.

9. Gene Sarazen's spectacular double eagle on the par-5 fifteenth hole in the last round of the 1935 Masters. By making par on the next three holes, he tied Craig Wood for first place. Sarazen then went on to win in the play-off.

10. Evonne Goolagong Cawley won the women's singles championship at Wimbledon, a feat she last accomplished in 1971. The name Goolagong means "tall trees by still waters" in an aboriginal language of her native Australia.

Government

■ ■

1. The name for which type of legislator is derived from the Latin word for old man?

2. What effect did an attempt to blow up the English Houses of Parliament have on American slang?

3. Which right is given to a government to take private property for public use, with compensation to the owner?

4. "The only thing necessary for the triumph of evil is for good men to do nothing." Who wrote this defense of the party system?

5. Who said: "I don't make jokes. I just watch the government and report the facts."?

6. Where would you find the Seym, the Oireachtas, the Storting, the Althing, and the Eduskunta?

7. Which English novelist described Parliament as "the houses of Parler and Mentir," the places of wordiness and lies?

8. Who is the only man to serve as Chief Justice of the United States as well as President?

9. Which part of the U.S. Constitution appears to contradict itself?

10. Two politicians described the job of Vice President of the United States as "inside work with no heavy lifting" and "not worth a pitcher of warm spit"? Can you identify them?

Government

1. A senator. *Senex* is Latin for "old man."

2. The failure of Guy Fawkes' Gunpowder Plot in 1605 is still celebrated on its anniversary, November 5, with fireworks and the burning of effigies called Guys. From this the word guy became a term for any male.

3. The right of eminent domain.

4. We do not know; though it has always been attributed to Edmund Burke, the British statesman and political philosopher, it has never been found among his writings. Similar but less telling passages have, and this appears to be an example of anonymous talent improving on known genius.

5. Will Rogers, American humorist.

6. They are the parliaments of Poland, Ireland, Norway, Iceland, and Finland respectively.

7. Charles Dickens, writing in the magazine *Household Words*.

8. William Howard Taft, who also had the distinction of being the largest U.S. President and Chief Justice.

9. In the 25th Amendment, providing for the succession to the Presidency, Section IV refers in Paragraph i to ". . . the principal officers of the executive departments . . ." and in Paragraph ii to ". . . the principal officers of the executive department . . ." Clearly the art of proofreading is a fading one, even at the highest levels.

10. Respectively, Senator Robert Dole, Republican candidate for Vice President in 1976, and John Nance Garner, Vice President for Franklin D. Roosevelt's first two terms (1933–41).

Graffiti

■■

Graffiti, which have been called the scrawl of the wild, have been with us at least since A.D. 79 when Pompeii, Herculaneum, and Stabiae were buried under cinders, ashes, and mud. Even Byron contributed by carving his name on the Temple of Poseidon on Cape Sounion in Greece. In Norman Mailer's opinion, "Some of the best prose in America is [sic] graffiti found on men's room walls"; judging from the level of much American prose, this observation may not be far off the mark. While graffiti are generally blatant vandalism and an affront to the eye, some evince a certain dark, grim humor. The following examples have provoked what responses?

1. Do not write on walls!

2. T. S. Elliot loves D. H. Lawrence.

3. Nietzsche is pietsche.

4. The meek shall inherit the earth.

5. Jesus saves.

6. My mother made me a homosexual.

7. Masturbation is habit-forming.

8. Legalize mental telepathy.

9. I love grils.

10. *Prière de ne pas jeter les mégots de cigarettes dans le pissoir*. (Please do not throw cigarette ends in the urinal.)

Graffiti

1. You want we should type maybe?

2. Eliot is spelled with one l, you ass.

3. But Sartre is smarter.

4. If that's OK with the rest of you.

5. Moses invests, but only Buddha pays dividends.

6. If I give her the wool, will she make me one?

7. Now he tells me.

8. I knew you were going to say that.

9. You mean girls, stupid!
   (and underneath)
   What about us grils?

10. *Ils seront trempés et difficiles à allumer.** (They get soggy and hard to light.)

*This addition to the notice in the men's room of "The Travellers" in Paris has been attributed to Alfred Duff Cooper, former British Ambassador to France.

Great Britain

■ ■

1. What has been described as "this extraordinary stone memory of the past—there is no other place in Europe where so much of history survives unbroken, unruined, unchanged, hauntingly evocative of passing time"?

2. According to the reassertion of Scottish independence, drawn up at Arbroath in 1320, from which area of the world do the Scots come?

3. Where was the last pitched ground battle in Great Britain?

4. Which famous part of London arrived at the docks in Long Beach, California, and was classified by the U.S. Customs as "a large antique"?

5. Why are there two stone slabs of different sizes at the curb outside the Athenaeum Club in London?

6. Caledonia is the poetic name for Scotland, but few Scots know whence it comes. Do you?

7. The infamous Tyburn Tree, which was in reality a three-legged structure with stands for spectators erected around it, was the gallows where prisoners from the jails of the county of Middlesex and the City of London were publicly hanged for nearly 600 years. Where in London did it stand?

8. How did London's Covent Garden get its name? What was its function until the recent past, and what has it now become?

9. Where in Great Britain is to be seen one of the most enormous examples of virility in the world?

10. Give the American equivalent of these British words and phrases.

a) Naught
b) Never-never
c) First floor
d) Crisps
e) Bespoke
f) Subway
g) Off-license
h) Table a motion
i) Chips
j) Short and curlies

Great Britain

1. The Tower of London, an ancient fortress perhaps of Roman origin, and certainly a stronghold for 900 continuous years. Once a royal residence, later a jail for state prisoners, it is now an arsenal, and the repository of the Crown Jewels.

2. Scythia, an ancient region of Eurasia north of the Black Sea, whence they arrived in Scotland by way of Spain.

3. The Battle of Culloden in 1746, on a large stretch of rough, upland country known as Drummossie Moor near Inverness in northeast Scotland, where the forces of George II under his son the Duke of Cumberland routed the Jacobites—Highlanders and Irish—under Prince Charles Edward Stuart (Bonnie Prince Charlie), ending the Jacobite "Rising of the 'Forty-five."

4. London Bridge, which was sold to American promoters and was re-erected in 1968 over a channel of Lake Havasu in Arizona. It is perhaps apocryphal that the promoters thought they were buying the far more colorful Tower Bridge, which still stands in London.

5. They were put there at the request of the Duke of Wellington so he could mount his horse easily.

6. It is the Roman name for part of Northern Britain, now associated with the Scottish Highlands or Scotland in general. The name was used by the Latin poet Lucan in the 1st century A.D.

7. A plaque, set in the roadway, where Oxford Street becomes the Bayswater Road at Marble Arch, marks the site.

8. The land was once a convent garden. With the dissolution of the monasteries by Henry VIII the property was given to the 1st Earl of Bedford. (The 5th Earl became a Duke in 1694.) Formerly the produce center for London, Covent Garden has now been transformed into a cluster of small, often expensive, shops and restaurants.

9. Outside the Dorset village of Cerne Abbas the Cerne Giant, carved into the underlying chalk and possibly dating from the Roman occupation, exhibits a huge erect phallus. The brush around it is trimmed regularly by the villagers.

10. a) Zero
b) Installment plan
c) Second floor
d) Potato chips
e) Made to order
f) Pedestrian underpass
g) Liquor store
h) Bring up for discussion
i) French fried potatoes
j) Short hairs

High and Low

■ ■

1. What is the highest civilian award that a United States citizen can receive?

2. Who occupied the highest position in the British Empire ever held by someone born a U.S. citizen?

3. Name the tallest bird that ever existed.

4. Which literary classic was subtitled *A Tale of Life Among the Lowly*?

5. Who is compared to the following?

> A Waldorf salad, a Berlin ballad,
> A Ritz hot toddy, a Brewster body,
> A Bendel bonnet, a Shakespeare sonnet,
> The National Gallery, Garbo's salary.

6. Which breed of horse is closest to the ground?

7. Who defined a highbrow as "the kind of person who looks at a sausage and thinks of Picasso"?

8. Where would you find Bottom, and The Bottom?

9. Whom did the playwright Christopher Marlowe make Doctor Faustus hold responsible for burning "the topless towers of Ilium"?

10. How did the Belgian physicist, Professor August Piccard, have it both ways, high and low?

High and Low

1. The Presidential Medal of Freedom, which was established in 1963 by President John F. Kennedy to continue and expand presidential recognition of meritorious service, and which, since 1945, had been granted as the Medal of Freedom.

2. Lady Curzon, Vicereine of India as the wife of the Viceroy, Lord Curzon of Kedleston. She was born Mary Victoria Leiter in Chicago, daughter of Levi Leiter, an early partner of Marshall Field.

3. The wingless moa, related to the ostrich, which was 13 feet tall. Native to New Zealand, it became extinct 400 years ago.

4. *Uncle Tom's Cabin*, a novel by Harriet Beecher Stowe. An instant best seller when it was published in 1852, it had a powerful antislavery influence.

5. You, because "You're the Top," Cole Porter's smash hit from his 1934 musical comedy *Anything Goes*.

6. The Falabella, which was developed over a period of 45 years by crossing a group of undersized English thoroughbreds with Shetland ponies. Falabellas stand about 30 inches at the shoulder. The upper limit accepted by the American Miniature Horse Breeders' Association is 34 inches.

7. A. P. Herbert, English author and member of parliament.

8. Bottom is a bewitched and bewitching weaver in Shakespeare's *A Midsummer Night's Dream*. The Bottom, located in the crater of an extinct volcano, is the chief settlement of the Dutch Leeward Island of Saba. (To the Dutch and the natives the islands of Sint Maarten, Saint Eustatius, also called Statia, and Saba are known as the Netherlands Antilles Windward Islands.)

9. Helen, one of the most beautiful of women in Greek mythology, who was married to Menelaus, King of Sparta. Her abduction by Paris, a Trojan prince, precipitated the Trojan War and the destruction of Troy, which is also known by the more poetic names of Ilium or Ilion.

10. He is known for his balloon ascents into the stratosphere and his dives into the ocean depths in a bathyscaphe of his own design.

Hills and Mountains

■■

1. Three mountains—Nebo, Sinai, and Pisgah—were the settings for important events in the life of Moses. What happened on each?

2. Why is the name of Edward Whymper remembered in the annals of Alpine pioneering?

3. Which unusual gift did Queen Elizabeth II receive on her Coronation Day?

4. Who uttered the following lines?

> Night's candles are burnt out, and jocund day
> Stands tiptoe on the misty mountain-tops.

5. What were Sir Henry Curtis, Commander Goode, R.N. (Ret.), Allan Quartermain, and Umbopa seeking when they traveled over the mountains known as "Sheba's Breasts"?

6. How did the English writer Gilbert Keith Chesterton, a gentleman of goodly girth, invoke the 121st Psalm when asked if he would like to go mountain climbing?

7. Who was known as the "Grand Old Tramp of the Sierras"?

8. Beverly Johnson was the first woman to complete a solo climb of the El Capitan peak in Yosemite National Park. What was the comment of one observer on her reason for making the climb?

9. Which classical scholar wrote these verses?

> Into my heart on air that kills
>   From yon far country blows:
> What are those blue remembered hills,
>   What spires, what farms are those?
>
> That is the land of lost content,
>   I see it shining plain,
> The happy highways where I went
>   And cannot come again.

10. Give the literal English meaning of Grand Tetons, the name of a range of the Rocky Mountains in southeastern Idaho and northwestern Wyoming, which were named by the French.

Hills and Mountains

1. Moses viewed the Promised Land from Mt. Nebo, received the Ten Commandments on Mt. Sinai, and went to Mt. Pisgah to die in sight of the Promised Land.

2. In 1865, Edward Whymper, an English illustrator, led the first party to scale the Matterhorn, or Mont Cervin (Mount of the Horn) as it is called in French. A small museum commemorating this event may be seen today in Zermatt. The descent was marred by an accident when a frayed rope caused the death of four in the party of seven. In the past century, the Matterhorn has claimed more climbers' lives than any other mountain. Since Whymper's ascent, which he described in his book *Scrambles Amongst the Alps*, more than 125,000 people have climbed the Matterhorn via the relatively easy Hörnli ridge.

3. News of the conquest of Mount Everest by Edmund Hillary and his Sherpa guide Tenzing Norkay. After the climb Hillary said, "We've done the bitch!" He was later knighted for his exploit.

4. Romeo in Shakespeare's *Romeo and Juliet*.

5. King Solomon's mines, in the book of the same title by H. Rider Haggard.

6. He replied, "I will lift up mine eyes unto the hills, but I will not lift up my body thither."

7. John Muir, the Scottish-born American naturalist, who was famed as a conservationist and crusader for national parks and reservations. Muir Glacier in Alaska is named after him.

8. "She wanted something sheer next to her skin."

9. A. E. Housman, a poet noted for economy of words and directness of thought, in *A Shropshire Lad*.

10. The name is an American simplification of the spelling and pronunciation of "big tits" in French.

Hodge and Podge

■ ■

1. What seems to be the principal reason for the Sybarites, ancient inhabitants of a city in Sicily, acquiring such a reputation for decadent luxury that they became proverbial?

2. Which renowned motorist was thrown into "the remotest dungeon of the best-guarded keep of the stoutest castle in all the breadth of Merrie England" and escaped dressed as a washerwoman?

3. Give the origin of the slightly contemptuous phrase "son of a gun."

4. Who, in a letter to H. G. Wells, coined the phrase "the bitch-goddess SUCCESS"?

5. What connection is there between Lady Chatterley and Snoopy in the "Peanuts" comic strip?

6. Which thoroughfare is indirectly named after the starched ruffs fashionable at court in the days of James I?

7. Who wrote: "You see things, and you say 'Why?' But I dream things that never were, and I say 'Why not?'"?

8. How did it arise that one class at West Point was 50 percent Jewish?

9. In *Candide*, Voltaire noted that from time to time the British find it desirable to shoot an admiral *"pour encourager les autres"* (to put heart into the others). Name two British admirals who were shot on quarterdecks.

10. The novelist Michael Arlen was born Dickran Kuyumjian and called "a case of pernicious Armenia." What was the epitaph he proposed for himself?

Hodge and Podge

1. They invented the chamber pot.

2. Mr. Toad in Kenneth Grahame's *The Wind in the Willows*.

3. It dates back to the time when shore women were allowed on training vessels and warships. In the latter case their hammocks were slung on the gun decks, and a boy born there was called "a son of a gun." In some instances a gun was fired to speed a difficult delivery.

4. The American philosopher William James, who wrote, "The moral flabbiness born of the exclusive worship of the bitch-goddess SUCCESS. That—with the squalid cash interpretation put on the word success—is our national disease."

5. Her creator, D. H. Lawrence, was married to Frieda von Richtofen, a cousin of the Red Baron.

6. London's Piccadilly, which is named after Piccadilly House, the home of a tailor, Robert Baker, who made a fortune from the sale of these ruffs, or pickadill collars as they were known.

7. George Bernard Shaw, in his play *Back to Methuselah*, puts these words into the mouth of the serpent addressing Adam and Eve. Robert F. Kennedy later used the epigram in his campaign for the Presidential nomination.

8. The first class at West Point, in 1802, had only two members—Joseph Goodman Swift and Simon Magruder Levy.

9. Byng and Nelson. Admiral Byng was executed on the quarterdeck of the *Monarque* in 1757 on a charge of neglect of duty arising from his inaction and retreat when ordered to relieve the French siege of Minorca. (He had protested at the prospect of being shot on the foredeck, as a bad precedent for executing admirals in the future.) Admiral Nelson, who insisted on wearing all his decorations into battle, provided an inviting target to a French musketeer perched in the fighting top of a French ship and was shot during the Battle of Trafalgar. He died below-decks shortly after.

10. "Here lies Michael Arlen, as usual."

Horse Sense

■ ■

1. Which breed of American light-harness horse descends from a single progenitor?

2. Marengo and Copenhagen were ridden by which commanding figures on what historic occasion? Why were they so named?

3. The famed relay mail service known as the pony express, where riders changed horses every 10 to 15 miles, operated between which two points? For how many years did the service last?

4. What was the name of the only horse to defeat the legendary Man O'War?

5. Name the famous young knight who came out of the West riding a remarkably fine horse.

6. Where do the famous Lipizzaner stallions execute the intricate maneuvers of an equestrian art perfected in Greece around 400 B.C.?

7. Harness racing features two differently gaited horses—pacers and trotters. Explain the difference between their gaits.

8. Who first wrote, "For want of a nail the shoe is lost, for want of a shoe the horse is lost, for want of a horse the rider is lost."?

9. In which equine activity are these French dancing terms used—*lavade, capriole,* and *courbette*?

10. Which was the only horse in the history of Saratoga racing to win two $100,000 stakes races at the same meeting?

Horse Sense

1. The Morgan horse, which is descended from a stallion named in memory of its first owner. Morgan horses are used as all-purpose light horses, and are very popular on cattle ranches for their agility, strength, and intelligence.

2. Napoleon and Wellington at the Battle of Waterloo in 1815. Marengo was named after Napoleon's victory in Italy in 1800, and Copenhagen was so called because Wellington had commanded land forces on an expedition to Denmark in 1807.

3. Between St. Joseph, Missouri, the western end of the telegraph line, and Sacramento, California. The service began in April 1860, but in October 1861 the first telegram was transmitted to San Francisco. The pony express was gradually discontinued, having lasted about two years.

4. An appropriately named horse called Upset in the Sanford Memorial Stakes at Saratoga in 1919.

5. Lochinvar in Sir Walter Scott's song of that title from his long poetic work *Marmion*:

> Oh, young Lochinvar is come out of the West,
> Through all the wide Border his steed was the best.

6. At the Spanish Riding School, which is housed in the baroque riding hall of the Imperial Palace in Vienna.

7. Pacers are laterally gaited: they bring the right front and right hind legs forward in unison, and move with a swaying motion. Trotters are diagonally gaited: they bring the right front and left rear legs forward at the same time, and move with a high-stepping, straight-ahead gait.

8. George Herbert, the English metaphysical poet, in *Jacula Prudentum*. Writing on the subject of neglect, Benjamin Franklin imitated Herbert in *Poor Richard's Almanack*.

9. *Haute école*, or "Airs above the ground," an advanced form of dressage in which the horse is guided through a series of complex movements of the hands, legs, and weight.

10. The splendidly named New York-bred "Quintessential," owned by Dr. Charles Pettigrow, trained by John Campo, and ridden by Frank Lovato, Jr., in 1980. (Johnny Campo also trained Pleasant Colony, who in 1981 won the Kentucky Derby and the Preakness but came in third in the Belmont Stakes, misssing his chance for the Triple Crown.)

Hotels and Inns
■ ■

1. In the Middle Ages which association provided a hostel at Jerusalem for the reception of pilgrims to the Holy Land?

2. What is a ryokan?

3. At which inn did Billy Bones take lodging and receive the "black spot" from Blind Pew?

4. What notice was posted in the dining room of a leading hotel in Colombo, Sri Lanka, after a typhoid scare?

5. Name the *grande luxe* hotel that was known as the Mivart, after a French chef who founded it in 1815, until it was taken over in 1838 by a former butler, who gave it his name.

6. Where did George Washington bid farewell to his officers in 1783?

7. Who was the proprietress of a famous if slightly raffish London hotel that had all the charm of an English country house? She has been immortalized in a novel by Evelyn Waugh, biographies by Daphne Fielding and Anthony Masters, and a British television series.

8. Which hotel, originally built as a palace for a maharajah, sits on an island in the middle of a lake in the old town of Udaipur in India?

9. What stood on the site of New York's Empire State Building, which is also known as "the house that Al built" for Alfred E. Smith, its first president?

10. Where in Paris did Oscar Wilde find himself "dying beyond my means" in 1900?

Hotels and Inns

1. The Knights Hospitallers of St. John of Jerusalem, also called Knights of St. John, Knights of Rhodes, and, later, Knights of Malta.

2. A traditional Japanese inn, a beautiful reminder of Imperial Japan.

3. The Admiral Benbow Inn, which was kept by the parents of Jim Hawkins, the hero of Robert Louis Stevenson's *Treasure Island*. (John Benbow was an English admiral who died after a naval engagement with the French in 1702.)

4. "All vegetables in this establishment have been washed in water specially passed by the manager."

5. Claridge's, on Brook Street, in London's Mayfair.

6. At Fraunces Tavern at the corner of Broad and Pearl Streets in lower Manhattan. This landmark is still standing, though bombed by Puerto Rican terrorists, and contains a restaurant and a George Washington museum.

7. The "unconquerable Cockney," Rosa Lewis, a former cook and reputed mistress of Edward VII, who owned and ran the Cavendish Hotel on the corner of Jermyn and Duke Streets. In Waugh's *Vile Bodies*, Rosa appears as Lottie Crump and the hotel as Shepherd's. In the TV series *The Duchess of Duke Street* she is Louisa Trotter and the hotel the Bentinck. (Cavendish-Bentinck is the family name of the Dukes of Portland.) The new Cavendish Hotel which stands on the same site bears no resemblance to the original, although a nod to Rosa Lewis' memory is made by naming the bar Sub Rosa.

8. The Lake Palace Hotel, one of the truly unique hospices of the world. Udaipur is about halfway between New Delhi and Bombay.

9. The old Waldorf-Astoria Hotel.

10. At the Hôtel Alsace on the Left Bank rue des Beaux-Arts, an establishment now known simply as L'Hôtel.

House and Home

■ ■

1. Which lofty room in a house has a classical origin?

2. Who displayed in her living room a pillow embroidered with the words, "If you can't say something good about someone, sit right here by me"?

3. What is the purpose of the widow's walk, the railed rooftop gallery seen on many early American houses?

4. Who defined home as follows:

Home is the place where, when you have to go there,
They have to take you in.

5. What was Joe E. Lewis' comment on the song "Home on the Range"?

6. Some old castles in France had a room called an *oubliette*. What precisely was it?

7. Dorothy Parker's apartment in New York was hardly pretentious, but, according to her, all she needed was enough space to do what?

8. In certain vast intellectual wastelands of the United States a popular item of patio furniture is known as a chaise lounge. What is the correct term?

9. Of whose poem are these lines by Ogden Nash titled "A Heap o' Livin'" a parody?

But meanwhile I ask you to believe that
It takes a heap of other things besides
A heap o' livin' to make a home out of a house,
To begin with it takes a heap o' payin'.

10. Why does the much-married Zsa Zsa Gabor claim to be a marvelous housekeeper?

House and Home

1. The attic, originally called the Attic story, with square columns in a style characteristic of ancient Attica, of which Athens was the metropolis.

2. Alice Roosevelt Longworth, eldest daughter of President Theodore Roosevelt and widow of Nicholas Longworth, Speaker of the House, in her house on Massachusetts Avenue, Washington, D.C.

3. Not, as generally supposed, to provide a vantage point to catch sight of ships returning from sea (many houses with widow's walks are miles from the water), but rather to fight fires in the chimney, which then was in the center of the house.

4. The farmer in Robert Frost's "The Death of the Hired Man."

5. "Show me a home where the buffalo roam and I'll show you a messy kitchen."

6. A dungeon with a trap-door in the ceiling as its only means of access. The word derives from the French *oublier*, to forget.

7. "To lay a hat—and a few friends."

8. Chaise longue, which in French means simply long chair.

9. "Home" by Edgar A. Guest, whose poems were extremely popular with the people he called "folks" for their homely saccharine morality. The lines that Nash parodies are:

It takes a heap o' livin' in a house t' make it home,
A heap o' sun an' shadder, an' ye sometimes have t' roam
Afore ye really 'preciate the things ye lef' behind,
An' hunger fer 'em somehow, with 'em allus on yer mind.

10. "Every time I leave a man," she explains, "I keep his house."

Hunting, Shooting, and Fishing

■ ■

1. In which of the above would the services of a priest be employed?

2. During the controversy over *Lady Chatterley's Lover*, what did a certain peer reply, according to Viscount Gage, when asked if he would show the book to his daughter?

3. Auceps, Piscator, and Venator—representing a fowler, a fisherman, and a hunter respectively—are to be found in which book?

4. In fox hunting "tallyho" is shouted when the fox is sighted. How did this term supposedly arise?

5. What is meant by "burning the water" in Scotland?

6. In which celebrated fantasy does George Proteron, "one of the ten or twelve best shots in the kingdom," turn into a grouse?

7. How did Dr. Johnson contrast fly-fishing with angling?

8. What was Landseer's *Monarch of the Glen*?

9. How did the Irish fox hunt known as the Galway Blazers get its name?

10. Why is the 2nd Marquess of Ripon remembered?

Hunting, Shooting, and Fishing

1. Fishing. A priest is a mallet or other instrument used to "give the last rites" to a fish when spent. The term originated in Ireland.

2. "My daughter, certainly, but my gamekeeper, never!"

3. *The Compleat Angler*, by Izaak Walton.

4. It is believed to be a contraction of the French phrase "*Il est haut*," meaning "He is up."

5. Spearing salmon illegally with the aid of a flashlight.

6. *The Twelfth*, by J. K. Stanford. The title refers to August 12 when the grouse season in Britain opens.

7. "Fly-fishing may be a very pleasant amusement, but angling or float fishing I can only compare with a worm at one end and a fool at the other."

8. A painting of a fine, twelve-pointed or royal stag in the Scottish Highlands.

9. From the fact that the house in which they once held their annual hunt ball burned to the ground the same night.

10. For being one of the best shots in England and keeping game books to prove it. The record of the game he killed in the period 1867 to 1923 is framed in the showrooms of the gunsmiths James Purdey & Sons in London and is found in *The Big Shots*, by J. G. Ruffer. In his best year, 1893, Lord Ripon bagged 2,611 grouse, 8,732 partridges, 5,760 pheasants, and 166 "various." (In his 66-year shooting career he recorded 124,193 partridges and 241,224 pheasants.) The grand total—which included deer, woodcock, snipe, wild duck, black game, capercaillie, hare, rabbit, and "various"—came to 556,813. Lord Ripon died in 1923—as he undoubtedly would have wished, whilst on a grouse shoot.

Inner Space
■ ■

1. What is the body's largest organ?

2. Why was Napoleon feeling considerably below par on the day of his defeat at Waterloo?

3. Who defined a human being as "an ingenious assembly of portable plumbing"?

4. The human body can digest literally tens of thousands of substances. Apart from water, there is only one nonorganic compound among these. What is it?

5. In 1980 the United States Supreme Court ruled in a genetic-engineering case that new life forms created in the laboratory can be patented. What name has been given to such entities?

6. Which literary figure, whose name is similar to that of a member of the onion family, remarked on a normal female physiological occurrence?

7. What did Oliver Cromwell's face have in common with Tom Sawyer's hands?

8. Describe a steatopygous woman.

9. One out of every two hospital beds in the United States is occupied by a patient with what form of illness?

10. Who described a part of his body as follows: "'Tis a rock—a crag—a cape. A cape? Say rather, a peninsula"?

Inner Space

1. The skin, which in adults accounts for about 16 per cent of body weight. It is the body's first line of defense against germs. The liver comes next, weighing 3½ pounds, five times the weight of the heart.

2. He was suffering from an acute case of swollen hemorrhoids, and he was groggy both from lack of sleep and the opium that had been administered to ease his pain.

3. Christopher Morley, the American editor and author, in *Human Being*.

4. Salt, which is simply sodium chloride. Every other compound digestible by the human body is organic—that is to say, containing carbon atoms.

5. Designer genes.

6. The Lady of Shalott in Alfred, Lord Tennyson's poem of the same name:

> Out flew the web, and floated wide;
> The mirror crack'd from side to side;
> "The curse has come upon me," cried
> The Lady of Shalott.

7. Both had warts. When Cromwell had his portrait painted, he said, "Mr. Lely, I desire you would use all your skill to paint my picture truly like me, and not flatter me at all; but remark all those roughnesses, pimples, warts, and everything as you see me, otherwise I will never pay a farthing for it." Hence the phrase "warts and all."

8. She has an ample fundament, or, in other words, a fat ass. This is considered a mark of beauty in parts of Africa. Anthropologically, it shows she comes from good stock that enables her to sit on her haunches for the long periods necessary for preparing food.

9. Psychiatric disorders, including alcoholism, schizophrenia, and acute emotional problems.

10. Cyrano de Bergerac, in Edmond Rostand's play of the same name, characterizing his prominent nose.

The Inscrutable East

■■

1. What historic event occurred at Shimoda, Japan, in March 1853?

2. If Japan is the Land of the Rising Sun, what is the Land of the Morning Calm?

3. Who successively became king of his country, then abdicated, making his father king, in order to become Prime Minister; and then, when his father died, became the Chief of State without becoming king again?

4. Which city is known as the Venice of the East?

5. From what precisely is the Chinese delicacy known as bird's nest soup made?

6. Who in Japan is literally an "art person"?

7. For what is the colossal Indian temple at Konarak in the state of Orissa noted?

8. Sir Run Run Shaw of Hong Kong is so well remembered for being one of the world's largest producers of motion pictures, chiefly for the Oriental market. How did he get the name Run Run?

9. Why are Mrs. Leonowens and Mongkut famous today?

10. "Imagine a person, tall, lean and feline, high-shouldered with a brow like Shakespeare and a face like Satan, a close-shaven skull and long, magnetic eyes of the true cat green. Invest him with all the cunning of an entire Eastern race, accumulated in one giant intellect, with all the resources of science past and present. Imagine that awful being, and you have a mental picture of _____." Who is the author of this passage, and whom is he describing?

The Inscrutable East

1. Commodore Matthew Perry's arrival opened up Japan to American trade.

2. Korea.

3. Norodom Sihanouk of Cambodia.

4. Bangkok, which has over 600 canals.

5. The salivary secretions of some Oriental swifts with which they form their nests instead of using straw.

6. A geisha girl—*gei* meaning art, and *sha*, person. Geisha girls, unique to Japan, are trained to provide entertainment in the form of dancing, singing, or amusing conversation, usually for men only.

7. The "Black Pagoda," as it is called, is famous for erotic sculptures, and its walls are covered with carvings of hundreds of them. It is the greatest temple to sexual love that has ever been built.

8. When he began in the movie business, he and his brother Run Me had two movie houses. When they had only one film to show, they would run with the various reels between the two theaters.

9. They have proved to be a redoubtable pair and are known in the book world as *Anna and the King of Siam*. On the stage and screen they figure as *The King and I*. The historical King Mongkut was also known as Rama IV and had 9,000 wives and concubines.

10. Sax Rohmer, author of *The Insidious Dr. Fu Manchu* and other thrillers about the sinister Oriental doctor.

Insects

■■

1. The shape of which insect has not changed markedly in 350 million years?

2. Name the famous writer, politician, and statesman who said as a young man, "All men are worms, but I believe I am a glowworm."

3. Identify the speaker of these lines:

As flies to wanton boys, are we to the gods;
They kill us for their sport.

4. The French, Italians, and Spanish have the following words, pleasing to the ear, for butterfly—*papillon, farfala,* and *mariposa.* What is the German equivalent?

5. Which king profited greatly from the study of arachnology?

6. Who noted the problems of a flea in the following lines?

So, naturalists observe, a flea
Hath smaller fleas that on him prey;
And these have smaller still to bite 'em;
And so proceed *ad infinitum.*

7. What student of the gall wasp—his researchers preserved and measured over three million of them—achieved even greater fame with his sensational later studies?

8. Why is the black widow spider aptly named?

9. Which famous international banker has a bad case of beetlemania—not in the Liverpudlian sense?

10. Which bug was considered sacred by the Egyptians?

Insects

1. The cockroach.

2. Winston S. Churchill, who said this in 1906 in his first conversation with Violet Asquith, later Lady Violet Bonham-Carter, and ultimately Baroness Asquith. (A glowworm, another name for a firefly, is not a fly but a type of nocturnal beetle.)

3. The Earl of Gloucester in William Shakespeare's *King Lear*

4. *Schmetterling*.

5. Robert I the Bruce of Scotland. While hiding out on Rathlin Island off the Antrim coast in 1306, he watched a spider persevere with the spinning of its web, which so inspired and strengthened his resolve that he eventually freed Scotland from English rule. (Arachnology is the study of spiders—which are insects only in popular classification.)

6. Jonathan Swift, in "On Poetry."

7. Dr. Alfred Kinsey, whose two books, *Sexual Behavior of the Human Male* and *Sexual Behavior of the Human Female*, achieved considerable popularity.

8. Because of the female's proclivity for devouring her mate after mating. This can happen, and does, as many as 25 times in a single day.

9. David Rockefeller, former Chairman of the Board of the Chase Manhattan Bank, who has a collection of more than 50,000 species of beetle.

10. The scarab beetle, which would reappear periodically in great numbers on the surface of the Nile mud flats. This led the Egyptians to associate the sacred scarab with resurrection and immortality.

In Vino Veritas
■ ■

1. What two things is the blind Benedictine monk Dom Pierre Pérignon credited with inventing?

2. Who laid it down that: "Claret is the liquor for boys; port for men; but he who aspires to be a hero must drink brandy"?

3. What is considered the only great grape of Germany?

4. In England it was long a tradition to "lay down" a pipe of port for one's eldest son to be opened on the occasion of his twenty-first birthday. What precisely is a pipe of port?

5. Which alcoholic and debt-ridden poet wrote these lines in his poem: *"Vitae Summa Brevis Spem Nos Vetat Incohare Longam"* (Life's Short Span Forbids Us to Enter on Far-Reaching Hopes)?

> They are not long, the days of wine and roses:
>> Out of a misty dream
> Our path emerges for a while, then closes
>> Within a dream.

(The Latin title of this poem is from an ode by Horace.)

6. What is the significance of the following: 1963, 1965, and 1968?

7. Kir has been called the ultimate apéritif of France and is becoming increasingly popular elsewhere. How is it made, and for whom is it named? Finally, what is a Kir Royal?

8. How did a sheep and a shield come together to make oenological history in 1973?

9. Explain the connection between wine and the word fiasco.

10. Ambrose Bierce defined a connoisseur as "a specialist who knows everything about something and nothing about anything else." As an example of this, he recounted the story of an elderly wine bibber who was injured in a railway crash and had wine poured down his throat to relieve his pain. According to Bierce, what were the gentleman's last words before he died?

In Vino Veritas

1. The cork and the first true sparkling champagne. The firm of Moët et Chandon named its most famous champagne after Dom Pérignon.

2. Dr. Samuel Johnson, according to Boswell's *Life of Johnson*.

3. The Riesling, a white grape from which is produced all the significant wines of the Rhine and Mosel valleys.

4. It is a cask having a capacity of 126 gallons—half a tun—used both in fermenting and aging port.

5. The consumptive Ernest Dowson, who died of tuberculosis at the age of 33.

6. They are the worst years for claret in the last two decades.

7. Kir, also known as *vin blanc cassis*, is a mixture predominantly of chilled white Burgundy, preferably an aligoté, with crème de cassis, a black currant liqueur. The drink was named in honor of Canon Félix Kir, a World War II Resistance hero and mayor of Dijon, the capital of Burgundy, where black currants are a crop second in importance only to Burgundy's famous wines. A Kir Royal simply involves the substitution of a *brut* Champagne for the Burgundy.

8. In that year Baron Philippe de Rothschild's superb claret Château Mouton-Rothschild was finally classified as the fifth of the *premiers crus classes*, joining Haut Brion, Lafite, Latour, and Margaux—all of which had been so classified in 1855. (*Mouton* means sheep and Rothschild red shield, from the coat of arms on the ancestral house in 17th-century Frankfurt.)

9. The connection lies in the ancient art of glass blowing. When failure occurred in the fashioning of a fine and more delicate vessel, the reject became a wine bottle, known in Italy as a *fiasco*, or flask, which thus became synonymous with a mistake. Such *fiascos* are often covered with raffia.

10. "Pauillac, 1873."

Island Hopping

■ ■

1. During World War II what was known as "the unsinkable aircraft carrier"?

2. Which famous island is now the internally self-governing nation of Kalaatllit Nunaat?

3. Does *South Pacific*'s Bali Ha'i really exist? If so, where is it?

4. What is the most recent island on the earth?

5. Can you name the island that has been divided peacefully between two European nations for over 300 years?

6. Who represented the only surviving kingdom in the South Pacific at the coronation of Queen Elizabeth II?

7. What was the setting for J. M. Synge's play, *The Playboy of the Western World*?

8. Which island gives its name to the word serendipity, meaning "the faculty of making fortunate but unexpected discoveries by accident"?

9. Which Caribbean island has, in light of its climate, an extremely unlikely name? Who was its most important native son?

10. Who delivers this passage and in which play?

This royal throne of kings, this scepter'd isle,
This earth of majesty, this seat of Mars,
This other Eden, demi-paradise,
This fortress built by Nature for herself
Against infection and the hand of war,
This happy breed of men, this little world,
This precious stone set in the silver sea,
Which serves it in the office of a wall,
Or as a moat defensive to a house,
Against the envy of less happier lands,
This blessed plot, this earth, this realm, this England,
This nurse, this teeming womb of royal kings,
Fear'd by their breed and famous by their birth.

Island Hopping

1. The island of Malta, which lies south of Sicily. After being subjected to 2,000 intensive air raids, the Maltese people in 1942 were collectively awarded the George Cross for gallantry by King George VI—the only group to be so honored. The George Cross, given to civilians, is Britain's second highest decoration, ranking just below the Victoria Cross.

2. Greenland, which, with the advent of home rule, changed its name from the Danish Grønland to the aboriginal Inuit name meaning "Land of the People."

3. It is the small, lovely island of Moorea, northwest of Tahiti, in the Society Island group of French Polynesia.

4. The volcanic island of Surtsey, south of Iceland, which appeared dramatically from the ocean in 1963 and continued to grow for the next four years. The name Surtsey derives from Surtur, the ancient Norse god of fire. This refutes Mark Twain's observation that "God made the earth, and He's not making any more."

5. Saint Martin, also Sint Maarten, one of the Leeward Islands of the Caribbean, which has been shared by the French and Dutch since 1648. The northern part, with the capital at Marigot, belongs to French Guadeloupe; the southern part has its chief town at Philipsburg and is administered by the Netherlands Antilles.

6. Queen Salote of the island group of Tonga, which has been called the place where time begins, or the Islands of Tomorrow, because the International Date Line passes just to the east. When the enormous Queen Salote attended the coronation of Queen Elizabeth II, she rode in an open carriage with the minute Premier of Malta, Dr. Borg Olivier. When asked who he was, Noël Coward replied, "He's her lunch."

7. The Aran Islands off the west coast of Ireland.

8. Sri Lanka, which was formerly named Ceylon and before that was known to Arab merchants as Serendib. This word was coined by Horace Walpole after the characters in the fairy tale, *The Three Princes of Serendip* [sic], who made such discoveries.

9. The small Leeward Island of Nevis, originally called *Nieves*, the Spanish word for snow, after the clouds that swirl about the 3,596-foot Nevis Peak. Alexander Hamilton was born there in 1755.

10. John of Gaunt in William Shakespeare's *Richard II*.

Jazz and Pop
■ ■

1. Which famous bandmaster said, "Jazz will endure just as long as people hear it through their feet instead of their brains."?

2. What has been cited as the first rock 'n' roll record?

3. Name the songwriter and band leader who wrote "St. Louis Blues" and "Beale Street Blues."

4. Where did the music of reggae originate and what is ska?

5. "Man, if you gotta ask you'll never know" and "Lady, if you got to ask you ain't got it" were whose responses to what questions?

6. Which rock group went longest without a change of members?

7. "Bix" Beiderbecke was a legend in the jazz world of his time. What instruments did he play?

8. How is Deborah Harry better known?

9. Why was Lee Wiley atypical of jazz singers?

10. Of which popular idol was it written, "That he himself never did or said anything remotely outrageous, significant or even interesting has only added to the purity of his myth"?

Jazz and Pop

1. John Philip Sousa, composer of over 100 marches including his most renowned one, "The Stars and Stripes Forever."

2. "Rocket 86," with Turner's Band and Jackie Breston, its saxophonist, singing lead, became the number-one rhythm and blues hit in 1951.

3. W. C. Handy, "the Father of the Blues."

4. Jamaica, where it was popularized by the Rastafarians, a local religious group. Ska, or bluebeat, is a Jamaican rhythm and blues form that was the precursor of reggae.

5. The first was Louis "Satchmo" Armstrong's reply when asked what jazz is, and the second was "Fats" Waller's when asked to explain rhythm.

6. The Who. The group's first change since their formation in 1962 was occasioned by the death of their drummer Keith Moon in 1978.

7. The cornet, his playing of which was noted for brilliant phrasing and clarity of tone, and the piano, on which he recorded his greatest composition, "In a Mist." He was solo cornetist with various jazz bands during the 1920s and joined Paul Whiteman from 1928 until 1931, when he died of pneumonia.

8. She is the blonde in the New Wave group "Blondie."

9. Lee Wiley was an American Indian with blonde hair who was also a composer. Possessing a husky voice with a wide vibrato, she performed with Eddie Condon and many other jazz groups in the 1940s. She was extremely selective about what she sang; her distinctive voice and phrasing have led some critics to compare her with Billie Holiday and Ella Fitzgerald.

10. Elvis Presley, in his obituary in *The Times* of London.

Journeys

■ ■

    1. How did a little girl, a small piebald mare, and the Mother of God join up for a historic trip?

    2. Why did W. Somerset Maugham prefer sailing on non-British ships?

    3. Who observed that solo travel was expeditious?

    4. What is the number-one tourist attraction in the world today?

    5. Which Inca deity sailed across the Pacific in 1947?

    6. What is Sir Ranulph Twistleton-Wykeham-Fiennes attempting to do the hard way?

    7. In the following passage who was "I"?

> Two roads diverged by a wood, and I—
> I took the one less traveled by,
> And that has made all the difference.

    8. What was Robert Benchley's opinion of going on a trip with children?

    9. Which famous traveler said, "I am a part of all that I have met"?

    10. Name the traveling companions of: a) Richard I Lion-Heart, b) Don Quixote, c) Bonnie Parker, d) Mr. Pickwick, e) Viola, f) Captain Hook?

Journeys

1. They were Columbus' three ships—*Niña*, *Pinta*, and *Santa Maria*—on his famous voyage in 1492.

2. Because, as he put it, "There's none of that nonsense about women and children first."

3. Rudyard Kipling in his poem "The Winners":

> Down to Gehenna or up to the Throne,
> He travels the fastest who travels alone.

4. Walt Disney World in Orlando, Florida.

5. Kon Tiki, the Inca sun god, who gave his name to the primitive balsa raft that Thor Heyerdahl, the Norwegian explorer and anthropologist, sailed from Peru to the Tuamotu islands to support his theory that the first settlers of Polynesia were of South American origin.

6. The unprecedented feat of circling the globe longitudinally via the North and South Poles, following as closely as possible the prime meridian, the imaginary line running north and south around the world that passes through the original site of the Royal Observatory at Greenwich, England. The equipment of the Transglobe Expedition includes amphibious rubber boats, snowmobiles, self-knotting ropes, and shoes that walk on water.

7. Robert Frost, in his poem "The Road Not Taken."

8. He said, "It corresponds roughly to traveling third class in Bulgaria."

9. Ulysses, in the poem of the same name by Alfred, Lord Tennyson.

10. a) Blondel de Nesle, b) Sancho Panza, c) Clyde Barrow, d) Sam Weller, e) Sebastian, f) Smee.

Kings and Queens

■■

1. If the delicacy of her exquisite bust in the Aegyptisches Museum in Berlin is to be believed, she was one of the most beautiful women of antiquity. Who was she, and who was her more famous nephew?

2. Who was in the habit of saying, "Off with her head!"?

3. Which unfinished English epic begins in this fashion?

A Gentle Knight was pricking on the plaine . . .

4. Which debauched king got a kick out of wearing low-cut women's dresses?

5. George III of England, who was considered insane during his later years, seems actually to have been the victim of what disease?

6. Which sovereign was alive at the same time as the next four rulers, a total of four generations?

7. During World War I which fictitious queen attempted to torpedo the German gunboat *Königin Luise*?

8. Name the Scottish-born writer who said:

The world is so full of a number of things,
I'm sure we should all be as happy as kings.

9. What was the remarkable thing about Alfonso XIII of Spain's accession to the throne in 1886?

10. Who succeeded to the throne when literally up a tree?

Kings and Queens

1. Nefertiti, a queen of ancient Egypt. She was the aunt of Tutankhamun, whose only claim to fame arises from the discovery of his accidentally hidden royal tomb in the Valley of the Kings, the first to be unearthed almost intact. An exhibit of his funerary objects, on loan from Cairo, has attracted enormous crowds throughout the world.

2. The Queen of Hearts in Lewis Carroll's *Alice's Adventures in Wonderland*.

3. *The Faerie Queen* by Edmund Spenser. In this sense, "pricking" means riding at a gallop.

4. Henry III, the weak and ineffective French king who was the last male member of the house of Valois.

5. Acute intermittent porphyria, which is manifested by recurrent attacks of abdominal pain, gastrointestinal dysfunction, and neural disturbances.

6. Queen Victoria, whose son, grandson, and great-grandsons became Edward VII, George V, Edward VIII (later the Duke of Windsor), and George VI.

7. The *African Queen*, a river steamer in the charge of Charlie Allnut, a Cockney engineer employed by a Belgian gold-mining company, in C. S. Forester's novel. After a perilous trip down the Ulanga with Rosie Sayers, a missionary's sister, Allnut constructs crude torpedoes from cylinders of oxygen and hydrogen, but the *African Queen* founders. The *Königin Luise*, however, later strikes the *Queen*'s semi-submerged bow and sinks. (The film version starred Humphrey Bogart and Katharine Hepburn, and Bogart received an Oscar for Best Actor as Charlie Allnut in 1951.)

8. Robert Louis Stevenson in "Happy Thought" from *A Child's Garden of Verses*.

9. It occurred the moment he was born, his father having died six months before.

10. Queen Elizabeth II, who was staying at Treetops Hotel near Nyeri in Kenya when she received news of the death of her father, George VI. Treetops is built in an immense fig tree so that the wild animals at the nearby salt lick can be viewed undisturbed.

Law and Order

■ ■

1. What was the Judgment of Solomon?

2. "The first thing we do, let's kill all the lawyers" is a sentiment that has often been repeated. Who said it first?

3. Who called himself "the law West of the Pecos" and named his saloon after which English actress?

4. Which noted Supreme Court Justice delivered the opinion of the court in the following terms: "The most stringent protection of free speech would not protect a man in falsely shouting fire in a theatre and causing panic."?

5. Who defined litigation as "a machine which you go into as a pig and come out as a sausage"?

6. Does the corpse in a murder case constitute *corpus delicti*?

7. In which work are the following lines found?

The hungry judges soon the sentence sign
And the wretches hang that jury-men may dine.

8. What does the Latin root *testis*, testicle, mean as used in such words as testify, testimony, and testament?

9. Explain the difference between assault and battery.

10. Is it legal for a man in South Carolina to marry his widow's sister?

Law and Order

1. A judgment displaying remarkable acumen, exemplified by King Solomon's settling a dispute over a child between two women who each claimed to be its mother. When Solomon proposed to cut the baby in half, the false claimant acquiesced, while the true mother identified herself by being willing to surrender the child altogether.

2. Dick Butcher in Shakespeare's *Henry VI, Part II*.

3. "Judge" Roy Bean, who dispensed justice with the aid of one law book and a six-shooter. He called his saloon "The Jersey Lily" in honor of Lillie Langtry, with whom he was infatuated but had never met. The town that grew up around his saloon was renamed Langtry (originally Vinegaroon) and is located in southwest Texas on the Mexican border.

4. Oliver Wendell Holmes in *Schenck* v. *United States*, March 3, 1919. The case involved a conspiracy to distribute an inflammatory circular denouncing conscription.

5. Ambrose Bierce in *The Devil's Dictionary*.

6. It may, but the terms "corpse" and *corpus delicti* are not synonymous. *Corpus delicti*, meaning "body of the crime," is the material evidence of the fact that a crime has been committed.

7. "The Rape of the Lock," by Alexander Pope.

8. Witness—for example, a testicle is a witness to the deponent's being a man. In ancient times, when testifying, the hand was placed on the testicles, just as we now place the hand on the Bible. (In those days, women did not swear oaths as they were merely considered chattels.)

9. Assault is the threat of force or violence, whereas battery is the actual employment of physical force.

10. It is not illegal; it is impossible.

Literary Endings

■ ■

*Name the authors and titles of the literary works which end as
follows.*

1. "To the high fantasy here power failed; but now my
desire and my will were resolved, like a wheel which is moved
evenly, by the Love that moves the sun and the other stars."

2. "So I awoke, and behold it was a dream."

3. "It was among the ruins of the Capitol that I first
conceived the idea of a work which has amused and exercised
nearly twenty years of my life, and which, however inadequate to
my own wishes, I finally deliver to the curiosity and candour of the
public."

4. "L—d, said my mother, what is all this story about?—A
COCK and a BULL, said Yorick—And one of the best of its kind I
ever heard."

5. "So we beat on, boats against the current, borne back
ceaselessly into the past."

6. ". . . he was like a man who stands upon a hill above
the town he has left, yet does not say 'The town is near,' but turns
his eyes upon the distant soaring ranges."

7. "But I reckon I got to light out for the territory ahead of
the rest, because Aunt Sally she's going to adopt me and sivilize
me, and I can't stand it. I been there before."

8. "I lingered round them, under that benign sky: watched
the moths fluttering among the heath and hare-bells; listened to
the soft wind breathing through grass; and wondered how any one
could ever imagine unquiet slumbers for the sleepers in that quiet
earth."

9. "That might be the subject of a new story—our present
story is ended."

10. "Vale."

Literary Endings

1. Dante Alighieri, *The Divine Comedy*.

2. John Bunyan, Part One of *The Pilgrim's Progress*.

3. Edward Gibbon, *The Decline and Fall of the Roman Empire*.

4. Lawrence Sterne, *Tristram Shandy*.

5. F. Scott Fitzgerald, *The Great Gatsby*.

6. Thomas Wolfe, *Look Homeward, Angel*.

7. Mark Twain, *The Adventures of Huckleberry Finn*.

8. Emily Brontë, *Wuthering Heights*.

9. Feodor Dostoevsky, *Crime and Punishment*.

10. Miguel de Cervantes, *Don Quixote*.

Long and Short of It

■ ■

1. Give the derivation of the word "laconic," meaning terse, concise, or succinct.

2. What is the longest street in the world?

3. Who is the only American poet to have his bust placed in Poets' Corner of Westminster Abbey?

4. In the Dempsey-Tunney rematch fight in Chicago in 1927, when Dempsey tried to regain his heavyweight crown, how long was the famous "long count" which gave Tunney extra time on the canvas?

5. What dissolved itself in 1660?

6. What is the longest athletic event in the Olympic Games?

7. Which somewhat bizarre author described himself in these terms to an interviewer: "I'm about as tall as a shotgun—and just as noisy," adding, "I think I have rather heated eyes."?

8. What distinction attaches to the title of a poem by William Wordsworth that has these opening lines?

There was a time when meadow, grave, and stream,
The earth, and every common sight,
To me did seem
Apparelled in celestial light,
The glory and the freshness of a dream.

9. Who wrote, "That lyf so short, the craft so long to lerne . . ."?

10. Which great French novelist is credited with composing one of the longest sentences ever published?

Long and Short of It

1. It comes from Laconia, itself a contracted form of Lacedaemonia, an ancient region of the Peloponnesian peninsula in Greece, of which Sparta was the metropolis. The Spartans were noted for their brevity of speech.

2. Broadway, which extends 150 miles from Bowling Green near the foot of Manhattan Island to Albany, New York.

3. Henry Wadsworth Longfellow, author of such long narrative works as *Evangeline*, *The Song of Hiawatha*, and *Paul Revere's Ride*.

4. Fourteen seconds. It took the referee, Dave Barry, about five seconds to wave Dempsey to a neutral corner before he could begin to count. Gene Tunney rose from the canvas at the count of nine and went on to win the bout on a decision.

5. The Long Parliament which, summoned by Charles I in 1640, had intermittently governed England with or without him for the next 20 years: it is the only Parliament to have enacted a law that it could only be dissolved by itself.

6. The 50-kilometer walk, which covers just over 31 miles. (The marathon run is only 26 miles, 385 yards.)

7. Truman Capote, who was born Truman Streckfus Persons.

8. The title of this poem—"Ode. Intimations of Immortality from Recollections of Early Childhood"—is considered to be the longest title of any work by a major author.

9. Geoffrey Chaucer, in *The Parliament of Fowls*. The thought was expressed much earlier by Hippocrates in his *Aphorisms* as "Life is short and the art long," referring in his case to medicine.

10. Victor Hugo, in *Les Misérables*, which contains 823 words, 93 commas, 51 semicolons, 4 dashes, and runs for three pages. Hugo is also remembered for sending the shortest letter. Like most authors anxious about sales, he wrote his publisher, "?". The reply came back, "!". (The beautiful last chapter of James Joyce's *Ulysses*, wholly without punctuation, is even longer but grammatically is hard to construe as a sentence.)

Manners and Mores

■ ■

    1. What do anthropologists say is the significance of a bride throwing her bridal bouquet?

    2. How can most Americans be instantly recognized in a British restaurant?

    3. What delicate rebuke did Louis XIV deliver when his coach arrived merely at the moment that he needed it; and conversely, what did his great-great-great-grandson Louis XVIII say about his own obligations in such matters?

    4. What custom do the Greeks employ to express pleasure at dancing and singing?

    5. When the mob dragged her from the jail and "strung her up upon the old willow across the way," what were Miss Otis' last words?

    6. To which of the guests at a diplomatic reception would you not offer your hand?

    7. Is it correct for an 80-year-old bride to wear a traditional wedding dress?

    8. How did the Duke of Somerset make his special contribution to the annals of hospitality at Bath around 1760?

    9. Who is reputed to have said, "I must decline your invitation owing to a subsequent invitation"?

    10. How did Oliver Herford define a gentleman?

Manners and Mores

1. It is the visual and symbolic enactment of her deflowering, or loss of virginity.

2. By their ridiculously inefficient habit of shifting the fork from the left to the right hand. This is a throwback to the days before forks appeared, around 1600, when food was eaten with the left hand or speared by a knife with the right. The European custom of retaining the fork in the left hand after cutting the meat is simplicity itself.

3. Louis XIV: *"J'ai failli attendre."* (I almost had to wait.) Louis XVIII: *"L'exactitude est la politesse des rois."* (Punctuality is the politeness of kings.)

4. They throw plates on the floor.

5. "Miss Otis regrets she's unable to lunch today." from Cole Porter's 1934 song. "Miss Otis Regrets" was sung by Monty Woolley, who was at Yale with Cole Porter, in the 1946 film *Night and Day*.

6. Royalty. They must always make the first move toward such physical contact.

7. No—it is worn only up to the age of forty.

8. He gave a large dinner party where none of the guests knew any of the others, but all stammered.

9. Oscar Wilde. In his play *The Importance of Being Earnest* Wilde describes another evasive ploy: "I have invented an invaluable permanent invalid called Bunbury, in order that I may be able to go down into the country whenever I choose."

10. "A gentleman is one who never hurts anyone's feeling unintentionally."

"Matters Mathematical"
■ ■

1. Describe a prime number, and name the only even prime number. In this connection what strange generalization did the German mathematician Christian Goldbach make 200 years ago, to which no exception has ever been found?

2. How is four depicted on the face of a clock or watch with Roman numerals?

3. What is a googol? A googolplex?

4. This verse from Emma Rounds' "Plane Geometry" parodies what?

> 'Twas Euclid and the theorem pi
>   Did plane and solid in the text,
> All parallel were the radii,
>   And the ang-gulls convex'd.

5. Can you define a perfect number?

6. What is missing in the Roman numeral system?

7. What do the European viper and Blaise Pascal, the French theologian and mathematician, have in common, and why does the name Elmer Rice come to mind?

8. In mathematics, what does "i" denote?

9. How did Albert Einstein react when the first experimental tests of general relativity appeared to disprove his theory?

10. Describe a polymath.

"Matters Mathematical"

1. A prime number is one that has no factors (numbers which can be multiplied to form it) but itself and 1. Two is the only even prime number. The first few prime numbers are 2, 3, 5, 7, 11, 13, 17, and 19. Goldbach hypothesized that every even number from 6 on is the sum of two primes.

2. IIII, not IV.

3. A googol is the number 10 raised to the power 100, or the number 1 followed by 100 zeroes. The word "googol" was coined by the American mathematician Edward Kasner from a sound made by his nine-month-old nephew. A googolplex is the number 10 raised to the power googol (formed from "googol" and *-plex* meaning folded, or twined).

4. Lewis Carrol's "Jabberwocky" from *Through the Looking Glass*:

'Twas brillig and the slithy toves
  Did gyre and gimble in the wabe;
All mimsy were the borogoves,
  And the mome raths outgrabe.

The point of the parody is that Lewis Carroll, under his real name of Charles Lutwidge Dodgson, was a distinguished mathematician who wrote *Euclid and His Modern Rivals*.

5. A number like 6 where the sum of its divisors equals the number itself—for example, its divisors (1, 2, 3) add up to six. From 1 to 40 million, there are only seven perfect numbers: 6, 78, 496, 8128, 130816, 2096128, and 33550336.

6. It has no symbol for zero, which comes from India through the Arabic numerical system.

7. A viper is an adder, and Blaise Pascal, in 1642 at the age of 19, invented a machine that could add, and also subtract. *The Adding Machine* is the title of a play by Elmer Rice.

8. The square root of -1, used in electronics and mathematics as part of complex-number theory.

9. He simply said, "If the results contradict me, so much the worse for the results."

10. A polymath is a person of great and varied learning.

Medicine

■ ■

1. What do the initials P.C. mean after a physician's name?

2. Paregoric is often prescribed for diarrhea and intestinal pain. What are its active ingredients?

3. By what other term is scopolamine known?

4. To whom did Father Damien minister and where?

5. Which medical man, on taking a patient's pulse, is remembered for saying, "Either he's dead or my watch has stopped."?

6. What major medical discovery was made in 1930 when people went to bars after working in rubber plants?

7. Who said before he was beheaded, "'Tis a sharp medicine [the axe], but a sure cure for all ills"?

8. Which debilitating disease, endemic throughout the tropics, is caused by infestation with a parasitic worm of the genus *schistosoma*?

9. The 1979 Nobel Prize for Physiology and Medicine went to two men who are not physicians, nor do they hold doctorates of any sort; and one of them never went to a university at all. For what did they receive the award?

10. Who drew a cartoon showing a man dragging his friend into a doctor's office and announcing, "I've got Bright's disease and he has mine"?

Medicine

1. Professional Corporation. Many doctors incorporate themselves because of certain tax benefits and favorable pension-plan provisions. Being a professional corporation does not limit a physician's liability in malpractice suits.

2. It is a camphorated tincture of opium.

3. Truth serum. It was widely used by the Germans in World War II when interrogating prisoners of war.

4. The lepers on Molokai, one of the Hawaiian islands. He went there at his own request and labored for sixteen years before dying of leprosy in 1889.

5. Dr. Hugh Z. Hackenbush, as played by Groucho Marx in the 1937 film *A Day at the Races*.

6. When they became violently nauseated, it was discovered that the compound sulfiram, used in the industrial treatment of rubber, was so incompatible with alcohol that it became used as the alcohol-aversion drug Antabuse.

7. Sir Walter Raleigh, English courtier, navigator, historian, and poet.

8. Bilharziasis, which was discovered by the German parasitologist Theodor Bilharz. The host body for the worms are snails found on the beds of freshwater ponds and streams, and the organisms usually enter the body through cracks between the toes.

9. For developing the incredible new diagnostic tool, the CAT scanner, which gives physicians precision pictures inside the body without invading it. (CAT is an acronym for Computerized Axial Tomography.) The laureates were Allan MacLeod Cormack, a physicist, and Godfrey Newbold Hounsfield, an electronics-computer engineer.

10. S. J. Perelman, who in 1979 wrote: "In the spring of 1927 . . . I drew cartoons that ultimately lowered the circulation of a weekly called *Judge* to the vanishing point." His captions for the cartoons became so long that he became a writer.

Meetings

■ ■

1. Who, according to whom, had a "rendezvous with destiny"?

2. Explain the significance of the French phrase "*cinq à sept*" (five to seven)?

3. Who met Jesus on His way to Calvary and offered Him her handkerchief?

4. Which Irish bard wrote these lines?

> I know that I shall meet my fate
> Somewhere among the clouds above;
> Those that I fight I do not hate,
> Those that I guard I do not love;
> My country is Kiltartan Cross,
> My countrymen Kiltartan's poor,
> No likely end could bring them loss
> Or leave them happier than before.

5. To whom was Queen Victoria referring when she complained that "he speaks to Me as if I was a public meeting"?

6. What meets what at a place once known as Fort Duquesne to form what?

7. Who had an important meeting on board ship in Placentia Bay off the southern coast of Newfoundland in August 1941, and which famous document emerged from this meeting?

8. Can you name the author of the following?

> When Spring trips north again this year,
> And I to my pledged word am true,
> I shall not fail that rendezvous.

9. The servant of a rich merchant in Baghdad told his master he had to leave immediately for Samarra because Death had just frightened him in the marketplace. Death later explained to the merchant that he did not mean to frighten his servant, but that he was startled to see him in Baghdad. What was Death's explanation for being startled?

10. A gushing admirer, on meeting the American novelist Henry James at a party, said, "Mr. James, we haven't met in five years." What was James' response?

Meetings

1. "This generation of Americans." These words were spoken by President Franklin D. Roosevelt in a speech accepting renomination in 1936.

2. It means an assignation with one's mistress or lover between work and going home.

3. Veronica, from the Latin *vera iconica* meaning "truly depicted." The cloth which retained the print of His face is a relic preserved in St. Peter's in Rome and is commonly called Veronica's veil.

4. William Butler Yeats, "An Irish Airman Foresees His Death."

5. Prime Minister William Gladstone.

6. The Allegheny and the Monongahela Rivers flow together to shape Pittsburgh's Golden Triangle and form the Ohio River.

7. Prime Minister Churchill and President Roosevelt, where they drew up a statement of principles and aims known as the Atlantic Charter. In 1942 the signatory powers of the United Nations pledged allegiance to the principles of the charter.

8. Alan Seeger, the American poet who enlisted in the French Foreign Legion and was killed on the Western Front in 1916. The lines are from his most celebrated poem, "I Have a Rendezvous with Death," which only appeared in *The North American Review* three months after he had fallen in action. His nephew, Pete Seeger, became a famous folk singer.

9. "For I had an appointment with him tonight in Samarra." This is from an Arabian Nights story as adapted by W. Somerset Maugham in his 1933 play *Sheppy*. John O'Hara used it as an epigraph for his novel *Appointment in Samarra*.

10. "A very suitable interval, I think."

Middle East

■ ■

1. To the Europeans, why were the countries bordering on the eastern Mediterranean known as the Levant?

2. Which is the largest of the sheikhdoms that make up the United Arab Emirates, formerly known as the Trucial States?

3. What is the expansion of the word Wog, used as an acronym, which is generally considered a racial slur throughout the Middle East?

4. Who said, "One man's Mede is another man's Persian"?

5. For a Moslem, what is the surest way to paradise?

6. Identify the author of the following lines:

Now, it is not good for the Christian's health
    to hustle the Aryan brown,
For the Christian riles, and the Aryan smiles,
    and he weareth the Christian down;
And the end of the fight is a tombstone white,
    with the name of the late deceased,
And the epitaph drear: "A fool lies here
    who tried to hustle the East."

7. According to an old Middle Eastern adage, if a woman is for children, what are boys and goats for?

8. Who journeyed to Mecca and Medina in various disguises and wrote about it afterward in his *Personal Narrative of a Pilgrimage to Al Madinah and Mecca*?

9. What does Mahdi mean in Arabic? Name one who became famous in Western history.

10. Which Middle Eastern political leaders were unusually associated with dynamite in 1978?

Middle East

1. It comes from the Old French *levant*, rising (referring to the sun).

2. Abu Dhabi. The temporary capital of the United Arab Emirates is also called Abu Dhabi.

3. Worthy, or wily, oriental gentleman. The word is believed originally to have derived from "golliwog," a black male doll of grotesque appearance. Wog was an encompassing British imperialist term for people with dark complexions, unfamiliar languages, strange habits, and odd food. The more fatuously Blimpish of the English upper classes used to say, "Wogs begin at Calais."

4. George S. Kaufman, American playwright and wit.

5. To perish in a *jihad*, or holy war against infidels. According to the Koran, those slain in such wars are not dead but "alive with their Lord."

6. Rudyard Kipling in *The Naulahka: A Story of West and East*. (Naulahka, the name of a fabulous jewel, was used by Kipling as the name of his house in Vermont where he lived for four years and wrote *The Jungle Book, The Second Jungle Book, Kim, Just So Stories* and *Captains Courageous*.)

7. "A boy is for pleasure, but a goat is for ecstasy."

8. Sir Richard Burton, English explorer and linguist, who is famous for his remarkably literal translation of the *Arabian Nights* in sixteen volumes.

9. "He who is rightly guided." In 1881 Mohammed Ahmad declared himself to be the Mahdi; he destroyed the Egyptian garrison of Khartoum under General "Chinese" Gordon in 1885. The decisive defeat of the forces of his successor, the Khalifa Abdallahi, did not occur until Kitchener's victory in 1898 at Karari outside the Mahdist capital and holy city of Omdurman, the twin city of Khartoum across the White Nile. (The film *Khartoum* starred Charlton Heston as Gordon and Laurence Olivier as the Mahdi.)

10. Menachem Begin, the Prime Minister of Israel, and Anwar al-Sadat, the President of Egypt, were jointly awarded the Nobel Peace Prize in that year. (Alfred Nobel invented dynamite.)

Mixed Bag

■ ■

1. Which goddess' name is doubled?

2. Which 17th-century swordsman with a large nose wrote *Histoire comique des états et empires de la lune* (Comic History of the Estates and Empires of the Moon), describing how man used rockets to build a flying machine?

3. Can you identify K2?

4. How did Churchill, speaking with the authority of a man who had been First Lord of the Admiralty in both World Wars, silence an admiral who protested that some reforming proposal was "contrary to the traditions of the Navy"?

5. What savagely cold evening did John Keats vividly describe?

6. "Pumping iron" is a term synonymous with body building. What is meant by "hanging iron," and who in New York City are expert at it?

7. What are netsuke and for which purpose were they used?

8. After World War I how did Mayor "Big Bill" Thompson of Chicago ensure getting the German and Irish vote?

9. Whose address was simply "Number One, London"?

10. What was Marilyn Monroe's reply when asked if she had anything on when she posed, apparently nude, for the famous calendar photograph?

Mixed Bag

1. Isis, an ancient Egyptian goddess of fertility and sister and wife of Osiris, who is identified with Dionysus, the Greek god of wine.

2. Savinien Cyrano de Bergerac, a French novelist and swordsman, who was the model for Edmond Rostand's famous fictional character. His 1657 work is curious because Newton's third law of motion (for every action there is an equal and opposite reaction), on which rocketry is based, was not promulgated until thirty years later.

3. With a height of 28,750 feet, it is the second highest mountain in the world after Everest. Rising in the Karakorum Range in the Hindu Kush, it is also known as Mt. Godwin-Austen after the English topographer who surveyed it.

4. "Don't talk to me about naval tradition. It's nothing but rum, sodomy, and the lash."

5. The Eve of St. Agnes in the poem of that name:

St. Agnes' Eve—Ah, bitter chill it was!
The owl, for all his feathers, was a-cold;
The hare limp'd trembling through the frozen grass.
And silent was the flock in woolly fold.

6. "Hanging iron" refers to erecting the girders in skyscraper construction, a trade at which the Mohawk Indians are past masters.

7. They are miniature Japanese carvings depicting mythological and real animals, household gods, nuts, and fruits. The small toggles were made to serve as counterweights for the tobacco pouches and medicine boxes that the Japanese hung from their kimono sashes.

8. He said, "If George V ever comes to Chicago, I'll punch him in the snoot."

9. The Duke of Wellington's Apsley House, which stands on Piccadilly near Hyde Park Corner. It now houses the Wellington Museum and a private flat for the current duke on the top floor.

10. "Just the radio."

Money

■ ■

1. What search for treasure has proved literally "the pit"?

2. A man has two U.S. coins which total 55 cents. One is not a nickel. What are the two coins?

3. Which friend of Gilbert Keith Chesterton characteristically wrote the following?

> I'm tired of Love: I'm still more tired of Rhyme.
> But Money gives me pleasure all the time.

4. What is the highest-denomination U.S. bill ever printed, and whose likeness appears on it?

5. Where would you go in order to spend: a) *sucres,* b) *korunas,* c) *gourdes,* d) *bolivars,* e) *kwachas*?

6. Who said, "His money is twice tainted: 'taint yours and 'taint mine"?

7. The American economist and social critic Thorstein Veblen, in *The Theory of the Leisure Class*, made the phrase "conspicuous consumption" a household phrase. What did he have to say about it?

8. In which poem do these lines appear?

> The world is too much with us; late and soon,
> Getting and spending, we lay waste our powers:
> Little we see in Nature that is ours;
> We have given our hearts away, a sordid boon!

9. How does thirteen, representing the 13 original states, enter the picture eight times on a U.S. one-dollar bill?

10. When F. Scott Fitzgerald observed that "the rich are different than us," who replied, "Yes, they have more money"?

Money

1. The famous Money Pit on Oak Island, Nova Scotia, where for 200 years innumerable expeditions, including one partly financed by Franklin D. Roosevelt, have been baffled by a deep shaft transected by an incredibly sophisticated series of flood channels. This search continues, but whatever lies below remains as much a mystery as ever.

2. One is not a nickel, but the other is: the two coins are a nickel and a fifty-cent piece.

3. The English author Hilaire Belloc. The lines are titled "Fatigue" from his book *Sonnets and Verse*.

4. The $100,000 gold certificate of 1934, which featured the portrait of President Woodrow Wilson. This note was intended only for official transactions, and none of them ever circulated outside Federal Reserve banks. (The Federal Reserve System was founded under Wilson.)

5. a) Ecuador, b) Czechoslovakia, c) Haiti, d) Venezuela, e) Zambia or Malawi.

6. Mark Twain, American humorist, speaking of Henry H. Rogers, an associate of John D. Rockefeller in Standard Oil.

7. "Conspicuous consumption of valuable goods is a means of reputability to the gentleman of leisure."

8. "The World Is Too Much With Us," by William Wordsworth.

9. In the Great Seal of the United States, both sides of which are shown on the reverse side of the bill, there are, starting from the right, a constellation of 13 stars inside the Glory of God, a ring of luminous clouds; 13 stripes in the shield; 13 arrows symbolizing war; 13 olive leaves and berries representing peace; and on the left, 13 rows in the unfinished pyramid. There are also 13 letters in each of the mottoes *E Pluribus Unum* (Out of Many, One) and *Annuit Coeptis* (He [God] Favors Our Undertakings). On the obverse side of the bill on the right within the Treasury Department seal is a chevron of 13 stars.

10. Ernest Hemingway, according to a footnote by Edmund Wilson to Fitzgerald's Notebooks published in *The Crack-up*; but Hemingway himself seems to have got the observation from Mary Colum, the critic.

Movies

■ ■

1. What triumph of *kitsch* opened on Hollywood Boulevard in May 1927?

2. In the following year, who starred in *Steamboat Willie*?

3. What did the following have in common: Stan Laurel, Charlie Chaplin, Bob Hope, Cary Grant, Elizabeth Taylor, and Alfred Hitchcock?

4. How did Fred Allen define an associate producer?

5. In *Casablanca* what did Captain Louis Renault (Claude Rains) reply when Rick Blaine (Humphrey Bogart) said that he had a loaded pistol pointed at his heart?

6. Of the following, who can be detected as being one up on the others: Robert Montgomery, George Montgomery, James Garner, Robert Mitchum, Dick Powell, and Humphrey Bogart?

7. In which film did Cuthbert J. Twillie and Flower Belle Lee make an implausible pair as an itinerant purveyor of "novelties and notions," and a woman who has just been run out of town?

8. Who played the part of the Pink Panther in the first film of the Blake Edwards series?

9. Which hilarious French farce has as its central characters two delightful "fairy queens"?

10. What was Constance Bennett's comment when she first observed Marilyn Monroe undulating across the lot?

Movies

1. Grauman's Chinese Theater, which was traditionally used for the big Hollywood premieres. Its minarets of burnished copper, jade-green pagoda roof, ornate obelisks, and enormous stone dragons were sufficiently vulgar to please everyone. Its forecourt contained the footprints and signatures of the stars, the first of whom to be so enshrined were Mary Pickford, Douglas Fairbanks, Norma and Constance Talmadge. The theater still exists as Mann's Chinese.

2. Walt Disney's Mickey Mouse, who made his initial appearance in the first synchronized sound cartoon.

3. They were all born in England.

4. "The only guy in Hollywood who'll associate with a producer."

5. "Believe me, Rick, that is my least vulnerable spot."

6. Robert Mitchum. They all have played Raymond Chandler's famous private eye Philip Marlowe on the screen, but Mitchum is the only one to have played him twice—first in *Farewell, My Lovely* and then in a new version of *The Big Sleep*.

7. *My Little Chickadee*, starring W. C. Fields and Mae West, who are jointly credited with the original screenplay.

8. No one. The Pink Panther was the name of the fabulous diamond that was stolen by the Phantom.

9. *La Cage aux Folles*, the largest-grossing foreign film to date.

10. "That girl's got a great future behind her."

"Murder Will Out"
■■

1. Which mystery story grips the reader with this compelling lead: "Some women give birth to murderers, some go to bed with them, and some marry them. Lina Aysgarth had lived with her husband for nearly eight years before she realized her husband was a murderer"?

2. Who was done in by Ingram Frisar at a brawl in a Deptford tavern in 1593?

3. What happened one cold morning in 1692 at the Pass of Glencoe in the Highlands of Scotland?

4. T. S. Eliot's verse drama *Murder in the Cathedral*, concerns the murder of Thomas à Becket, Archbishop of Canterbury, by followers of Henry II, who had cried, "Who will rid me of this turbulent priest?" What dilemma did Eliot pose in these lines?

> The last temptation is the greatest treason:
> To do the right deed for the wrong reason.

5. What is wrong with the sequence "hanged, drawn, and quartered"?

6. Who was unsuccessfully fed poisoned cakes and wine; then shot, emasculated, and pushed through the ice of a frozen river?

7. Which heir to the British throne has been mentioned as a possible suspect in the Jack the Ripper murders that shocked London in 1888?

8. Which literary heroine commits a murder in Bournemouth, is arrested at Stonehenge, and is hanged at Winchester?

9. In which poem do the following lines appear?

> Yet each man kills the thing he loves,
>   By each let this be heard,
> Some do it with a bitter look,
>   Some with a flattering word,
> The coward does it with a kiss,
>   The brave man with a sword!

10. What unsavory pair of millionaire teenagers tried to commit a perfect crime, or "thrill murder," in Chicago in 1924?

"Murder Will Out"

1. *Before the Fact*, by Francis Iles, whose real name was Anthony Berkeley Cox. Alfred Hitchcock's film *Suspicion*, starring Cary Grant and Joan Fontaine, who won an Oscar as Best Actress for her role in it, was based on this book, except for the movie's contrived happy ending.

2. The dramatist Christopher Marlowe, apparently in an argument over a bill, but possibly for political reasons—Marlowe was certainly an agent of the English intelligence service, and perhaps a double agent.

3. A troop of the Clan Campbell were entertained by a village of Macdonalds for ten days, then massacred 36 of their hosts in the night. The violent Highlands were horrified, not at the killing but at the breach of hospitality, and because it had been ordered by the Government as a cold-blooded exemplary atrocity to cow potential Jacobites.

4. The question is: was it Becket's principled defiance of encroaching royal power that caused his death, or did his sense of the heroic compel him to seek martyrdom in the prospect of heavenly glory?

5. The correct order of business was "drawn, hanged, and quartered."

6. Rasputin, the Russian monk and "holy man" who exercised a sinister influence over the court of Nicholas II. A group of noblemen murdered him at the house of Prince Felix Yussupov in Petrograd (now Leningrad) in 1916. (The Prince's palace in the Crimea was Stalin's headquarters at the Yalta Conference.)

7. Prince Albert Victor, Duke of Clarence, the eldest son of the future Edward VII. On his death in 1892 his brother Prince George, Duke of York, became heir apparent and later George V. In an unprecedented move Buckingham Palace has officially stated that the Duke of Clarence was not staying in London at the time of each of the Ripper's murders.

8. Tess Durbeyfield in Thomas Hardy's *Tess of the D'Urbervilles*.

9. "The Ballad of Reading Gaol," by Oscar Wilde.

10. Nathan F. Leopold, Jr., and Richard A. Loeb killed Loeb's cousin, Robert Franks. Leopold left his glasses behind, providing the clue that led to their conviction.

Musical Interlude

■ ■

1. The great Franco-Italian composer Jean Baptiste Lully is the only conductor to have died in the line of duty. How did this come about?

2. Where did Beethoven first hear his Ninth Symphony?

3. Many popular songs are derived from the classics. Can you name the sources of the following?
   - a) "A Stranger in Paradise"
   - b) "All My Love"
   - c) "Goin' Home"
   - d) "I'm Always Chasing Rainbows"
   - e) "When the Lights Go on Again"
   - f) "Tonight We Love"

4. What is considered to be the Rolls-Royce of pianos?

5. Who, by the time he was 8 years of age, had sat on the knee of the Empress Maria Theresa, delighted the court of George III, composed four sonatas, and was buried in a pauper's grave when he died insolvent at 35?

6. What, besides being musical compositions, do the following have in common: Dukas' "The Sorcerer's Apprentice," Schubert's "Ave Maria," Moussorgsky's "Night on Bald Mountain," and Stravinsky's "The Rites of Spring"?

7. Explain the connection between Handel and Gibraltar.

8. Can you name the song most frequently sung in the English-speaking world?

9. What do the following have in common apart from being symphonies: the Rhenish, the Polish, the Scottish?

10. The beer-stained manuscripts, unearthed by Professor Schickele, of which composer included such masterworks as "Perückenstück" (hair piece from *The Civilian Barber*), *The Stoned Guest* (an opera in one-half unnatural act), and the newly-discovered cantata "Blaues Gras" (bluegrass)?

Musical Interlude

1. Enraged by the obtuseness of an orchestra, he drove his six-foot baton into his foot, causing an abscess from which he died. On his deathbed he composed an exquisite *Miserere*.

2. Nowhere. He finished it in 1824 but had become totally deaf in 1819. The symphony was first performed in Vienna.

3. a) Borodin, "Polovtsian Dance No. 2"
   b) Ravel, "Bolero"
   c) Dvořák, "New World Symphony"
   d) Chopin, "Fantasie Impromptu"
   e) Beethoven, "Minuet in G"
   f) Tchaikovsky, "Piano Concerto No. 1"

4. The Bösendorfer Imperial Grand, which is manufactured only in Vienna.

5. Wolfgang Amadeus Mozart. Toward the end of his life, he composed three symphonies in 42 days: No. 39 in E Flat, No. 40 in G Minor, and No. 41 in C, known as the Jupiter Symphony.

6. They are all heard (and seen) in Walt Disney's classic feature-length film *Fantasia*.

7. He composed a "Jubilate" and the "Utrecht Te Deum" to celebrate the Peace of Utrecht in 1713, by which England kept Gibraltar.

8. "Happy Birthday to You," written in 1936 by Mildred Patty Hill, whose estate still collects royalties on it.

9. They are all third symphonies—by Schumann, Tchaikovsky, and Mendelssohn respectively.

10. P.D.Q. Bach, the 21st child of Johann the Elder and a twig on the family tree, who overcame the most staggering obstacle ever placed before a composer—absolute and utter lack of talent—and ignored handicaps that would have sent other men into teaching or government. He was catapulted into obscurity with works like "Iphigenia in Brooklyn," a cantata featuring spirited solos on P.D.Q.'s favorite instrument, the wine bottle. Like the man, the initials P.D.Q. stand for nothing.

Naval and Nautical Lore

■ ■

1. From which port in Spain did the Spanish Armada sail, and who commanded the English fleet when it faced the Armada in 1588?

2. Where is the Plimsoll line located, and what does it indicate?

3. Lord Nelson, victor over the combined French and Spanish fleets at the Battle of Trafalgar in 1805, lost his right arm at Santa Cruz de Tenerife in 1797. Where did he lose his right leg?

4. Why is a ship's latrine known as the head?

5. Name the Scottish-born sailor who has a dance named after him, became a rear-admiral in the Russian navy, and died in Paris, where he was originally buried, his body only being recovered when the U.S. ambassador had a tunnel driven into the cemetery by mining engineers.

6. If you sailed due east from Cape Horn, what would be your next landfall?

7. Which golden rule did the Right Honourable Sir Joseph Porter, K.C.B., follow to become the First Lord of the Admiralty?

8. For what period of time was a ship originally quarantined for fear of spreading contagious disease?

9. On what infamous day did who say, "Praise the Lord and pass the ammunition," a line which caught the public's imagination and provided Frank Loesser with the title of a popular wartime song?

10. Being "three sheets to the wind" is synonymous with being drunk. How did the phrase arise?

Naval and Nautical Lore

1. La Coruña in northwest Spain, where it was forced to seek shelter from a storm on the voyage from Lisbon. Charles, Lord Howard of Effingham, later Earl of Nottingham, was in command of the English fleet, and the English captains included Sir Francis Drake, Sir John Hawkins, and Sir Martin Frobisher.

2. The Plimsoll line, introduced after agitation by Samuel Plimsoll, is a circled, horizontal line drawn amidships on both sides of a ship, indicating the legal limit of submergence to prevent overloading.

3. He never did. Nelson lost most of the sight of his right eye at the siege of Calvi on the northwestern coast of Corsica.

4. Because this facility in the past was located in the forward part of the ship.

5. John Paul Jones (John Paul until he changed it to avoid a murder investigation), who is considered the greatest of American naval heroes and founder of the American naval tradition. Among his famous sayings is: "I wish to have no connection with any ship that does not sail fast, for I intend to go in harm's way." He is now buried in a Napoleon-like sarcophagus in the crypt beneath the Naval Academy Chapel at Annapolis, Maryland.

6. Cape Horn—you would encounter no other land at that latitude.

7. According to Sir Joseph in Gilbert and Sullivan's light opera H.M.S. *Pinafore:*

> Be careful to be guided by the golden rule—
> Stick close to your desks and never go to sea,
> And you all may be Rulers of the Queen's Navee!

8. For forty days, the Italian equivalent of which is *quarantina giorni*, which was believed to be the incubation period for the black plague.

9. Chaplain Howell M. Forgy, aboard the cruiser *New Orleans* at the time of the Japanese attack on Pearl Harbor on December 7, 1941.

10. The ropes attached to the lower part of the sail are called sheets. When all three sheets are loosened, the ship tends to reel in the wind.

North of the Border

■ ■

1. Who is generally regarded as the first great pioneer of what is now Canada?

2. Who were the *coureurs des bois*, and why were they renowned in the early days of Canadian history?

3. Where are the Plains of Abraham, and what important event occurred there in 1759?

4. What were the North American campaigns of the Seven Years War called, and why did the settlement of this war at the Treaty of Paris in 1763 result in possibly one of the worst real estate deals of all time?

5. Name the four Maritime Provinces of Canada.

6. Which governor-general of Canada wrote biographies of Montrose, Scott, and Cromwell, as well as a number of adventure novels?

7. Which are the only two rivers that form part of the border between the United States and Canada?

8. What is *la langue de joual*?

9. Why was Kenneth B. Taylor considered a hero by the American people in 1980?

10. What is the national tree of Canada?

North of the Border

1. Jacques Cartier, first European explorer of the Gulf of St. Lawrence and discoverer of the St. Lawrence River, in the period from 1534 to 1542.

2. They were the woodsmen who used the rivers as highways and hunted beaver and other animals for the European market.

3. Overlooking Québec city; here the British under General Wolfe defeated General de Montcalm's French garrison. Both commanding officers were mortally wounded in the battle.

4. Called the French and Indian War in America, it marked the end of French domination over Canada and the emergence of Great Britain as the world's chief colonial empire. For ceding all its North American possessions, which Voltaire called "a few acres of snow," with the exception of the tiny islands of St. Pierre and Miquelon, France recovered the sugar islands of Martinique and Guadeloupe—a bargain which may charitably be termed shortsighted.

5. Nova Scotia, New Brunswick, Prince Edward Island, and, since 1949, Newfoundland.

6. John Buchan, 1st Baron Tweedsmuir.

7. The St. Lawrence and the Niagara Rivers. The latter flows between Lake Erie and Lake Ontario, and separates Ontario and New York State.

8. Canadian French, so called because of its characteristic deformation of *cheval*, horse, into *joual*.

9. He was the Canadian Ambassador to Iran who hid six American members of the U.S. Embassy staff there in the Canadian Embassy, and then spirited them out of the country, after militants seized the U.S. Embassy in Tehran in November 1979.

10. The sugar maple, a representation of a leaf of which forms the centerpiece of the Canadian flag.

Olla Podrida
■■

1. Name the most famous literary work of the Greek philosopher Socrates that has come down to us.

2. Who actually gave the alarm that the British were coming "on the eighteenth of April, in Seventy-five"?

3. "Occam's razor" is named after the 14th-century philosopher William of Occam, who is widely regarded as the last of the great medieval thinkers. What does the phrase mean?

4. Which famous swasher of bucklers was born in Tasmania, and where is it?

5. Who "dined on mince and slices of quince,/Which they ate with a runcible spoon"?

6. Which sovereign country is digging itself away so fast that it is likely to disappear altogether, forcing its citizens to find themselves another country?

7. Name the only U.S. Indian tribe to have a written language.

8. Can you otherwise identify a) Prince Siddhartha Gautama, b) Florence Nightingale Graham, c) C.3.3.?

9. The name of what game, popular during the reign of Charles II, lends itself to two London streets?

10. When Louis XIII lay dying, he heard someone moving about the room and asked who was there. What reply was given?

Olla Podrida

1. Socrates left no writings of his own. All we know of his teachings comes indirectly from certain dialogues and memoirs of his disciples Plato and Xenophon.

2. Samuel Prescott. Of the three horsemen riding to give the alarm, William Dawes turned back and Paul Revere was briefly detained by British pickets, but Prescott got through to Lexington. Prescott was later captured and died in prison so obscurely that the date is not known. His achievement was eclipsed by Revere's later distinction.

3. "Occam's razor" means the principle of parsimony in logic, or the economy of assumptions in logical formulation. In other words, the analysis requiring fewer assumptions is preferable to those requiring more.

4. Errol Flynn. (Swash means "to bang together," and a buckler is a small round shield.) Tasmania lies just south of the mainland of Australia, of which it is a state.

5. "The Owl and the Pussycat," according to Edward Lear's poem.

6. The island nation of Nauru in the Pacific, an enormous block of fossilized guano phosphate, so valuable to the world's chemical and fertilizer industry that it has become one of the richest and one of the most perishable areas in the world.

7. The Cherokee, whose syllabic alphabet of 85 characters was invented by their chief Sequoya.

8. a) Buddha, a Sanskrit word for Awakened (that is, Enlightened) One; b) Elizabeth Arden, a leading figure in the field of cosmetics and fashion; c) Oscar Wilde, who signed the first edition in 1898 of his most celebrated poem, *The Ballad of Reading Gaol*, in this fashion. (C.3.3. was Wilde's jail number, indicating cellblock C, floor 3, cell 3.)

9. Pall Mall, after which the Mall (and from this all malls) and Pall Mall derive their names. Pall was the ball and mall the mallet. A descendant of the game has survived and is called croquet.

10. The tiny voice of a five-year-old boy said, "Louis XIV."

Openers

■ ■

Identify the authors and titles of the literary works whose opening lines appear below.

1. "Gather ye rosebuds while ye may,
   Old Time is still a-flying . . ."
2. "Stately, plump Buck Mulligan came from the stairhead, bearing a bowl of lather."
3. "The Mole had been working very hard all morning."
4. "What dire offense from am'rous causes springs . . ."
5. "Hazel Morse was a large, fair woman of the type that incites some men when they use the word 'blonde' to click their tongues and wag their heads roguishly."
6. "Just now the lilac is in bloom,
   All before my little room . . ."
7. "I am standing on the Pont des Arts in Paris."
8. "It was not until several weeks after he had decided to murder his wife that Dr. Bickleigh took any active steps in the matter. Murder is a serious business."
9. "I strove with none, for none was worth my strife."
10. "Sir Walter Elliot, of Kellynch-hall, in Somersetshire, was a man who, for his own amusement, never took up any book but the Baronetage; there he found occupation for an idle hour, and consolation in a distressed one; . . . this was the page at which the favourite volume always opened: ELLIOT OF KELLYNCH-HALL."

Openers

1. Robert Herrick, "To the Virgins, to Make Much of Time."

2. James Joyce, *Ulysses*.

3. Kenneth Grahame, *The Wind in the Willows*.

4. Alexander Pope, "The Rape of the Lock."

5. Dorothy Parker, "Big Blonde."

6. Rupert Brooke, "The Old Vicarage, Grantchester."

7. Kenneth Clark, *Civilization*.

8. Francis Iles (Anthony Berkeley Cox), *Malice Aforethought*.

9. Walter Savage Landor, "Finis."

10. Jane Austen, *Persuasion*.

Opera

■ ■

1. "O Freiheit," the stirring hymn to freedom, is sung in which opera?

2. For what historic occasion was Giuseppe Verdi commissioned to write *Aïda*?

3. In the first act of Wagner's great opera, Lohengrin arrives on stage in a boat drawn by a swan. When at one performance the swan was pushed on too soon, what did the unruffled tenor, Leo Slezak, ask the stagehand?

4. In which German opera, ostensibly set in Egypt, does the hero, according to the libretto, enter in an Oriental hunting outfit?

5. Who delivers this patter song from which light opera?

I am the very model of a modern Major-Gineral,
I've information vegetable, animal and mineral;
I know the kings of England, and I quote the fights historical,
From Marathon to Waterloo, in order categorical;
I'm very well acquainted too with matters mathematical
I understand equations, both the simple and quadratical,
About binomial theorem I'm teeming with a lot o' news—
With many cheerful facts about the square of the hypotenuse.

6. Which novel was adapted as the libretto for Verdi's opera *La Traviata*?

7. Apart from being the sopranos and heroines of their respective operas, what two things do the Puccini Mimi, Tosca, and Butterfly have in common?

8. Which social historian noted that "opera is like a husband with a foreign title: expensive to support, hard to understand, and therefore, a supreme social challenge"?

9. Which avant-garde opera is set in a fictitious, ultimately failed American utopia founded by escaped convicts and inhabited by the dregs of society?

10. Can you name the opera whose last words are *"La commedia è finita"*?

Opera

1. *Fidelio*, the only opera Beethoven ever wrote.

2. The opening of the Suez Canal. It was first performed at Cairo Opera House in 1871, two years after the canal had opened.

3. "What time does the next swan leave?"

4. *The Magic Flute*, by Wolfgang Amadeus Mozart.

5. Major-General Stanley in Gilbert and Sullivan's *The Pirates of Penzance*.

6. *La Dame aux Camélias*, by Alexander Dumas *fils*, son of the author of *The Three Musketeers*.

7. They are all heard offstage before they make their entrances, and they all die before the end of their respective operas: Mimi from tuberculosis, Tosca by drowning, and Butterfly by stabbing herself.

8. Cleveland Amory, author of *The Proper Bostonians*, *The Last Resorts*, and *The Trouble with Nowadays*.

9. *The Rise and Fall of the City of Mahagonny*, by Kurt Weill with libretto by Bertold Brecht. The grim, sardonic work reflects Weill's Germany of the 1920s with seedy cabarets, Nazi Brown Shirts, and economic despair. In one particularly haunting scene a man eats himself to death.

10. *I Pagliacci*, by Ruggiero Leoncavallo.

Oscars

■ ■

1. Who won Oscars as Best Actress for two consecutive years?

2. What was the first song to win an Academy Award, and in which film was it featured?

3. Name the last black and white picture to win an award for Best Picture.

4. Which father-and-son team was honored in 1948 for what picture?

5. Who is the only person in the history of the Academy to present himself with an Oscar?

6. In what film, for which he won a 1952 Oscar, was Jimmy Stewart unrecognizable?

7. Which star received four Oscars, yet was never nominated?

8. Only two films have won Academy Awards for Best Actor, Actress, Director, and Screenplay. Can you name them and the individual award winners?

9. Who spoke these lines about whom in which film that garnered six Oscars in 1950: "This is Miss Caswell. Miss Caswell is an actress. She is a graduate of the Copacabana School of Dramatic Art."?

10. The 1960s marked the first decade in which four musicals won Academy Awards for Best Picture. What are they?

Oscars

1. Luise Rainer for *The Great Ziegfeld* in 1936 and *The Good Earth* in 1937, and Katharine Hepburn for *Guess Who's Coming to Dinner* in 1967 and *The Lion in Winter* in 1968.
2. "The Continental" which was heard in the 1934 film *The Gay Divorcee*, starring Fred Astaire and Ginger Rogers.
3. *The Apartment* in 1960, starring Jack Lemmon and directed by Billy Wilder.
4. Walter Huston for Best Supporting Actor and John Huston for Best Direction and Best Screenplay in *The Treasure of Sierra Madre*.
5. Irving Berlin for "White Christmas" from *Holiday Inn* in 1942. This was in the days when presenters were not separated from the categories for which they were nominated.
6. *The Greatest Show on Earth*, directed by Cecil B. De Mille, in which Jimmy Stewart, playing a clown, was never seen without his makeup on.
7. Bob Hope, who received Special or Honorary Awards.
8. 1934's *It Happened One Night*, which starred Clark Gable and Claudette Colbert, was directed by Frank Capra and written by Robert Riskin; and 1975's *One Flew Over the Cuckoo's Nest*, which starred Jack Nicholson and Louise Fletcher, was directed by Milos Forman and written by Lawrence Hauben and Bo Goldman. (*Gone With the Wind*, which swept the Awards field in 1939, is not included because Clark Gable lost out as Best Actor to Robert Donat in *Goodbye, Mr. Chips*.)
9. George Sanders about Marilyn Monroe in *All About Eve*. Sanders won an Oscar in the film as Best Supporting Actor.
10. *West Side Story* in 1961, *My Fair Lady* in 1964, *The Sound of Music* in 1965, and *Oliver!* in 1968. All were originally stage musicals.

"Out Where the West Begins"

■ ■

1. If you were to saddle up to ride the Chisholm Trail, where would you be and where would you be going to or coming from? What about the Oregon Trail?

2. "Remember the Alamo" is a rallying cry for Texans who consider it "the cradle of Texas liberty." For what purpose was it first built?

3. Why would the song "Don't Fence Me In" not appeal to Joseph F. Glidden?

4. The 20-mule teams were famous for hauling wagonloads of borax. How many mules were used in a 20-mule team?

5. What is wrong with the following lines from "Home on the Range"?

> Oh, give me a home where the buffalo roam,
> Where the deer and the antelope play . . .

6. A maverick is one who refuses to conform, the name coming from a Texas cattle baron, Sam Maverick, who refused to brand his calves, thus giving his name to all unbranded cattle and hence to those who "wore no man's brand." What was his perfectly sound reason for so doing?

7. Who was the famous "hanging judge" of Fort Smith, Arkansas?

8. What is the name given to the heavy leather trousers without a seat, worn by cowboys over ordinary trousers to protect their legs?

9. Who developed Santa Gertrudis cattle, and what is the breed a cross between?

10. Name the most popular frontier and Western novelist of all time, whose sales far surpass those of Max Brand and Zane Grey combined.

"Out Where the West Begins"

1. In or between San Antonio, Texas, and Abilene, Kansas. The Oregon Trail branched off the Mississippi, usually around Independence, Missouri, and ran as far as Fort Vancouver in what was still called the Oregon Territory.

2. It was originally the Franciscan mission of San Antonio de Valera and was later converted into a fortress.

3. Because in 1874 he patented the first practical form of barbed wire, which began the gradual closing of the open range as the farmers enclosed ever-increasing expanses of grassland.

4. Eighteen—the two animals closest to the wagons were always horses, which were called wheelers. The muleskinner would occasionally ride on the left-hand horse.

5. Antelope, native to Africa and Asia, do not exist in America. Brewster Higley, the author of the song, was referring to the pronghorn, a small deer resembling an antelope and having small forked horns. It is also called pronghorn antelope. The American buffalo is correctly termed the American bison.

6. As his ranch was on an island, he saw no need to brand his calves.

7. Isaac C. Parker, who had final authority over judgments in all crimes in Indian Territory. In his 21 years on the bench, Judge Parker sent 160 men to their deaths on the huge gallows he had built outside his court designed to hang as many as 12 men at a time.

8. Chaps, which is the shortened form of *chaparejos*.

9. Santa Gertrudis cattle are derived from crosses between shorthorn cows and Brahma bulls. This breed of beef cattle was developed by Robert J. Kleberg, Jr., of the King Ranch in southern Texas, in the early 1900s. The breed is now widely distributed in the United States and has been extensively exported.

10. Louis L'Amour, with 79 titles in print which have sold something like 110 million copies in 19 languages. To date, 23 of his stories have become major motion pictures, and one of his fictional families, the Sacketts, gave its name to a four-hour TV mini-series.

Painting

••

1. Why is the brilliant 16th-century mannerist painter and sculptor Daniele de Volterra nicknamed *Il Branghettone* (The Breeches Maker)?

2. John Constable, famous for his English landscapes, described the work of which artist as being "airy visions painted with tinted steam"?

3. Which world-famous picture had to have its name changed after it was cleaned?

4. Who wrote of whose picture, "I have seen, and heard, much of Cockney impudence before now; but never expected to hear a coxcomb ask two hundred guineas for flinging a pot of paint in the public's face"?

5. Whose painting, *Déjeuner sur l'Herbe*, was turned down by the Academy of Fine Arts for their annual salon and was shown at the Salon des Réfusés?

6. Hoppner and Delacroix are supposed to have had what in common?

7. Which famous American artist painted a memorable picture of a lone black man on a disabled sloop surrounded by circling sharks with the sails of a large ship visible on the far horizon?

8. Name the huge (25 feet wide and 11 feet tall) black, gray, and white painting which was shipped in 1981 from the United States to Spain, a country which has never seen it.

9. Which American picture was rediscovered at an English boys' school and sold at auction in 1979 for $2.5 million—at the time more than twice as much as an American work had ever fetched?

10. Who said that "painting is the art of protecting flat surfaces from the weather and exposing them to the critics"?

Painting

1. He was employed to paint clothes on the nudes in Michelangelo's *Last Judgment* in the Sistine Chapel.

2. J. M. W. Turner. As his later style became increasingly free Turner encountered violent criticism, but he was passionately defended by the youthful Ruskin in the first volume of his *Modern Painters*. His painting, *Juliet and Her Nurse*, was sold for $6.4 million in 1980, a record price at the time.

3. Rembrandt's *Night Watch*, which, after it was cleaned in 1946–7, was proven by archival research to be a daytime picture of *The Shooting Company of Capt. Frans Banning Cocq*.

4. John Ruskin about James A. McNeill Whistler's *Nocturne in Black and Gold—The Falling Rocket*. Whistler promptly sued for libel. He was awarded one farthing—which he wore on his watch chain—but was bankrupted by the costs of the 1876 trial.

5. Édouard Manet, who is now considered the father of modern art. Among his other famous works are *Olympia* and *Bar aux Folies Bergère*.

6. It has been alleged that Hoppner was the illegitimate son of George III and Delacroix the illegitimate son of Talleyrand.

7. Winslow Homer. The painting, titled *The Gulf Stream*, is his best known painting and hangs in the Art Institute of Chicago.

8. *Guernica*, Picasso's masterpiece on the victims of war and fascism. It was named after the town of Guernica y Luno that is the spiritual center of the Basques and was savagely bombed by German warplanes in 1937 in support of Franco's advancing armies. Picasso stipulated that the picture should not hang in his native land until democracy raised its head there.

9. *Icebergs*, a long-lost work by Frederick Edwin Church, the 19th-century landscape painter—widely acclaimed as a luminist masterpiece.

10. Ambrose Bierce, in *The Devil's Dictionary*.

Pairing Off

■ ■

1. What was odd about the birth of Castor and Pollux, the twin heroes of classical mythology who were also called the Dioscuri?

2. With whom did Dismas and Gestas keep company at the end?

3. Who were Paolo and Francesca da Rimini, and who immortalized them?

4. Name the 19th-century German philologists who achieved fame in a more lighthearted field.

5. Tom and Jerry are known as cat and mouse cartoon characters and as a hot, spiced rum drink. Who were the original Tom and Jerry?

6. Who, during a marriage ceremony, said, "If any man can show just cause, why they may not joyfully be loined together . . ."?

7. Can you otherwise identify Nan, Burt, Flossie, and Freddie?

8. Who is reputed to have devised this punning epitaph for two rustic lovers struck by lightning?

> Here lye two Lovers, who had the mishap
> Tho' very chaste people, to die of a Clap.

9. Which two Southeast Asian brothers are commemorated by a fire fixture?

10. What does the biathlon pair?

Pairing Off

1. They were hatched from an egg laid by Leda, who was impregnated by Zeus when he approached her in the form of a swan.

2. Jesus. In medieval legend these were the names of the two thieves crucified on either side of the Savior.

3. They were the guilty lovers immortalized by Dante in the *Divine Comedy*.

4. The Brothers Grimm—Jacob and Wilhelm—who are remembered, apart from their great contributions to philology, for their collection of folk tales for children.

5. The two chief characters, Corinthian Tom and Jerry Hawthorn, in *Life in London*, by Pierce Egan, English sportswriter, about life in the metropolis in the early 19th century.

6. Canon Spooner, for many years Warden of New College, Oxford, who was famous for unintentional transpositions of (usually initial) word sounds, giving rise to the term "spoonerism." Once, when dismissing a student, he is reputed to have said, "You have deliberately tasted two worms and you can leave Oxford by the next town drain."

7. They were the two pairs of Bobbsey twins in a series of books for children by Edward Stratemeyer, who wrote under the pseudonym Laura Lee Hope.

8. Alexander Pope, in a 1718 letter to Lady Mary Wortley Montagu, an English author noted primarily for her spirited correspondence.

9. Chang and Eng, the original Siamese twins, who are commemorated by the Standpipe Siamese, a doubleheaded water pipe to which two hoses can be attached.

10. The biathlon is an Olympic event, started in 1960, which combines cross-country skiing and riflery. The Russians and Scandinavians excel in this event.

Phrase Origins

■ ■

Give the probable source of the following phrases or expressions:

1. Hold your horses!

2. Getting down to brass tacks

3. Hoist by his own petard

4. Keep your pecker up!

5. Apple-pie order

6. Naked truth

7. Win hands down

8. Lame duck

9. As queer as Dick's hatband

10. White elephant

Phrase Origins

1. When the circus came to town before the days of cars, the elephants would panic the horses, so the circus dispatched men before the parade to cry out, "Hold your horses!"

2. In country stores, the merchants hammered brass-headed tacks into the counter to measure lengths of cloth. This meant that bargaining was over and the sale made.

3. An allusion to someone brought to a sticky end by a strategem he plotted to ensnare others. In Renaissance warfare, a petar or petard was an explosive charge used to blow up a castle gate or wall. Occasionally it discharged prematurely, as Shakespeare noted in *Hamlet*: "For 'tis the sport to have the engineer/ Hoist with his own petar." (In French, *péter* means to break wind, or fart.)

4. A barnyard expression. When a chicken's pecker (its beak) is hanging down, it is a sign it is in poor health.

5. A corruption of the French phrase *nappe plié*, meaning neatly folded linen or table napkins.

6. In the old fable, Truth and Falsehood went swimming. Emerging first, Falsehood put on Truth's clothing, and Truth, not wanting to wear Falsehood's clothes, had to go naked.

7. The jockey of an easy winner finishes with both hands down on the horse's neck, not needing to use the whip.

8. Lame duck derives from a hunter's maxim: "Never waste powder on a dead duck," but the political "ducks" brought down at the polls go on waddling, sometimes very actively, until January. The phrase dates from the 19th century when the old Congress and President kept office until March.

9. Dick was Richard, son of the Lord Protector Oliver Cromwell, who ruled England from 1653 to 1658. On his father's death the amiable but ineffectual Richard inherited, but was forced to abdicate within a year. "Hatband" was a sardonic reference to his notional crown, and "queer" is used in the English sense of false or counterfeit, not homosexual.

10. In Siam (now Thailand) white—really, very pale gray—elephants were considered sacred and became the property of the king. If one of his courtiers displeased him, the king would give him a white elephant, which he then would be responsible for keeping and feeding.

Pick a Number

■■

1. It counts for nothing and cannot do what its companions can, but is able to make them greater. What is it?

2. What numerical comparison did Sir Galahad make about his strength, and why, in his opinion, was he so endowed?

3. How many degrees are there between S.S.W. and S.S.E.?

4. The name of which tragedy by Aeschylus contains a number?

5. In what numerical fashion do journalists customarily end an article, and how did this practice originate?

6. There are three books, of a hundred pages each with no covers, standing on a shelf. If a bookworm starts at page 1 of the first book and eats his way up to and including page 100 of the third, how many pages has it eaten through?

7. How many elusive cities of Cibola did the Spanish explorer Francisco Coronado seek in what is now the Zuñi country of New Mexico?

8. Complete this quotation from *Genesis*: "And all the days of Methuselah were . . ."

9. How many grooves does the long-playing record have?

10. Margaret Thatcher is Britain's first woman prime minister. How many other women prime ministers have there been?

Pick a Number

1. The number zero, which cannot be divided by itself.
2. Ten. Alfred, Lord Tennyson explains why in "Sir Galahad":

> My strength is as the strength of ten,
> Because my heart is pure.

3. Forty-five degrees.
4. *The Seven against Thebes.*
5. They use the term =30= to indicate the end. This custom arose with the early telegraphists who used =30= as a sign-off signal.
6. Only 102 pages. The worm does not have to eat its way through pages 100 to 2 of the first book or pages 99 to 1 of the third book because, standing on a shelf, page 1 of the first book and page 100 of the third are the only two pages that touch the middle book.
7. Seven. There was no fabled gold to be found, but the Indian pueblos looked golden in the sunset.
8. "Nine hundred sixty and nine years."
9. Two—one on each side.
10. By the end of 1981, six: Sri Lanka's Sirimavo Bandaranaike, India's Indira Gandhi, Israel's Golda Meir, Portugal's Maria da Lurdes Pintassilgo, Dominica's Mary Eugenia Charles, and Norway's Gro Harlem Brundtland.

Pirates

■ ■

1. What is the delectable derivation of the word buccaneer?

2. How did the legendary Captain Kidd meet his end?

3. Give the literal meaning of the term freebooter.

4. Who was Cap'n Flint, and what was his raucous cry?

5. Which island group has for its motto *"Expulsis Piratis Restituta Commercia."* ("With the pirates driven out, trade is restored.")?

6. Which royal personage issues the following manifesto?

> Oh, better far to live and die
> Under the brave black flag I fly,
> Than play a sanctimonious part,
> With a pirate head and a pirate heart.
> Away to the cheating world go you,
> Where pirates all are well-to-do;
> But I'll be true to the song I sing,
> And live and die a pirate king.
> For I am a Pirate King.

7. Which infamous freebooters' hangout, now drowned under the sea, was called the wickedest spot in the Caribbean? Near which capital city was it located?

8. By which name is Edward Teach better known?

9. How is the hymn of the U.S. Marine Corps connected with piracy?

10. Which colorful figure threw in his lot with General Andrew Jackson in the War of 1812?

Pirates

1. The buccaneers, precursors of the Caribbean pirates, cured their meat on *boucans*, which was the French word for barbecue frames.

2. William Kidd, who once owned considerable property in lower Manhattan, was a British privateer turned pirate. He was hanged in 1701 for killing his mate with a bucket and was left dangling in an iron framework called a gibbet overlooking the Thames estuary as a grisly object lesson.

3. One who obtains his booty free—hence, a pirate.

4. Cap'n Flint is the parrot belonging to Long John Silver, the pirate leader in Stevenson's *Treasure Island*; he is named after a great pirate under whom Silver served. His habitual squawk is, "Pieces of eight! pieces of eight!"

5. The Bahamas. New Providence Island, especially the town of Nassau, had long been a pirate stronghold until the first governor, Woodes Rogers, restored order. (It was Rogers, incidentally, who rescued the marooned Alexander Selkirk, the original of Defoe's Robinson Crusoe.)

6. The Pirate King in Gilbert and Sullivan's *The Pirates of Penzance*.

7. Port Royal, near Kingston, Jamaica: the base of the pirate Henry Morgan, who was later knighted and made lieutenant-governor of the island.

8. The notorious Blackbeard. After his well-deserved end in North Carolina's Ocracoke Inlet in 1718, the Royal Navy impaled his severed head on a cutter's bowsprit to mark the virtual end of piracy in North American coastal waters.

9. Its line, "To the shores of Tripoli," refers to the Tripolitan War, one of the conflicts between the United States and the Barbary States (Tripoli, Tunisia, Algeria, and Morocco) arising from the U.S. refusal to buy immunity from piracy. Seven U.S. Marines spearheaded a motley army across 500 miles of desert to take the city of Tripoli from the rear, only to discover that a truce had been made.

10. Jean Laffitte. Because of his knowledge of the terrain, he was of inestimable help to Jackson in repulsing the British attack on New Orleans.

Plants and Trees

■ ■

1. Who, on which occasion, was made to wear what is now known as *Zizyphus Spina Christi*?

2. In the Bible, in which tree did Absalom get his hair caught, and what did Zaccheus climb to get a better view of Jesus?

3. Whose safety depended on trees not growing legs?

4. What is unique about the Glastonbury thorn, a species of hawthorn that is a legend in England?

5. Which English king found himself quite literally up a tree?

6. By what name is John Chapman better known?

7. Which four-time Pulitzer Prize winner for poetry wrote these lines?

> The woods are lovely, dark and deep,
> But I have promises to keep
> And miles to go before I sleep.

8. Explain the significance of the name given to the French guerrilla arm of the Resistance that fought against the German occupation forces during World War II.

9. Pound for pound and dollar for dollar, what is the most valuable crop legally grown in the United States?

10. Name the only country to have a national flag with a tree on it.

Plants and Trees

1. Jesus Christ on the day of His crucifixion. His crown of thorns was fashioned from this tree, which is noted for its long spines. The genus Zizyphus is also known as the jujube tree from which the fruit-flavored, chewy candy or lozenge takes its name.

2. An oak (II Samuel 18:9) and a sycamore (Luke 19:4).

3. Macbeth's in Shakespeare's play. In the words of the three witches:

> Macbeth shall never vanquish'd be until
> Great Birnam wood to high Dunsinane hill
> Shall come against him.

The forces of Macduff camouflaged themselves with branches when they marched against Macbeth, so it seemed as if Birnam Wood was moving.

4. It blooms every year at Christmas time, but experts are not sure why.

5. Charles II, who hid in a giant oak tree after his defeat by Oliver Cromwell at the Battle of Worcester in 1651.

6. Johnny Appleseed, of whom the poet Vachel Lindsay wrote "In Praise of Johnny Appleseed":

> Planting the trees that would march and train
> On, in his name to the great Pacific,
> Like Birnam Wood to Dunsinane,
> Johnny Appleseed swept on.

7. Robert Frost in "Stopping by Woods on a Snowy Evening."

8. The Maquis took its name from the French word meaning mountain thicket, alluding to the undergrowth as a hiding place from the enemy.

9. Tobacco leaves, used for cigar wrappers, which are extensively cultivated in the Connecticut River Valley.

10. Lebanon, symbolizing the cedars of Lebanon.

Political Leaders
■ ■

1. Who led the first successful black slave revolt in the New World and died in a frozen fortress in the Jura Mountains?

2. Which British statesman on becoming Prime Minister said, "I have climbed to the top of the greasy pole."?

3. Who in the words of whom was "transported in a sealed truck like a plague bacillus from Switzerland into Russia"?

4. In the field of travel what did Hitler and Kemal Atatürk have in common?

5. Who made the remarkable, and possibly unique, observation that "Gaiety is the most outstanding feature of the Soviet Union"?

6. Can you name the only head of state to have been an "extra" in Hollywood?

7. Which three political leaders edited newspapers whose titles are translated as *Forward, Spark,* and *Worker?*

8. Who characteristically wrote, "The great masses of people . . . will more easily fall victims to a great lie than to a small one"?

9. Which literary stylist said: "I affected a combination of the styles of Macaulay and Gibbon, the staccato antitheses of the former, and the rolling sentences and genitival endings of the latter; and I stuck in a bit of my own from time to time"?

10. How did Alice Roosevelt Longworth ridicule Thomas E. Dewey, Republican nominee for president in 1944 against Franklin D. Roosevelt?

Political Leaders

1. Toussaint L'Ouverture, who paved the way for the independence of Haiti. He was given the name L'Ouverture (the opening) because of his fast-moving campaigns.

2. Benjamin Disraeli, later 1st Earl of Beaconsfield. At country fairs, a prize was given for getting up a pole drenched with pigs' fat: the impatient tried, ruined their clothes, and fell off, but cleaned up the pole for some cooler competitor. Disraeli was reflecting on all the men who had had better chances than his but ruined themselves on the way.

3. Lenin. After the outbreak of the Russian Revolution in 1917, the German government allowed him to travel across Germany from Switzerland to Sweden, and thence to Russia, in the correct assumption that he would disrupt the Russian war effort. The quotation is from *The World Crisis* by Winston S. Churchill, who erred in saying "a sealed truck"; Lenin went in an ordinary railway coach.

4. Both their fathers were customs officials.

5. Joseph Stalin.

6. Fidel Castro, who appeared briefly in some early films featuring Xavier Cugat, the Cuban bandleader.

7. Mussolini edited *Avanti* (Forward); Lenin edited *Iskra* (Spark); and Pilsudski edited *Robotnik* (Worker).

8. Adolf Hitler, in *Mein Kampf* (My Struggle).

9. Winston S. Churchill, in *My Early Life*, which was subtitled *A Roving Commission*.

10. She said, "How can the Republican Party nominate a man who looks like the bridegroom on a wedding cake?"

Potpourri

■ ■

1. Who painted the famous picture *The Death of Actaeon*, now in London's National Gallery, of what happened to Actaeon, the boastful huntsman? And what did happen to him?

2. What is a virgule?

3. A Cockney might say, "I ain't got the bees to pay me Burton." How would this be translated?

4. What would be the color of the thing you were seeking if, en route, you had to pass an episcopal object and a saint?

5. Name the genial television personality who won a prize in a science fiction limerick contest with this entry:

> Salutations to Arthur C. Clarke
> Who's constantly hitting the mark.
>   He has a class act
>   In both fiction and fact
> And gives off more charm than a quark.

6. If you were privileged enough to be admitted to the Black Museum of Scotland Yard, what would you find?

7. What kind of specialist was Doctor T. J. Eckleburg?

8. Who wrote the short story ".007"?

9. Explain the meaning of these foreign terms: a) *ne plus ultra* (L.); b) *dolce far niente* (It.); c) *coup de foudre* (Fr.).

10. A *mohel* is the person who performs the surgery at ritual circumcisions. How is he recompensed for his services?

Potpourri

1. Titian. Actaeon surprised the goddess Artemis bathing naked, whereupon she turned him into a stag, and his own hounds tore him to pieces.

2. A diagonal mark, /, used to separate numerals in fractions such as ¼, to separate alternatives as in "and/or," to represent the word per as in "miles/hour," and to indicate the ends of verse lines printed continuously as in "Candy/Is dandy." It is also called a stroke, slash, shilling, and solidus.

3. This is an example of Cockney rhyming slang: "I ain't got the money *(bees and honey)* to pay me rent *(Burton-on-Trent)*."

4. Blue. The Blue Riband of the Atlantic was held by the liner making the fastest time, in either direction, between Bishop Rock, off the Scilly Isles of England, and Ambrose lightship in the Atlantic south of New York.

5. Hugh Downs, host of many television shows, including the popular and informative *20/20* television newsmagazine on ABC.

6. A collection of objects which have been played an important role in some of the classic cases handled by London's Metropolitan Police. These items range from Jack the Ripper's taunting letters to the authorities, written in red ink, to the matchbox carried by John Christie, the ghoul of 10 Rillington Place, which contained one pubic hair from each of his female victims.

7. The oculist whose advertisement of two gigantic blue eyes with "retinas [*sic*] . . . one yard high" in *The Great Gatsby* by F. Scott Fitzgerald.

8. Not Ian Fleming, but Rudyard Kipling: it is the tale of an American locomotive which proves its way into the brotherhood of engines by hauling a breakdown train.

9. No more beyond, beyond all others, acme, culmination: *ne plus ultra* was said to have been written on the Mediterranean side of the Pillars of Hercules in the days before the Atlantic was explored; b) sweet doing nothing, pleasant idleness; c) thunderclap, love at first sight.

10. It is said that "the rabbi gets the fees, but the *mohel* gets the tips."

Power of the Press

■ ■

1. The term "fourth estate" refers to the public press and journalism or journalists generally, and was formerly used jocularly for something outside the Three Estates of the Realm. What were these?

2. In what terms did Prime Minister Stanley Baldwin castigate the two British press lords, Rothermere and Beaverbrook?

3. Name the newspaper with the largest daily circulation in the United States.

4. *Sticks Nix Hick Pix* was a famous headline on July 17, 1935, from which publication? What does it mean?

5. According to the stylebook of which famous newspaper is "that forlorn, fatherless and motherless little word Ms. cast into the lexicographical outer darkness"? The paper goes on to say: "This is a rallying cry for common sense. There are several reasons why Ms. should be allowed no air. It is artificial, silly, means nothing and is rotten English. It is a faddish, middle-class plaything, and far from disguising the marital status of women, as is claimed, it draws attention to it. It is a vanity."

6. A tabloid is a newspaper of small format—like the old *Evening* (or *"Porno-"*) *Graphic*—giving the news in condensed form, usually illustrated and often sensational in nature. How did this name come about?

7. A twenty-five-pound reward was offered for the capture of which well-known war correspondent, dead or alive, during what war?

8. Who said about what, "We're yellow, but we're read and we're true blue"?

9. Which newspaperwoman conceived the title *Salt-free, Fat-free, Quick, Natural, Easy, Economical, Gourmet Diet Cookbook*, and what is it destined to become?

10. At the end of which famous play and motion pictures about the newspaper business does who say about whom, "That son of a bitch stole my watch"?

Power of the Press

1. The clergy, the nobility, and the commons, which included the knights and townspeople of substance—the burgesses or bourgeoisie.

2. "Power without responsibility, the prerogative of the harlot throughout the ages," a phrase, it is said, coined by Baldwin's cousin Rudyard Kipling.

3. *The Wall Street Journal*, which passed New York's *Daily News* in 1980.

4. It appeared in *Variety* and was written by Abel Green, editor for forty years of *Variety*, "The Bible of Show Business." Translated, the headline means that movies with rural themes do not appeal to the farming communities. The headline is often misquoted, even by the usually authoritative *Bartlett's*, which also misattributes it to Sime Silverman, *Variety's* founding editor, who died two years before.

5. *The Times* of London, which was known fondly as "the Thunderer," a nickname given by Thomas Carlyle, for its once-imperious editorials. For years it has been the bulletin board of the British Establishment.

6. It came from *Tabloid*, a trademark for a tablet of condensed medicine.

7. Winston S. Churchill, who, when covering the Boer War as a correspondent for London's *Morning Post*, was captured and had just escaped. Churchill's articles and subsequent book on his adventures raised him to the forefront of British journalists and, he considered, put him into Parliament years before he otherwise might have got there.

8. Harry Tammen, the legendary co-founder—in 1892, with Fred Bonfils—of the Denver *Post*.

9. Mimi Sheraton, the food and restaurant critic of *The New York Times*. Because of the contradictory motives people have for choosing the food they eat, she predicts it will be the single winning cookbook title of the next decade.

10. *The Front Page*, by Ben Hecht and Charles MacArthur. Walter Burns, the editor of the Chicago *Herald-Examiner*, had given his ace reporter Hildy Johnson a watch as a going-away present. The curtain line was Burns' way of getting the police to bring him back to the newspaper.

Put-Downs

■ ■

1. What was the rejoinder of the English politician John Wilkes to the notoriously dissolute 4th Earl of Sandwich when the latter predicted: "Sir, you will either die on the gallows or of the pox"?

2. To whom did Dr. Johnson address these words in a letter: "Is not a Patron, my Lord, one who looks with unconcern on a man struggling for life in the water, and, when he has reached ground, encumbers him with help? The notice which you have been pleased to take of my labors, had it been early, had been kind; but it has been delayed till I am indifferent, and cannot enjoy it; till I am solitary, and cannot impart it; till I am known, and do not want it"?

3. Mme. Récamier and Mme. de Staël, two of the most notable women of their time, were equally insulted when a gentleman at dinner observed, "I am now seated between wit and beauty." How did Talleyrand avenge the slur on both ladies?

4. What was Voltaire's reply after he received an impudent letter?

5. During the Civil War, Lincoln, exasperated by General George McClellan's inactivity, sent him what laconic note?

6. What was the observation of Sir William Schwenck Gilbert, the librettist of the popular light operas, when he heard a theatrical manager puffing an actress who was also the manager's mistress?

7. George Bernard Shaw sent Winston S. Churchill a telegram inviting him to the first night of his latest play, adding, "Bring a friend—if you have one." How did Churchill respond?

8. How did Dorothy Parker describe Katharine Hepburn's performance in the play *The Lake*?

9. What was the stripper Gypsy Rose Lee's retort when Mae West called her Lady Peel? (A malevolent pun, since Beatrice Lillie legitimately held that title by marriage to Sir Robert Peel.)

10. How did Groucho Marx acknowledge receiving an unsolicited copy of S. J. Perelman's first book, *Dawn Ginsbergh's Revenge*, from the author?

Put-Downs

1. "That, my Lord, depends on whether I embrace your principles or your mistress."

2. Lord Chesterfield, who had largely ignored Dr. Johnson when he appealed for Chesterfield's patronage during the writing of his famous *Dictionary of the English Language*, the first comprehensive work of its kind. When it was approaching completion after ten long years and still not dedicated, Chesterfield suggested in a periodical that Johnson be made dictator of the English language. This prompted Johnson's scathing reply.

3. He promptly remarked, "Yes, and without possessing either."

4. "I am seated in the smallest room in the house. I have your letter before me. Soon it will be behind me."

5. My dear McClellan:

   If you don't want to use the army, I should like to borrow it for a while.

   Yours respectfully,
   A. Lincoln

6. "That fellow," commented Gilbert, "is blowing his own strumpet."

7. Churchill wired back that he could not make the opening but would attend the second night, "if you have one."

8. "Katharine Hepburn ran the gamut of the emotions from A to B."

9. She referred to Mae West as "the weakest link in the Vassar daisy chain."

10. "From the moment I picked up your book until I laid it down, I was convulsed with laughter. Someday I intend reading it."

Quartets

■ ■

1. In medieval and Elizabethan physiology what were considered to be the four humors or bodily fluids, the dominance of any which one determined man's health and temperament?

2. Name the four national languages of Switzerland in order of common usage.

3. Who comprised the Virginia Dynasty?

4. "The Inns of Court" is the collective term for the four legal societies in London which have the exclusive right of admission to the junior bar. Can you name them?

5. Whose memoirs of which momentous event contain the following "Moral of the Work"?

> In War: Resolution
> In Defeat: Defiance
> In Victory: Magnanimity
> In Peace: Goodwill

6. Soft, semisoft, firm, and hard are four basic categories of what?

7. Where or what are Burnt Norton, East Coker, the Dry Salvages, and Little Gidding, and what is their collective significance?

8. Who were the "Big Four" in the early days of California's history as a state?

9. What are the names of the four principal Balearic Islands?

10. Who made the following inventory of her life?

> Four be the things I am wiser to know:
> Idleness, sorrow, a friend, and a foe.

> Four be the things I'd been better without:
> Love, curiosity, freckles, and doubt.

Quartets

1. Blood, phlegm, choler, and black bile. Accordingly, one's disposition might be sanguine, phlegmatic, choleric, or melancholic.

2. German (75 percent), French (20 percent), Italian (4 percent), and Romansch (1 percent).

3. George Washington, Thomas Jefferson, James Madison, and James Monroe. Of the first five presidents, only John Adams, who was born in Massachusetts, was a non-Virginian.

4. Lincoln's Inn, Gray's Inn, the Middle Temple, and the Inner Temple—all of which date from before the 14th century.

5. Winston S. Churchill's *The Second World War*. The six volumes are respectively entitled: *The Gathering Storm, Their Finest Hour, The Grand Alliance, The Hinge of Fate, Closing the Ring,* and *Triumph and Tragedy*.

6. Cheeses—once called poor man's meat, rich man's treat—of which there are over 5,000 varieties in the world. Of Brie, a soft cheese, editor and author Clifton Fadiman once parodied Joyce Kilmer's "Trees":

> Essays are writ by fools like me,
> But only God can make a Brie.

7. These titles of T. S. Eliot's "Four Quartets" weave together, like the poems themselves, memory and history, being and becoming: "Burnt Norton," from an English country house beloved by Eliot, symbolic of the social order of the land he had adopted; "East Coker," the village from which his ancestors went to America; "The Dry Salvages," desolate, haunting islands off Cape Ann, Massachusetts, near which British and American warships had fought; and "Little Gidding," where in the 17th century, about the time Eliot's Congregational ancestors left for America, there gathered an austere and beautiful semimonastic community of that Anglican church to which Eliot himself was converted.

8. Collis P. Huntington, Charles Crocker, Mark Hopkins, and Leland Stanford.

9. In order of size, they are Majorca, Minorca, Ibiza, and Formentera.

10. Dorothy Parker, in her poem "Inventory."

Quiz for All Seasons

■■

1. About whom did Thomas Bolt write the play *A Man for All Seasons*?

2. In Shakespeare's *Richard III*, what happened to "the winter of our discontent"?

3. In January 1776, Thomas Paine published *Common Sense*, appealing to the common man to rally to the cause of republicanism and national independence. Do you know the seasonal sentence that follows "These are the times that try men's souls"?

4. Who was derisively called the "Winter King" from his short tenure on the throne?

5. According to whom, when does a young man's fancy lightly turn to thoughts of love?

6. Who is the author of the following lines, and what does he mean by "snow"?

> And since to look at things in bloom
> Fifty springs are little room,
> About the woodlands I will go
> To see the cherry hung with snow.

7. In which musical would you hear the refrain, "Summertime, and the livin' is easy"?

8. When was the "Springtime of the Nations"?

9. Which English poet described autumn as a "season of mists and mellow fruitfulness"?

10. According to Noël Coward's *Bittersweet*, when will I see you again?

Quiz for All Seasons

1. St. Thomas More, the Roman Catholic martyr, who, because of his refusal to subscribe to the Act of Supremacy, which impugned the pope's authority and made Henry VIII—whose most trusted minister he had been—head of the Church of England, was beheaded for treason on Tower Hill in 1535.

2. It was "made glorious summer by this sun of York."

3. "The summer soldier and the sunshine patriot will, in this crisis, shrink from the service of their country . . ."

4. Frederick, the Elector Palatine, called in as King of Bohemia in 1619 by rebels against the Emperor Matthias, but driven from his throne after only a season's reign.

5. Alfred, Lord Tennyson, who wrote in "Locksley Hall":

> In the Spring a livelier iris
> changes on the burnish'd dove;
> In the Spring a young man's fancy
> lightly turns to thoughts of love.

6. A. E. Housman in Poem II from *A Shropshire Lad*. Snow refers to cherry blossoms.

7. *Porgy and Bess*, a folk opera about the blacks in Charleston, South Carolina, with music by George Gershwin and lyrics by his brother Ira, deriving from the book and play by DuBose Heyward. Porgy, Bess, and Sportin' Life were the three most prominent denizens of Catfish Row.

8. 1848, when the subject nations of Eastern and Central Europe—the Czechs, Hungarians, Italians—attempted to assert their independence in the Year of Revolutions.

9. John Keats in "To Autumn."

10. "I'll see you again,
> Whenever spring breaks through again."

Relatively Speaking

■ ■

1. At the Versailles Peace Conference in 1919 what did the French Premier Georges Clemenceau say when President Woodrow Wilson asked him if he did not believe that all men were brothers?

2. What was the name of Mohammed's favorite wife?

3. Name the prettier and younger step-sister of Anastasia and Drizella.

4. In Arthurian legend, what was the relationship between Arthur and Modred, who was slain in battle by Arthur, but not before fatally wounding the king?

5. Why is the face of the mother of Frédéric Auguste Bartholdi so widely known?

6. According to Rudyard Kipling's poem "The Ladies," what did the Colonel's Lady and Rosie O'Grady, who moved in different social circles, have in common?

7. What is Napoleon's connection with the F.B.I.?

8. In which line of work were the Everleigh sisters active?

9. Who did Professor Archimedes Q. Porter's daughter Jane marry?

10. In the film *The Corsican Brothers*, which was based on a short story by Alexander Dumas *père*, did Ronald Colman, Errol Flynn, or David Niven play the brother of the character portrayed by Douglas Fairbanks, Jr.?

Relatively Speaking

1. "Of course I do, Mr. President. Cain and Abel! Cain and Abel!"

2. Ayesha, who was married to the Prophet soon after the Hegira, the flight of Mohammed from Mecca to Medina in A.D. 622, from which year the Moslem era is reckoned.

3. Cinderella, whose story was given classic form by the French poet Charles Perrault.

4. Since Modred was the son of Arthur and Morgawse, Arthur's half-sister, he was also Arthur's nephew.

5. She was the model for her son's Statue of Liberty, originally known as *Liberty Enlightening the World*. The inner structure was designed by Alexandre Eiffel, who built the Eiffel Tower for the Paris Exposition of 1889. The statue stands on Liberty Island, formerly Bedloe's Island, in New York Bay.

6. They were "sisters under their skins."

7. As the Bureau of Investigation, it was founded in 1908 by Napoleon's grandnephew, Attorney General Charles J. Bonaparte, during the administration of Theodore Roosevelt.

8. They operated a famous *belle époque* brothel in Chicago.

9. Tarzan of the Apes, who was really Lord Greystoke, in the books by Edgar Rice Burroughs.

10. None of them. As the part called for identical twins who had physical telepathy (they were Siamese twins who were separated at birth), Fairbanks played both roles. This was the last film he made before joining the U.S. Navy, in which he served with great distinction during World War II, being highly decorated for gallantry and rising eventually to the rank of Captain, U.S.N.R. (Ret.).

Religion

■ ■

1. Whose birth was the result of immaculate conception?

2. Which Jewish holiday marks the gathering of the harvest and commemorates the desert wanderings of the ancient Israelites from bondage in Egypt to the Promised Land?

3. What are the two main branches, or fundamental divisions, of the Islamic faith?

4. Can you identify the name of the Pope's Cathedral Church in Rome?

5. Why is there an empty seat at the Passover Seder?

6. Who spoke thus to a priestess: "You pray in your distress and in your need; would that you might pray also in the fullness of your joy and in your years of abundance"?

7. What can a Roman Catholic cardinal do at the age of 79 that he cannot do at 80?

8. What is unquestionably the world's largest Shinto shrine?

9. Simony and the trade of a colporteur both involve selling what?

10. Ronald Knox, the English man of letters and future Monsignor, when an undergraduate at Balliol College, Oxford, pinned this limerick on Berkelian idealism to a tree in the front quadrangle of the college:

> There was once a man who said "God
> Must think it exceedingly odd
>   If he finds that this tree
>   Continues to be
> When there's no one about in the Quad."

What reply did he find the next morning?

Religion

1. The Virgin Mary's. The Roman Catholic dogma of the Immaculate Conception, promulgated by a bull of Pius IX in 1854, states that Mary was conceived in her mother's womb free from all stain of original sin. The doctrine has nothing to do with Christ's being born of a virgin.

2. Succoth, or the Feast of Tabernacles, which lasts eight days in the fall. Temples and synagogues erect succahs, tabernacles filled with autumnal fruits, vegetables, flowers, and plants.

3. The largest branch is the Sunnite, comprising 90 per cent of the Moslem world. The Shi'ites, centered chiefly in Iran, make up the remainder, comprising many other separatist sects including the Ismaili.

4. The church of St. John Lateran. (St. Peter's in Rome, the largest church in the world, is a basilica, not a cathedral.)

5. To await the arrival of the Prophet Elijah, who will announce the coming of the Messiah.

6. The Prophet of God in the Syrian-American Kahlil Gibran's immensely popular book *The Prophet*.

7. He cannot participate in those proceedings of the Sacred College of Cardinals leading to the election of a new pope.

8. Japan's Mount Fuji, because Jimmu, the first emperor, said to have been born about 660 B.C., supposedly descended on it from heaven. That he was a lineal descendant of the sun goddess and forebear of the present emperor was held as official dogma until 1946. Like all Shinto shrines, Mount Fuji is a place of great natural beauty.

9. Simony was the practice of buying and selling ecclesiastical benefices or pardons. A colporteur is a peddler, especially of religious tracts and periodicals.

10. A note on the tree read:

> Dear Sir, your astonishment's odd:
> *I* am always about in the Quad.
>   And that's why the tree
>   Will continue to be,
> Since observed by Yours faithfully, God.

Reptiles and Amphibians

■ ■

1. A hamadryad is better known by what regal title?

2. Which two land creatures particularly fascinated the English naturalist Charles Darwin when he visited the Galápagos Islands in 1835 during the course of a round-the-world voyage on H.M.S. *Beagle?*

3. Lewis Carroll wrote a book titled *The Hunting of the Snark.* What is a snark? And, when the hunters finally track it down, what do they discover they have?

4. Who was the most famous prisoner of Fort Jefferson in which group of islands named by Ponce de Léon after the plethora of sea turtles nesting there?

5. The scientific name for which much-maligned creature is *Bufo vulgaris?*

6. When education was firmly rooted in the classics, which college adopted an amphibious cheer from what ancient Greek comedy?

7. Its Greek name meant "worm of the pebbles" from its habit of basking in the sun. By which name do we know it?

8. During the Civil War, what reproachful term was given to the Northern sympathizers with the South?

9. Which nocturnal literary effort had a mixed bag of characters, including a defrocked Episcopalian clergyman acting as a cicerone and a nonagenarian with a penchant for reciting his own poetry?

10. In 1980 a group of urban guerrillas in Bogotá, Colombia, held 32 people, most of them diplomats, hostage at the embassy of the Dominican Republic after a reception held there. Among the group was a *largato,* which signifies what in Latin America?

Reptiles and Amphibians

1. The king cobra, a large venomous snake of tropical Asia. (It is also a wood nymph who lives in a tree, of which she is the spirit, and lives only as long as the tree is alive.)

2. The iguana and the giant tortoise.

3. A snark is a creature of Carroll's imagination, a portmanteau word combining both snake and shark. In the end the quarry turns out to be a "boojum," the dangerous variety of snark.

4. Dr. Samuel A. Mudd, who set the broken left leg of Lincoln's assassin, John Wilkes Booth. Fort Jefferson is located in the Dry Tortugas, a group of islands lying 60 miles west of Key West, Florida. Although Dr. Mudd was a Confederate sympathizer, he had nothing to do with the assassination and was finally pardoned by President Johnson in 1869 after his unjust punishment. (The derivation of the saying "His name is mud" has no connection with the unfortunate doctor.)

5. The common toad, a conceited yet lovable fellow, if one can believe some not quite disinterested lines of self-description quoted by Kenneth Grahame in *The Wind in the Willows*:

> The clever men at Oxford
>   Know all that there is to be knowed,
> But they none of them know one half as much
>   As intelligent Mr. Toad!

6. Yale. The cheer, "Brekekekex, ko-ax" is from *The Frogs*, by Aristophanes.

7. The crocodile.

8. Copperheads, because the snakes of that name give no warning before they strike.

9. *The Night of the Iguana*, by Tennessee Williams.

10. A gatecrasher. The term *largatos*—lizards in Spanish—is given to this group for their ability to slither into places where they do not belong, such as diplomatic functions.

Resorts

■ ■

1. Which resort became a generic term?

2. The Abstract Expressionist movement is associated with which seaside gathering place?

3. The queen of American winter resorts is named for something not indigenous to the country. What is it?

4. Name a continental resort which was so popular with English tourists that its main thoroughfare was named after them.

5. After which resorts are named a hat, a trunk, and a jacket?

6. An important conference during World War II was held at which famous health retreat?

7. Where would you find the oldest synagogue building in the United States, and the Tennis Hall of Fame?

8. Which repetitive name became that of a fashionable spa in the Edwardian era?

9. Name the development built and promoted by the present Aga Khan.

10. The initials S.B.M. are associated with which famous resort?

Resorts

1. Spa, in the Ardennes of East Belgium. Its mineral springs and baths, frequented from the 16th century, made it one of the most fashionable watering places in the world, and its name became so well known that the word *spa* now designates all similar health resorts.

2. East Hampton, Long Island, which was the home of such painters as Jackson Pollock, Willem de Kooning, Robert Motherwell, and Franz Kline.

3. Palm Beach, Florida, a barren offshore island until a shipment of coconuts bound for Cádiz out of Trinidad was washed ashore when the Spanish brig *Providencia* grounded there in 1878.

4. Nice, on the Cote d'Azur of France. Its main street is called Promenade des Anglais, though the English were attracted to the Côte d'Azur by a Scots lawyer, Lord Brougham.

5. The Homburg hat from Bad Homburg in West Germany; the Saratoga trunk from Saratoga Springs; and the tuxedo from Tuxedo Park, the latter two in New York State.

6. Yalta, the largest health resort in the Crimea, was the site of a conference among the "Big Three" of Roosevelt, Churchill, and Stalin in 1945.

7. Newport, Rhode Island, which is famous for what are called "cottages"; in reality they are elaborate copies of European châteaux. The Touro Synagogue, the oldest in the country, was built in 1763 by descendants of the Sephardic Jews from Spain and Portugal who had fled the Inquisition (originally to the Netherlands), and the International Tennis Hall of Fame was founded there by James H. Van Alen and is housed in the Newport Casino.

8. Baden-Baden, in the Black Forest of what is now West Germany, where one went to take the waters and rest the body from excesses of food and drink.

9. Costa Smeralda on the northeastern coast of Sardinia, where he built the Cala di Volpe Hotel, the Pitrizza, and the Cervo with the enormous yacht basin of Porto Cervo.

10. Monaco, where the Société des Bains de Mer (Sea Bathing Corporation) owns L'Hôtel de Paris, L'Hôtel Hermitage, the Old Beach Hôtel, Le Casino, Le Sporting d'Hiver, and Le Monte-Carlo Sporting Club, among other holdings. The majority of the S.B.M. shares are held by the Monégasque government.

R.I.P.
■■

1. Which famous movie star wrote his own epitaph: *"Feo, fuerte y formal"*?

2. What did Evelyn Waugh satirize in his novel *The Loved One*?

3. Who wept for Adonais, and whom was he eulogizing in the following?

> I weep for Adonais—he is dead!
> O, weep for Adonais! though our tears
> Thaw not the frost which binds so dear a head!

4. How did Ambrose Bierce define longevity in *The Devil's Dictionary*?

5. Potter's field is a burial place for indigent or unknown persons. Where did the phrase originate?

6. What Massachusetts belle did not play on graves?

7. In the churchyard of which village were the following lines written?

> The boast of heraldry, the pomp of pow'r,
>   And all that beauty, all that wealth e'er gave,
> Awaits alike th' inevitable hour,
>   The paths of glory lead but to the grave.

8. With what familiar words does Horatio bid farewell to the dying Hamlet?

9. In Mary Wollstonecraft Shelley's novel *Frankenstein*, where is the Creature last seen?

10. Calvin Coolidge slept 12 to 15 hours a day. What was Wilson Mizner's reaction to his death?

R.I.P.

1. John Wayne. The Spanish phrase means: "He was ugly, was strong, and had dignity."

2. The American funeral industry and particularly the enormous Forest Lawn Memorial-Park in Los Angeles, which he immortalized as "Whispering Glades."

3. Percy Bysshe Shelley, whose poem "Adonais" was subtitled "An Elegy on the Death of John Keats." Shelley was deeply moved both to sorrow by the death of Keats, whom he considered a genius of the age, and to indignation at the criticisms of Keats' work which Shelley believed had hastened his end. Byron concurred by penning these lines:

> Tis odd, the soul, that very fiery particle
> Should let itself be snuffed out by an article.

4. "An uncommon extension of the fear of death."

5. It came from the Bible, Matthew 27:7, which says, "And they took counsel and bought with them the potter's field, to bury strangers in." Washington Square in New York started as a potter's field, as did the site of the New York Public Library.

6. Emily Dickinson, in poem Number 467 in *The Complete Poems:*

> We do not play on Graves—
> Because there isn't Room—
> Besides—it isn't even—it slants
> And People come—

7. "Elegy Written in a Country Churchyard" was composed by Thomas Gray in the churchyard at Stoke Poges, a village then deep in the country but now being engulfed by the fringes of Greater London.

8. In the last act of *Hamlet*, Horatio says:

> Now cracks a noble heart. Good night, sweet prince,
> And flights of angels sing thee to thy rest!

9. After killing Frankenstein, he leaps over the ship's side onto an ice floe. The last line of the book is: "He was soon borne away by the waves and lost in darkness and distance." (The movie versions of the story bear little resemblance to the original.)

10. "How do they know?"

Salmagundi

■ ■

1. Which weapon enabled the English under Edward III and his son, the Black Prince, to defeat a much larger French army under Philip VI at Crécy in 1346 in the Hundred Years War?

2. Why was the paca-vicuña developed?

3. What was the unique record of Captain Bligh?

4. What epitaphs did W. C. Fields and Dorothy Parker propose for themselves in the old *Vanity Fair* magazine?

5. Charles J. Guiteau and Leon F. Czolgosz did something outrageous which what two others also did? Explain the difference between the first two and the second two.

6. How did William Cosgrave, Eamon de Valera's predecessor as President of the Irish Free State, describe the latter's smile?

7. Why does a whip emit a cracking sound when snapped?

8. With which organization is the Lutine Bell associated?

9. What was Phiz to Boz?

10. In Gibraltar at the start of World War II, the Royal Navy formed the powerful Force H under Vice-Admiral Sir James Somerville, K.B.E. It comprised the battleships *Hood*, *Resolution*, and *Valiant*, the carrier *Ark Royal*, two cruisers, and eleven destroyers. When Admiral Somerville later received the K.C.B. (Knight Commander of the Bath), what signal did "Cincmed" (Commander-in-Chief Mediterranean), Admiral Sir Andrew Cunningham, make to him?

Salmagundi

1. The English longbow, which demonstrated that weapons used in the age of chivalry were hopelessly outmoded.

2. The paca-vicuña, a new crossbreed between the South American alpaca and the vicuña, was developed to combine the length of the alpaca wool with the fine, silky fleece of the vicuña.

3. Having been deposed once by the mutiny on H.M.S. *Bounty,* he was deposed again in the general mutiny at the Nore, and, finally becoming a progressive Governor of New South Wales, he was overthrown by a mutiny of his militia. (He still became an admiral.)

4. Fields suggested, "I would rather be living in Philadelphia," and Parker, "Excuse my dust."

5. Guiteau and Czolgosz assassinated Presidents Garfield and McKinley respectively. The other pair were John Wilkes Booth who murdered President Lincoln, and Lee Harvey Oswald who assassinated President Kennedy. The difference between the two sets of assassins was that the first two were brought to trial and found guilty, while the other two were killed before they could stand trial.

6. "Like moonlight on a tombstone."

7. Because the tip actually moves faster than the speed of sound (760 miles per hour), resulting in the "crack" which is a miniature sonic boom.

8. Lloyd's of London. The Lutine Bell, salvaged from the French frigate *La Lutine* that sank in 1799, is rung before important announcements. Contrary to popular opinion, Lloyd's is not an insurance company and does not issue policies; it is a corporation consisting of some 300 individual insurance underwriting syndicates.

9. Phiz was the pseudonym of Hablot Knight Browne, who, at the age of 21, was chosen by Charles Dickens, who used to sign himself Boz, to illustrate *The Pickwick Papers* and, in due course, many more of Dickens' novels.

10. "Fancy, twice a knight and at your age. Congratulations."

Science

■ ■

1. Agricola (Georg Bauer), the 16th-century German scientist, is known as the father of mineralogy. His celebrated work, *De Re Metallica*, a standard text in metallurgy and mining for over a century, was translated into English by which future U.S. President and his wife?

2. Why is the name of Antoine Henri Becquerel included in the book *The 100, A Ranking of the Most Influential Persons in History*, by Michael H. Hart?

3. An electron repels another electron because like charges repel each other. What does an electron do to a neutron?

4. Who wrote, "If I have seen further it is by standing on the shoulders of Giants."?

5. James Watson and Francis Crick were largely responsible for discovering the molecular structure of something of which the genes are made. Can you give the short and long names of this substance?

6. Which *maniac* did indispensable work in enabling the United States to produce and test in 1952 the world's first hydrogen bomb?

7. What distinction do quarks seem to have, and whence does the word derive?

8. Explain the connection between a certain lightweight metal and a ruined limestone city.

9. Squid is an acronym for what electronic device?

10. Who once said, "the eternal mystery of the world is its comprehensibility," and wrote a historic letter to President Franklin D. Roosevelt in August 1939, outlining the steps the Germans had made in developing the atomic bomb and pleading for the creation of a similar program that could alter the course of the war?

Science

1. Herbert C. Hoover and Lou H. Hoover in 1912. Prior to entering government service, Hoover was a noted mining engineer.

2. Because in 1896 he was the first to discover radioactivity in uranium. The Curies made further investigations of the phenomenon and shared with Becquerel the 1903 Nobel Prize for physics.

3. It has no effect because a neutron has no charge.

4. Sir Isaac Newton, English physicist, natural philosopher, and mathematician, in a letter to a fellow physicist, Robert Hooke.

5. DNA, or deoxyribonucleic acid. Watson's memoir, *The Double Helix*, describes this discovery.

6. *Maniac* is an acronym for "mathematical analyzer numerical integrator and computer" developed by John von Neumann, the Hungarian-American mathematician.

7. Quarks are that group of subatomic particles hypothesized to have the smallest electrical charges yet imagined and are widely believed to be the basic building blocks of matter. The name comes from a line in James Joyce's *Finnegans Wake*: "Three quarks for Muster Mark!"

8. Bauxite, the principal ore of aluminum, was first found at Les Baux in southern France.

9. Superconductive quantum interference device, which is the most sensitive instrument used to measure magnetic fields.

10. Albert Einstein, who wrote the letter with two other Princeton scientists, Leo Szilard and Eugene P. Wigner, but signed it alone to ensure the President read it. Roosevelt immediately created an atomic bomb study group as a result.

Sculpture

■ ■

1. The head of the Great Sphinx at Al Jizah (formerly Gizeh) is atop the body of which animal?

2. Why is a plated statuette named "The Spirit of Ecstasy" seen around and about?

3. Of which northern capital has *The Little Mermaid* by Edward Erikson been the symbol since 1913?

4. On the grounds of the Mormon Temple in Salt Lake City is the stone figure of which bird atop a tall shaft? Explain its historical significance.

5. What stands out rockily in South Dakota?

6. Which peripatetics were "talking of Michelangelo"?

7. The first statue cast in aluminum is also one of the most famous in the world. What and where is it?

8. Which sculptor was commissioned by the city to create the group *The Burghers of Calais*, six prominent citizens whom Edward III proposed to hang for the city's bitter resistance to a siege but spared at the intercession of his wife?

9. Why is there a statue to a dog named Balto in New York City's Central Park?

10. Of which statue of an American general is it said, "Trust a Yankee to make a lady walk"?

Sculpture

1. A lion.

2. Known also as the Flying Lady mascot, she forms, with the entwined initials and the Grecian radiator, the three symbols of Rolls-Royce motorcars. Charles Sykes, who created her in 1911, said she was a girl who "has selected road travel as her supreme delight and has alighted on the prow of a Rolls-Royce to revel in the freshness of the air and the musical sound of her fluttering draperies."

3. Copenhagen. The lovely statue of a mermaid sitting on a rock overlooking the harbor was presented to the city by the Carlsberg Brewing Company. The Little Mermaid is the heroine of one of Hans Christian Anderson's tales.

4. A seagull, which commemorates the huge clouds of gulls that arrived to save the Mormons by devouring crickets destroying their crops in 1848.

5. The immense carvings, by Gutzon Borglum and his son Lincoln, on Mount Rushmore of the faces of Presidents Washington, Jefferson, Lincoln, and Theodore Roosevelt.

6. The women, in T. S. Eliot's poem "The Love Song of J. Alfred Prufrock":

> In the room the women come and go
> Talking of Michelangelo.

7. The 8-foot statue of Eros by Alfred Gilbert. The winged figure with a drawn bow stands on one foot atop a fountain in the center of London's Piccadilly Circus and commemorates the 7th Earl of Shaftesbury, who devoted his life to social reform. (Contrary to some opinion, this figure does not represent the Angel of Christian Charity, nor is there a sculptured pun intended on the siting of the statue "burying a shaft" near Shaftesbury Avenue.)

8. Auguste Rodin. A bronze casting of the group may be seen in the gardens of the British Houses of Parliament.

9. Balto was the lead dog in a sled team that battled a blizzard in the winter of 1925 to bring diphtheria serum to Nome, Alaska, to halt an epidemic among the Eskimos.

10. The statue of Victory leading the mounted Union General William Tecumseh Sherman at the southeastern corner of Central Park in New York City.

Sea Creatures

■ ■

1. Which special feature of a remora enables it to do what?

2. What is unique about the coelacanth?

3. Name the mammal that is known as "the unicorn of the sea."

4. Which gentleman from Trinidad gave his name to a small, brightly colored fish that is popular for home aquariums?

5. What is a mermaid's purse, a black rectangular object found on the seashore?

6. In which poem by whom do these lines appear?

And in that Heaven of all their wish,
There shall be no more land, say fish.

7. How was sepia, the fine brown pigment used in drawing and painting, first obtained?

8. Which mollusk shares a connection with a Greek sailor, Jules Verne, a poem by Oliver Wendell Holmes, and a painting by Andrew Wyeth?

9. When the cry "Thar she blows" goes out, what is the whale doing?

10. Who observed that "One man's fish is another man's *poisson*"?

Sea Creatures

1. A remora, also called a suckerfish, has a sucking disk on the head with which it attaches itself to sharks, whales, sea turtles, or the hulls of ships. The name derives from the Latin, *re*, back, and *mora*, delay, as remoras were believed to slow ships down by sticking to them.

2. Long thought to be extinct and known only in fossil form, a living coelacanth was caught in 1938 in deep water off South Africa. It is the closest fish relative of the amphibians.

3. The narwhal, the one-spiral-tusked member of the whale family that is seldom seen by anyone except Eskimos, explorers, and occasional whalers.

4. R. J. L. Guppy, who introduced these colorful little fish into England. His descendants now live at The Pond, Haddenham, Cambridgeshire.

5. It is the egg case of the shark, skate, ray, or dogfish.

6. "Heaven," by Rupert Brooke. This is a play on the Biblical vision of Heaven in the *Book of Revelation:* ". . . and there was no more sea."

7. It was found in the fluid from the "ink bag" of some species of cuttlefish.

8. The nautilus. Nautilus is Latinized Greek for sailor, and is also the name of the submarine in Jules Verne's *20,000 Leagues Under the Sea*. "The Chambered Nautilus" is the title of a poem by Oliver Wendell Holmes, and *Chambered Nautilus* that of Andrew Wyeth's sensitive tempera painting owned by the actor Robert Montgomery. (The chambered nautilus, known for its beautiful spiral shell, can fill its compartments and swim at ocean depths of 1,800 feet.)

9. Exhaling not water but pressurized air and water vapor through nostrils on the top of its head. When these gases hit the outside atmosphere, the expanding air cools and condenses to form the dramatic column of mist and spray.

10. Carolyn Wells, American humorous writer.

Seconds

■■

1. In Milton's *Paradise Lost*, who was the chief of the fallen angels and second to Satan in power?

2. Next to "e," what is the second most commonly used letter in the English language?

3. Sherlock Holmes considered Professor Moriarty "the most dangerous man in Europe." Whom did he call "the second most dangerous man in London"?

4. Everyone knows that St. Peter's in Rome is the largest church in the world, but do you know the second largest?

5. What was the second cheapest real estate purchase the United States ever made?

6. What observation did Victor Hugo make about the Battle of Waterloo in *Les Misérables*?

7. Name the second oldest city in the United States.

8. What did Samuel Johnson have to say about a second marriage?

9. Which metropolis has long billed itself as "the second largest French-speaking city in the world"?

10. What was Oscar Wilde's comment after visiting Niagara Falls?

Seconds

1. Beelzebub.

2. "t," although more words begin with "s" than with any other letter.

3. Colonel Sebastian Moran, formerly 1st Bangalore Pioneers. He and the air gun, "noiseless and of tremendous power," constructed for Professor Moriarty by the blind German mechanic Von Herder, figured in A. Conan Doyle's tale "The Adventures of the Empty House."

4. St. John the Divine, the seat of the Protestant Episcopal Bishop of New York, located on Morningside Heights in New York City. The first stone was laid in 1892, but the fabric has yet to be completed.

5. The Louisiana Purchase—100 million acres at four cents an acre. The best real estate deal the United States ever made was Alaska—350 million acres at two cents an acre.

6. "Waterloo is a battle of the first rank won by a captain of the second."

7. Sante Fe, New Mexico, which was founded in 1609. The oldest is St. Augustine, Florida, founded in 1565.

8. He defined it as "the triumph of hope over experience." Johnson was referring to an unhappily married man who had remarried the moment he was widowed.

9. Montréal, Canada, with a population of 2.8 million.

10. "This must be the second greatest disappointment in marital life."

Sex

■ ■

1. Who was embraced so closely that his own nature was changed?

2. In which 16th-century play are these memorable lines exchanged?

Friar Barnadine: Thou hast committed—
Barnabas: Fornication? but that was in another country: and besides, the wench is dead.

3. Which castrating instrument symbolizes the passage of time?

4. In Victorian days, what advice was given to brides on their wedding night?

5. What did Mrs. Patrick Campbell, the celebrated English actress, have to say about marriage?

6. Under the Napoleonic code what was the *"injure grave"*?

7. What did Lytton Strachey reply to the chairman of a tribunal for conscientious objectors who asked him what he would do if he saw a German about to violate his sister?

8. Buggery is the slang term for sodomy—that is, anal copulation or copulation with animals. The word sodomy derives from the ancient Biblical town of Sodom, but how did the word buggery originate?

9. How many collective nouns can you think of for a group of prostitutes?

10. What, according to Alfred Kazin, has happened to the Victorian concept of the love that dared not speak its name?

Sex

1. Hermaphroditus, the son of Hermes and Aphrodite, who became united in one body with the nymph Salmacis. Hence, a hermaphrodite is one having the sex organs and many of the secondary sex characteristics of both male and female.

2. *The Jew of Malta,* by Christopher Marlowe.

3. The sickle. The Titan Kronos castrated his father Uranus with a sickle, which later turned into a scythe and became the symbol of Father Time.

4. "Close your eyes and think of England."

5. She said, "Marriage is the result of the longing for the deep, deep peace of the double bed after the hurly-burly of the chaise-longue."

6. Bringing one's mistress under the matrimonial roof, which constituted a woman's only grounds for divorce at that time.

7. In his most flagrantly homosexual accent: "Oh, sir, I would endeavor to interpose my body."

8. In the Middle Ages the Catharist heretics, who regarded the body as sinful, were accused of homosexuality because they disapproved of marriage. The sect was especially strong among the Bulgars. Hence its members were often called in French *Bougres*, which passed into English as the common noun "buggers."

9. How about a jam of tarts, a pride of loins, a flourish of strumpets, an anthology of pros, a cunning array of stunts, or a chapter of trollops?

10. "It has become the love that refuses to shut up."

Shakespeare

■■

1. On which island does *The Tempest* take place?

2. In which plays by Shakespeare would you find: a) a moated grange, b) a handkerchief spotted with strawberries, c) a bloody sergeant, d) a clock anachronistically striking, e) a chink in the wall?

3. Who pontificates to whom on the dangers inherent in borrowing or lending money?

4. Who is missing from the following list: Cassius, Regan, Macduff, King Lear, Ophelia, Julius Caesar, Hamlet, Iago, Macbeth?

5. Cobweb, Moth, Mustardseed, and Peaseblossom are the names of four fairies in *A Midsummer Night's Dream*. Can you name three others?

6. Who, in which of Shakespeare's plays, utters the following?

    a) "The game is up."
    b) "I am but mad north-north-west."
    c) "All the world's a stage."
    d) "Childe Roland to the dark tower came."
    e) "I kiss'd thee ere I kill'd thee."
    f) "The better part of valor is discretion."

7. In the line "O Romeo, Romeo! wherefore art thou Romeo?" what does the word "wherefore" mean in modern English?

8. When Hamlet's father died, why did not Hamlet become king?

9. When Mercutio reminds Romeo of the "fine foot, straight leg, quivering thigh,/And the demesnes, that there adjacent lie," belonging to the latter's lady, of whom is he speaking?

10. Name the last and one of the least-performed of all Shakespeare's plays, and the only one of which part seems to have survived in his own handwriting.

Shakespeare

1. Shakespeare does not name the island, but it is believed that he based the locale on reports of the shipwreck of Sir George Somers on Bermuda while transporting settlers to Virginia. In the play the spirit Ariel refers to "the still-vexed Bermoothes."

2. a) *Measure for Measure*, b) *Othello*, c) *Macbeth*, d) *Julius Caesar*, e) *A Midsummer Night's Dream*.

3. Polonius to his son Laertes in the first act of *Hamlet*:

Neither a borrower, nor a lender be;
For loan oft loses both itself and friend,
And borrowing dulls the edge of husbandry . . .

4. Othello. The list is of the titles of plays and a character in each: Cassius appears in *Julius Caesar*; Regan in *King Lear*; Macduff in *Macbeth*; Ophelia in *Hamlet*; and Iago in *Othello*.

5. Puck, Oberon, and Titania.

6. a) Belarius in *Cymbeline*, b) Hamlet in *Hamlet*, c) Jaques in *As You Like It*, d) Edgar in *King Lear*, e) Othello in *Othello*, f) Falstaff in *Henry IV, Part I*.

7. It means "why." Juliet is asking plaintively why he is a Montague and she a Capulet, members of two feuding families.

8. The Danish throne was elective, and Hamlet failed to be elected—as he explains:

[Claudius] hath kill'd my king and whored my mother,
Popp'd in between the election and my hopes . . .

9. Not Juliet, but Romeo's mistress Rosaline, before he crashed the famous Capulet party.

10. *Henry VIII*, written in 1612, probably in collaboration with John Fletcher. It is just possible, however, that Fletcher's collaboration *The Two Noble Kinsmen*, produced about 1612, may have been Shakespeare's last literary effort.

Ships and Boats
■ ■

1. Where is the world's oldest fully identified and refitted warship to be seen?

2. With what are the ships *Susan Constant*, *Godspeed*, and *Discovery* identified?

3. For which feat is Captain Joshua Slocum remembered?

4. The Royal Navy's first "all big-gun" battleship, mounting 11-inch guns and 12-inch armor, and Britain's first nuclear-powered submarine were given the same name. What was it?

5. What great maritime disaster occurred off Ireland's Old Head of Kinsale?

6. Can you describe the Q-ships?

7. In World War II what had more firepower for its size than any other vessel?

8. In which works did: a) the *Cotton Blossom* ply the Mississippi under the command of Captain Andy Hawks; b) the corvette H.M.S. *Compass Rose* escort North Atlantic convoys during World War II; c) a case of missing strawberries cause consternation in the wardroom; d) U.S.S. *Reluctant*, known to its crew as The Bucket, a Naval Auxiliary (cargo ship) carrying such necessities as dungarees, toothpaste, and toilet paper, make a regular run from Tedium to Apathy and back, an occasional run to Monotony, and once a run all the way to Ennui, a distance of two thousand nautical miles from Tedium?

9. What is meant by the abbreviation VLCC?

10. Which vessel made history in 1958 by making the first underwater transit from the Pacific to the Atlantic Ocean across the North Pole?

Ships and Boats

1. At a special museum in Stockholm lies the salvaged and restored *Wasa*, a magnificent 16-gun man-of-war. At her launching in 1628, she was caught by a squall which allowed sea water to pour through her lower gunports, capsizing and sinking her.

2. Jamestown, then a peninsula, now an island in the James River near Williamburg, Virginia, was the first permanent English settlement in America, established in 1607. The settlers came over on these three ships, replicas of which are exhibited at Jamestown.

3. He was the first man to circumnavigate the world alone, between April 1895 and July 1898, in his 36-foot gaff-rigged yawl *Spray*.

4. H.M.S. *Dreadnought*. (In a 1939 speech Churchill said, "For each and for all, as for the Royal Navy, the watchword should be, 'Carry on, and dread nought!'")

5. The sinking without warning in May 1915 of the unarmed Cunard liner R.M.S. *Lusitania*, by a German submarine, with a loss of almost 1,200 lives.

6. Q-ships were artfully disguised armed tramp steamers, coastal freighters, fishing trawlers, and even sailing ships which were sent out to decoy German U-boats into range in the western approaches to the British Isles from 1915 to the end of the First World War.

7. The PT boat powered by three 12-cylinder Packard engines. Its armament consisted of four torpedoes, two depth charges, two twin 50-caliber machine guns, a 20- and a 40-millimeter gun. Later a 37-millimeter gun and rockets were added.

8. a) Edna Ferber's *Show Boat*, b) Nicholas Monserrat's *The Cruel Sea*, c) Herman Wouk's *The Caine Mutiny*, d) Thomas Heggen's *Mister Roberts*.

9. Very Large Crude Carriers—large supertankers for shipping crude oil.

10. The world's first nuclear-powered submarine, U.S.S. *Nautilus*, was capable of cruising around the world without surfacing.

Sporting Life

■ ■

1. Which sport originated in India, where it was called *poona*?

2. The Olympic symbol consists of five interlocking colored rings. What do the circles and the colors stand for?

3. Name the only four world heavyweight boxing champions to retire undefeated.

4. It is doubtful whether the Duke of Wellington ever said that the Battle of Waterloo was won on the playing fields of Eton, but who did say: "Upon the fields of friendly strife are sown the seeds which, on other days, in other fields, will bear the fruits of victory."?

5. Why is an athletic supporter generally known as a jockstrap?

6. Who is the only man to win Olympic gold medals in both the summer and winter Olympics, and in which sports did he participate?

7. What is the official national sport of Canada?

8. Who wrote a treatise on polo, which proved immensely popular, and signed it Marco? What is the origin of the word polo?

9. What was the sportswriter Bob Considine's less than enthusiastic comment about covering the America's Cup races off Newport, Rhode Island? And what is curious about the America's Cup itself, which is bolted down in a showcase at the New York Yacht Club?

10. In the XIII Winter Olympics held at Lake Placid, New York, in 1980, speed skater Eric Heiden became the first man ever to do what?

Sporting Life

1. Badminton, whose name comes from the seat of the Duke of Beaufort in England, where it became popular in the 1870s. The game was also called "battledore and shuttlecock" after the racquet and the small rounded piece of cork with a crown of feathers (the "bird") respectively.

2. The rings, or circles, represent the five major continents: Europe, Asia, Africa, Australia, and the Americas. They are linked together to denote the sporting friendship of all peoples. The colors—blue, yellow, black, green, and red—were chosen because at least one of them appears on the flag of every nation on earth.

3. James L. Jeffries, Gene Tunney, Joe Louis, and Rocky Marciano.

4. Douglas MacArthur, when he was superintendent of the U.S. Military Academy, West Point, after the First World War. The words are inscribed over the entrance to the Academy's gymnasium.

5. Because jock is slang for penis.

6. Lake Placid's Eddie Eagan won the light-heavyweight boxing title at the 1920 Games in Antwerp and then was a member of the championship four-man bobsled team at Lake Placid in 1932.

7. Lacrosse. The game was developed as a war-training exercise by the North American Indians, who called it "baggataway" and played it in a battering manner without many fixed rules. The first organized lacrosse game took place between Iroquois and Algonquin teams at a Montreal horse track in 1834.

8. Lord Louis Mountbatten, later 1st Earl Mountbatten of Burma, who was assassinated by Irish terrorists in 1979. Polo comes from *pulu*, the willow root from which polo balls were first made in Tibet around 650 B.C.

9. "It's about as exciting as watching grass grow." The term America's Cup is a bit of a misnomer, as it has no bottom.

10. Eric Heiden was the first person to win five gold medals individually in a single year. He won in the 500-, the 1,000-, the 1,500-, the 5,000-, and the 10,000-meter races. In the 1972 Olympics the swimmer Mark Spitz won seven gold medals, but three were with relay teams.

States of the Union

■ ■

1. Explain the connection between Archimedes and the State of California.

2. Who was Button Gwinnett, and what did he do that is so valuable?

3. Why is the title of the official state song of Florida so appropriate?

4. Name the only state over whose territory no foreign flag was ever flown.

5. Did the American flag always have thirteen stripes denoting the original states?

6. Which is the Sooner State, and why was it so named?

7. Which state has been described as "a vale of humility between two mountains of conceit"?

8. Where is the inscription "What's Past Is Prologue" to be found? Who is the author?

9. What was Fred Allen's observation on the Golden State?

10. Who were the only three persons to be made Honorary Citizens of the United States?

States of the Union

1. The motto of the State of California is *Eureka*, from the Greek, meaning "I have found [it]." It can apply either to the gold strike at Sutter's Mill in 1848 or the admission of California to the Union in 1850. *Heureka!* was Archimedes' cry when he discovered a method of testing the purity of gold.

2. A Georgian, he signed the Declaration of Independence and not much else, possibly because he was killed in a duel a year later, which imparts an insanely high value to his signature.

3. Because the title of the song is "The Old Folks at Home," which begins "Way down upon the Swanee River," by Stephen Foster. Florida now has the largest percentage of old people in its population of any state in the Union.

4. Idaho.

5. No. In 1794, after the admission of Vermont and Kentucky to the Union, Congress began to add a stripe and a star for each state. In 1818, the thirteen stripes were restored, the feeling being that new states could be accommodated on the flag more easily by stars alone.

6. Oklahoma, because the old practice of illegally entering public lands, about to be opened, ahead of time (hence "Sooner") reached its climax in the land rush on Indian Territory, now Oklahoma, in 1889.

7. North Carolina, bordered by Virginia and South Carolina.

8. It is a quotation from Shakespeare's *The Tempest* inscribed on the pedestal under the female figure outside the National Archives Building in Washington, D.C.

9. "California is a fine place to live—if you happen to be an orange." A more current comparison is of California to granola cereal: when you remove the nuts and fruits, only the flakes are left.

10. The Marquis de Lafayette, Sir Winston Churchill, and Raoul Wallenberg. The Act proclaiming Churchill's Honorary Citizenship read in part: "In the dark days and darker nights when Britain stood alone . . . he mobilized the English language and sent it into battle. The incandescent quality of his words illuminated the courage of his countrymen."

Superlatives

■ ■

1. Can you name the oldest golf club in the world?

2. Where is the waterfall which has both the highest total drop and the longest uninterrupted leap in the world?

3. For its size and weight, what is the most valuable single object in the world?

4. Which religion has the most followers?

5. What is the oldest Greek-letter society in the United States?

6. Where is the oldest university in the world?

7. Which is the most expensive item you can buy in a gourmet food store?

8. Who wrote the song which has become the best-selling phonograph record?

9. What is the largest private yacht ever built?

10. Who said, "I am a very simple man and I am perfectly willing to accept anything the good Lord has to offer; and the best is none too good."?

Superlatives

1. The Honourable Company of Edinburgh Golfers, at Muirfield, which was formed in 1744. It was also the club that first promulgated a code of rules to govern its competitions.

2. Venezuela, where the Salto Angel, or Angel Falls, has a total drop of 3,212 feet, and single drop of 2,646 feet. It was named for Jimmy Angel, the bush pilot who brought it to the attention of the world.

3. The sole surviving 1856 British Guiana provisional 1-cent stamp—a crudely printed black-on-magenta octagon—that was sold at auction in 1980 for $850,000.

4. Christianity, with over 1,070 million adherents. The largest non-Christian religian is Islam (the Muslim faith) with about 550 million followers.

5. Phi Beta Kappa, which was founded in 1776 at the College of William and Mary in Williamsburg, Virginia. It soon became a scholarship honor society, a position it retains today. The initials ΦΒΚ are from the Greek phrase *Philosophia Biou Kubernetes*, "The love of knowledge is the guide of life," which is the motto of the society.

6. The University of Karneein, founded in 859, in Fez, Morocco. Oxford, which came into being around 1167, is the oldest European university.

7. Spanish saffron, which retails for over $5 per gram, which is the equivalent of more than $2,500 per pound. It takes 75,000 crocus blossoms, or 225,000 dried stigmas, to make one pound of saffron, which is used to color foods and as a cooking spice.

8. Irving Berlin, who wrote "White Christmas." Over 135 million copies have been sold, including 25 million of the Bing Crosby single, recorded in 1942.

9. The *Savrona*, built for Mrs. Emily Roebling Cadwalader in 1931, with an overall length of 408 feet. It later became a Turkish naval training ship.

10. It was a favorite saying of Winston S. Churchill.

Superquiz

■ ■

1. The Reggie candy bar is named after Reggie Jackson, the Yankee slugger. After whom is the Baby Ruth bar named?

2. What is the similarity between a misogamist and an epithalamium?

3. Sir Christopher Wren drew the original masterly plan of Willis' Circle, which can still be seen where?

4. In the "Song of the Pelagian Heresy," Hilaire Belloc wrote:

> Oh, he didn't believe in Adam and Eve—
> He put no faith therein;
> His doubts began with the fall of man,
> And he laughed at original sin.

Give a one-word definition of original sin.

5. During the Sepoy Rebellion of 1857–58, Sir Colin Campbell was ordered to relieve the siege of Lucknow in northern India. How did he report the success of his mission?

6. Name Leonardo Vinci's most famous work.

7. What famous event started at Pudding and ended at Pie?

8. In *Man and Superman* George Bernard Shaw called it "the brandy of the damned"; Joseph Addison in "A Song for St. Cecelia's Day" said it was "the greatest good that mortals know." What is it?

9. How, from reading a 17th-century satire, did Robert Browning come to make a truly dreadful mistake in these lines from "Pippa Passes"?

> Then owls and bats
> Cowls and twats,
> Monks and nuns, in cloister's moods . . .

10. When Voltaire, the French philosopher and author, was staying at the court of Frederick the Great of Prussia, he received an invitation in the form of a rebus which he replied to in a like manner. How would you interpret this exchange?

$$\text{``}\frac{p}{a}\text{''} \quad \text{à} \quad \frac{ci}{100} \text{?''} \qquad \text{``G} \quad \text{al''}$$

Superquiz

1. Not Babe Ruth, who was probably nicknamed after it, but Grover Cleveland's eldest daughter Ruth, born in 1891 in the interval between his two terms. (His second daughter Esther became the first and only President's child to be born in the White House.)

2. They are both "averse" to marriage: a misogamist is a hater of marriage, and an epithalamium is a verse praising marriage. (The more commonly used word misogynist means a woman-hater.)

3. In anyone's head: it is the great arterial circle at the base of the brain, named for Thomas Willis, the English physician. Besides being a great architect, Wren was a distinguished anatomical illustrator.

4. Disobedience—not sex—which Adam having defied God's command, passed on to his heirs. *Paradise Lost* begins:

> Of Man's first disobedience, and the fruit
> Of that forbidden tree, whose mortal taste
> Brought death into the world, and all our woe,
> With loss of Eden.

5. He sent the terse Latin message: *"Nunc fortunatus sum."* (I am in luck now.)

6. The opera *Astianatte*. The Italian composer was not related to Leonardo da Vinci.

7. The Great Fire of London in 1666 started in a bakeshop on Pudding Lane and ended three days later at Pie Corner, destroying 89 churches; 13,200 houses; and encompassing 436 acres. It is commemorated by the Monument topped by a gilt-bronze urn of flames, 202 feet high, and 202 feet from the site of the outbreak of the fire.

8. Music.

9. The satire *Vanity of Vanities* says, "They talk'd of his having a Cardinalls Hat,/ They'd send him as soon an Old Nuns Twat." Browning innocently assumed a twat to be a nun's wimple.

10. The King invited Voltaire to dine with him: *"A souper à Sans Souci,"* his palace of Potsdam, outside Berlin, and Voltaire accepted by replying: *"J'ai grand appetit!"*

Television

■ ■

1. Why is color TV reception in western Europe so much better than it is in the United States?

2. In the television business for what are Clios awarded?

3. Which popular series are spun off from the British shows *Steptoe and Son*, *Till Death Do Us Part*, and *Man About the House*?

4. Whose many faces developed into the characters of Freddy the Freeloader, Clem Kadiddlehopper, and Cauliflower McPugg?

5. The distinguished commentator Alistair Cooke, once the host of the *Omnibus* and *America* series, abhors one adjective generally used to describe him. When he became host of *Masterpiece Theatre* how did the critic John Crosby use this word in an article about Cooke?

6. Name the television personality of whom Kenneth Tynan wrote as follows: "Squatly built, rather less bald than Mussolini, his bulbous face running the gamut from jovial contempt to outright nausea, he looks like an extra in a crowd scene by Hieronymus Bosch."

7. Where did Alfred Pennyworth work as a butler for a strange twosome who went to work in funny clothes?

8. What was the subject of the harrowing three-hour television movie *Friendly Fire*?

9. The title of which long-running TV series, deriving from a highly successful anti-war film starring Donald Sutherland, Elliot Gould and Sally Kellerman, makes extensive use of asterisks? What does the title mean?

10. What is the most popular half-hour feature in PBS television history?

Television

1. Western European television has 625 lines on the screen as opposed to 525 lines on American sets, resulting in a sharper and more pleasantly subtle image.

2. The best television commercials, which must be the ultimate degradation ever suffered by Clio, the distinguished Muse of history. The Greek root from which Clio derives means teller or praiser, which seems apt enough.

3. *Sanford and Son, All in the Family,* and *Three's Company* respectively.

4. Red Skelton, whose biography was written by Arthur Marx.

5. He titled the article "Urbane Renewal."

6. That master maligner, the comedian Don Rickles, "the man you love to hate," who is otherwise known as "the Merchant of Venom" and "Mr. Warmth." Johnny Carson has said of him: "He'll always work—if there's no one around with talent." Orson Welles observed, "underneath that rough exterior there really is a rabid shark," and Frank Sinatra has said, "I like him. I have no taste, that's why I like him."

7. In stately Wayne Manor, the home of millionaire Bruce Wayne, better known as Batman, who with his young ward Robin fought crime in Gotham City where they were known as the Dynamic Duo or the Caped Crusaders.

8. It was the true-life story of a patriotic Iowa farm couple who became transformed into radical activists by the Army's handling of the accidental death of their son during the Vietnam War. The television film won an Emmy Award.

9. *M*A*S*H,* which is an acronym for Mobile Army Surgical Hospital. The program, which stars Alan Alda, Wayne Rogers, McLean Stevenson, and Loretta Swit, has been judged by a national survey of television critics to be the best TV series produced in this country.

10. *Wall Street Week,* hosted by Louis Rukeyser, which has an audience of over 10 million.

Theater

■■

1. Who was called "the Prince of Players," and who was the first actor to be knighted?

2. According to the tale told by Alexander Woollcott, what did the actor say to the streetwalker when they were both sitting down and out on a park bench?

3. What did the rivalry between the English actor William Macready and the American actor Edwin Forrest lead to?

4. Who was Sarah Siddons, and who won the 1980 award given by the Sarah Siddons Society of Chicago?

5. What connection did the American theatrical producer and manager David Belasco have with Puccini?

6. How did Eugene Field once review the performance of Creston Clark's portrayal of the title role in *King Lear*?

7. Name the longest-running play in the world.

8. What did Sarah Brown and Barbara Undershaft have in common?

9. How did Clive Barnes put down *Oh! Calcutta!*?

10. Which half-French satirist elaborated on Jacques' famous speech in this sonnet?

> The world's a stage. The light is in one's eyes.
> The Auditorium is extremely dark.
> The more dishonest get the larger rise;*
> The more offensive make the greater mark.
> The women on it prosper by their shape,
> Some few by their vivacity. The men,
> By tailoring in breeches and in cape.
> The world's a stage—I say it once again.
>
> The scenery is very much the best
> Of what the wretched drama has to show,
> Also the prompter happens to be dumb.
> We drink behind the scenes and pass a jest
> On all our folly; then, before we go
> Loud cries for "Author" . . . but he doesn't come.

*a larger raise.

Theater

1. Edwin Booth, the brother of John Wilkes Booth, who shot Lincoln in Ford's Theater in Washington, D.C. He was the first president of the Players' Club in New York and bequeathed his house on Gramercy Park to the organization. (On the day of his death in June 1893, Ford's Theater, turned into government offices, collapsed.) Sir Henry Irving, manager of London's Lyceum Theatre, was knighted in 1895 and is buried in Westminster Abbey.

2. "Ah, madam, the two oldest professions in the world—ruined by amateurs."

3. The Astor Place Riots, in which their quarreling supporters were quelled by the militia at the cost of 31 lives.

4. A famous English actress, whose portrait as *The Tragic Muse* by Joshua Reynolds hangs in California's Huntington Art Gallery. Claudette Colbert won the 1980 award for her 55 years in the theater. The award consists of a sculpture derived from the Reynolds painting.

5. He wrote the plays *Madame Butterfly* and *The Girl of the Golden West*, which became better known as operas by Puccini.

6. "All through the five acts of that Shakespearean tragedy he played the king as though under the momentary apprehension that someone else was about to play the ace." Being the target of this review seems to be Creston Clark's chief claim to fame.

7. Agatha Christie's *The Mousetrap*, which opened in London in 1952 and is still running. The longest-running Broadway show in this country was *Grease*, followed by *Fiddler on the Roof*.

8. They were both members of similar spiritual organizations. Undershaft was "Major Barbara," of the Salvation Army, in Shaw's play of that name, while Sarah Brown was a member of the Save a Soul Mission in *Guys and Dolls*, written by Jo Swerling and Abe Burrows, with music and lyrics by Frank Loesser.

9. "It is the sort of show that gives pornography a bad name."

10. Hilaire Belloc, in *Sonnets and Verse*.

Three of a Kind

■ ■

1. Hitler's New Order for Germany, which was supposed to last for a thousand years, was called the Third Reich. What were the first two?

2. Who were Flopsie, Mopsie, and Cottontail?

3. Who enumerated her permanent "possessions" as follows:

> Three be the things I shall have till I die:
> Laughter and hope and a sock in the eye.

4. Where do Enderby, Wilkes, and Queen Maude lie together?

5. Identify the missing member of a threesome that also included hydrogen and tritium.

6. Who are the three Rhinemaidens in Wagner's opera *Das Rheingold*?

7. Explain the academic origin of the word trivia.

8. What do the three stripes on the uniforms of British sailors signify?

9. Can you name King Lear's three daughters and their husbands?

10. What did Thomas Jefferson, John Adams, and James Monroe have in common that was reversed in the case of Calvin Coolidge?

Three of a Kind

1. The first was the Holy Roman Empire (962–1806), the second the Hohenzollern Empire that lasted from 1871 to 1918.

2. Peter Rabbit's siblings in Beatrix Potter's *The Tale of Peter Rabbit*.

3. Dorothy Parker, in her poem "Inventory."

4. They are adjoining tracts of land in Antarctica.

5. Deuterium, the second of the three isotopes of hydrogen.

6. Woglinde, Wellgunde, and Flosshilde.

7. It is the plural of the Latin *trivium*, a crossroads or a place where three roads meet. Later it came to mean the threefold way of the "liberal" arts—grammar, logic, and rhetoric—classified in medieval schools as the lower group of such studies. A *quadrivium* was the fourfold way—arithmetic, music, geometry, and astronomy—forming the course for three years of study between the B.A. and M.A. degrees.

8. The three great victories of Nelson—the Nile in 1798; Copenhagen, or, more grandiloquently, "the Baltic" in 1801; and Trafalgar in 1805.

9. Goneril was the wife of the Duke of Albany; Regan the wife of the Duke of Cornwall; and Cordelia, the youngest, the wife of the King of France.

10. They all died on July 4: Jefferson and Adams in 1826, the 50th anniversary of the Declaration of Independence; and Monroe in 1831. Coolidge, on the other hand, was born on July 4, 1872.

Titles

■ ■

Give the quotations from which the following titles are taken, naming also the work and the author.

1. *Vanity Fair*, by William Makepeace Thackeray

2. *The Dogs of War*, by Frederick Forsyth

3. *Tender Is the Night*, by F. Scott Fitzgerald

4. *Clouds of Witness*, by Dorothy L. Sayers

5. *Bell, Book, and Candle*, by John Van Druten

6. *The Sun Also Rises*, by Ernest Hemingway

7. *The Wings of the Dove*, by Henry James

8. *Antic Hay*, by Aldous Huxley

9. *A Rage to Live*, by John O'Hara

10. *From Here to Eternity*, by James Jones

Titles

1. "It beareth the name of Vanity-Fair, because the town where 'tis kept, is lighter than vanity."

    —*The Pilgrim's Progress*, by John Bunyan

2. "Cry, 'Havoc!' and let slip the dogs of war."

    —*Julius Caesar*, by William Shakespeare

3. "Already with thee: tender is the night . . ."

    —"Ode to a Nightingale," by John Keats

4. ". . . we also are compassed about by so great a cloud of witnesses . . ."

    —Hebrews, 12:1

5. "Bell, book, and candle shall not drive me back,
    When gold and silver becks me to come on."

    —*King John*, by William Shakespeare

6. "The sun also ariseth, and the sun goeth down, and hasteth to his place where he arose."

    —Ecclesiastes 1:5

7. "For years fleet away with the wings of the dove."

    —"The First Kiss of Love," by Lord Byron
    (This line itself refers to Psalm 55:6.)

8. "My men, like satyrs grazing on the lawns,
    Shall with their goat feet dance an antic hay."

    —*Edward II*, by Christopher Marlowe

9. "You purchase pain with all that joy can give,
    And die of nothing but a rage to live."

    —*Moral Essays*, Epistle II, by Alexander Pope

10. "Gentlemen-rankers out on the spree
    Damned from here to Eternity . . ."

    —"Gentleman-Rankers" from Rudyard Kipling's *Barrack-Room Ballads*. (Gentleman-rankers were "broken gentlemen"—ruined or disgraced men of social standing—who had lost themselves by enlisting as privates in the Army.)

Transportation

■ ■

1. With the exception of walking, what is the most frequently used form of transportation in the world?

2. What follows this sequence—quarter-less-three, half-twain, quarter-twain? If you had heard these terms, where would you have been?

3. Who are gandy dancers, and how did the term arise? And on what did John Henry's fame rest?

4. Which medical man wrote "The Deacon's Masterpiece," which starts as follows?

> Have you heard of the wonderful one-hoss shay
> That was built in such a logical way
> It ran a hundred years to the day?

5. What was the purpose of the picturesque covered bridges seen in New England and elsewhere throughout the country?

6. Why was the Conestoga wagon responsible for the U.S. custom of driving on the right?

7. What was Mrs. August Belmont's reaction to having a private railroad car?

8. Between which two points does the world's fastest train operate?

9. Which Secretary of the Bank of England created the character of a celebrated motorist who had a coach house filled with "fragments of motor cars, none of them bigger than your hat!"?

10. In big-city traffic motorists become trapped in an intersection when the light turns red. What name is given to this problem, and what term applies when the traffic is frozen in all directions because of totally blocked intersections?

Transportation

1. Elevators and escalators—which, according to estimates made by the Otis Elevator Company, carry about 1.8 billion passengers every day.

2. Mark twain, which means "river running clear and two fathoms beneath the keel," the cry of the leadsman on the old Mississippi River steamboats, and the origin of Samuel L. Clemens' nom de plume.

3. Railroad workers were called gandy dancers because of their rhythmic movements working with tools produced by the long-defunct Gandy Manufacturing Company in Chicago. Legendary among gandy dancers was John Henry who is said to have been born with a hammer in his hand and who could drive steel faster than a machine.

4. Oliver Wendell Holmes, Sr., who Sir William Osler told Dr. Harvey Cushing was "the most successful combination the world has ever seen, of physician and man of letters."

5. Simply to protect the structural members of the bridge from the rigors of winter weather; it was easier to repair the roof than to replace rotten bridge timbers.

6. Because horses are traditionally mounted from the left, Conestoga drivers sat on, or walked beside, the left rear animal. When oncoming traffic was met, the wagons kept to the right so the drivers on foot could see the other vehicles and walk on the drier center of the road. This started the custom of right-side driving.

7. "A private railroad car is not an acquired taste," she said, adding, "One takes to it immediately."

8. Paris and Lyons, a distance of 264 miles. The new T.G.V. (*Très Grande Vitesse*, or very high speed) trains, France's answer to Japan's "Bullet Train," make this trip in under three hours, traveling at a top speed of 165 m.p.h. When the entire line is fully operational in 1983, the time will be reduced to two hours and the speed of the train progressively increased to 190 m.p.h.

9. Kenneth Grahame, who gave us the immortal Mr. Toad of Toad Hall in *The Wind in the Willows*.

10. Spillback and grid lock. In New York City diagonally striped boxes are painted on the roadway at busy intersections to alleviate the problem, together with signs reading: "FIGHT GRID LOCK" and "DON'T BLOCK THE BOX," probably echoing the song "Don't Knock the Rock," popularized by Bill Haley and The Comets.

U.S. Presidency

■ ■

1. Seven of the first twelve Presidents were born in Virginia, which came to be known as "the Mother of Presidents." (Three were elected from other states.) Who was the last President born there?

2. Which Presidents were called "His Rotundity" and "His Accidency"?

3. Who was so gifted that he could simultaneously write Latin with one hand and Greek with the other?

4. Name the only President to renounce the Union.

5. How many Presidents have been bachelors when they entered the White House?

6. Abraham Lincoln once observed, "As for being President, I feel like the man who was tarred and feathered and ridden out of town on a rail." What was his punch line?

7. Why was Rutherford B. Hayes, a one-term President, sworn in twice?

8. Which President is responsible for a well-known advertising slogan still in use today and, with his family, contributed two eponymous terms to the language?

9. Which Presidential candidate first used the phrase "The New Frontier"?

10. Who was fond of saying, "The White House is the finest jail in the world," and, "If you can't stand the heat get out of the kitchen"? He also had a favorite sign on his desk which proclaimed what?

U.S. Presidency

1. Woodrow Wilson, who was born in Staunton, Virginia, in 1856. Although Virginia calls itself "the Mother of Presidents," she has not been pregnant since the 19th century.

2. The short and chubby John Adams, whose Presidency came between Washington and Jefferson, two six-footers; and Rutherford B. Hayes, because a special electoral commission decided by one vote that he had won a majority of one in the electoral college.

3. The ambidextrous classical scholar, James Madison, whose his skill in political science and persuasive logic made him "the master-builder of the Constitution."

4. John Tyler, who was a member of the Confederate Provisional Congress and died in 1862, just before taking his seat in the Confederate House of Representatives.

5. Two—James Buchanan, a lifelong bachelor, and Grover Cleveland, who was married during his first term in office. (Samuel J. Tilden, another bachelor, may well have been elected in 1876, but the Electoral Commission ruled against him.)

6. "When the man was asked how he liked it, he said, 'If it wasn't for the honor of the thing, I'd rather walk.'"

7. Since March 4, 1877, fell on a Sunday, a day on which no President has ever been inaugurated, he was secretly sworn in on the evening of Saturday, the third, and formally inaugurated the following Monday. His election had been so bitterly contested that there were fears that Southern irreconcilables might attempt a coup when there was no President to take action.

8. Theodore Roosevelt, who said, "Good to the last drop," after having coffee at the Maxwell House in Nashville, Tennessee. The teddy bear is named after him as he was once depicted as sparing a cub's life on a hunting trip; and alice blue was a shade made popular by his daughter, later Alice Roosevelt Longworth.

9. Alfred M. Landon, when he ran against Franklin D. Roosevelt in 1936, carrying only two states, Maine and Vermont. John F. Kennedy later copied the phrase.

10. Harry S Truman. (There is no period after the S because Truman had no middle name.) The sign on his desk read, "The buck stops here."

Variety Show

■ ■

    1. Who reported what surface was "fine and powdery"?

    2. Where are Pussy Galore and the Black Pussy Café to be found?

    3. Which celebrated football coach is remembered for saying, "Show me a good and gracious loser, and I'll show you a failure."?

    4. Why did the American writer John Jay Chapman observe that it would be more useful for a Martian to attend the worst Italian opera than to read Emerson?

    5. What does the inspiration for Sherlock Holmes have in common with three literary sisters? And what tenuous connection does Horatio, Viscount Nelson have with the latter?

    6. Explain the acronyms WASP, SPAR, and BAM as used during World War II.

    7. Samuel Guthrie made his name with an invention and a discovery which seem singularly well adapted to one another. What are they?

    8. Why does the first violin enter separately from the rest of the orchestra?

    9. How was Hans van Meegeren finally unmasked as the greatest art forger of all time?

    10. According to Professor Thomas Postlewait, "This is the Age of Jargon and to fight against it is about as wise as the Charge of the Light Brigade." Let us, however, take a stand. Put the following, which are just a few examples of "bafflegab" and "doublespeak," into plain, simple English: a) Retrograde maneuver, b) Text-processing analysis, c) Social-control engineer, d) The piscatorial biota exhibited a 100 per cent mortality response.

Variety Show

1. Neil Armstrong, on the occasion of man's first walk on the moon in 1969.

2. Pussy Galore was the leader of an all-girl flying circus in Ian Fleming's *Goldfinger*, and the Black Pussy Café was the favorite hangout of Egbert Sousé, as played by W. C. Fields in the film *The Bank Dick*.

3. Knute Rockne, who was head football coach at Notre Dame from 1913 until he was killed in an airplane crash in 1931.

4. Because it would at least find out that there were two sexes.

5. The name Bell. Joseph Bell was a Scottish surgeon whose powers of deduction impressed a medical student named A. Conan Doyle, while Charlotte, Emily, and Anne Brontë wrote a volume of verse under the pseudonyms of Currer, Ellis, and Acton Bell. Lord Nelson was given the title Duke of Brontë by the King of Naples and Sicily. The Brontë sisters' family name had originally been the very Irish Prunty, but it was changed by their socially aspiring father to that of Nelson's title.

6. A WASP was a member of a civilian group known as Women's Auxiliary Service Pilots, and a SPAR was a female reserve in the U.S. Coast Guard, the name being an acronym of S(emper) Par(atus), the Coast Guard's motto. BAM simply stands for Broad-Assed Marine.

7. He successively invented the percussion cap, thus making obsolete the flintlock musket and enormously increasing the efficiency of firearms, and then discovered chloroform which anaesthetized the victims of such efficiency.

8. In the 18th century he functioned as the conductor and retains some of the conductor's privileges.

9. He was forced to unmask himself to avoid prosecution by the postwar authorities as a collaborator for selling to the Nazis what were actually his own forgeries but which were believed to have been national treasures. He was prosecuted instead for selling forgeries to non-Nazis and died in jail.

10. a) Retreat, b) Reading, c) Bouncer, d) All the fish died.

"War Is Hell"
■■

1. Which historic piece of embroidery, measuring 231 feet in length, chronicles whose exploits?

2. Where was the Battle of Bunker Hill fought, and which side was the victor?

3. In what military circumstance did Napoleon Bonaparte say, "From the sublime to the ridiculous is but a step"?

4. A certain battle of the War of Independence was significant in that it brought France in on the American side. After the battle the defeated commander unsuccessfully sought a court-martial. The victorious general suffered a disgraceful defeat in a later battle. Name the battles and the commanders.

5. Who said, "War is much too serious to be left to the military"?

6. What is the feminine origin of the word *gun*?

7. How did the Duke of Wellington respond at the Battle of Waterloo to an eager young artillery officer's request to shell Napoleon and his staff, who were riding within range?

8. Which declaration of war against the United States has the United States never acknowledged, yet cost the country more lives than any other war?

9. How did the famous U.S. Rainbow Division, which was the first combat division to arrive in France in June 1917, get its name?

10. During which war was there an official communiqué issued which read, "The advance was continued all day without any ground being lost."?

"War Is Hell"

1. The Bayeux tapestry, now preserved at the Bayeux Museum in France, tells the story of King Harold and William the Conqueror from 1063 to 1066. During World War II Bayeux was the first city in France to be liberated by the Allies.

2. On Breed's Hill, where the battle monument now stands, somewhat to the southeast of Bunker Hill. Breed's Hill, occupied by American troops against orders, threatened the British fleet in Boston Harbor; American accounts have always placed the battle on harmless Bunker Hill. The British won but lost half their troops, more than double the American casualties.

3. The French retreat from Moscow. As Field Marshal Lord Montgomery once noted, "Rule One of the book of war is: 'Don't march on Moscow.'"

4. After the Battle of Saratoga in 1777, General Sir John ("Gentleman Johnny") Burgoyne sought a court-martial to prove that his superiors were responsible. The American general, Horatio Gates, was routed by the British at the Battle of Camden in 1780.

5. The French statesman Talleyrand, as quoted by the French Premier Aristide Briand to his British counterpart David Lloyd George during the First World War.

6. It probably comes from Gunne, a pet form of the Old Norse woman's name Gunnhild, itself a modification of *gunnhildr*, war-strife. This nickname seemed very apt for siege engines, and thence for other weapons.

7. "Certainly not! It is no business of commanding officers to fire upon one another."

8. The Civil War, where the Confederate States' declaration of war went unacknowledged because the United States considered the Confederacy merely an unlawful combination of U.S. citizens.

9. The 42nd Division of the U.S. Army included National Guard troops from a majority of the states. Colonel Douglas MacArthur, its first chief of staff and future acting commander, suggested the name because the outfit spanned the Union "like a rainbow."

10. This was an announcement of the Republican government during the Spanish Civil War.

"Water, Water, Every Where"

■ ■

1. On which river would you most likely be if you encountered two fellaheen in a felucca?

2. Who advised us to "Drink deep, or taste not the Pierian spring"?

3. Explain the uniqueness of the Lake of Menteith in Scotland?

4. What did one of Edgar Allen Poe's heroes have in common with Captain Nemo of Jules Verne's *20,000 Leagues Under the Sea*?

5. On whose back did the "Old Man of the Sea" ride?

6. Name four rivers of Switzerland that flow to four different seas.

7. What went "five miles meandering with a mazy motion"?

8. Which graduate in surgery wrote these lines:

The same that oft-times hath
Charm'd magic casements, opening on the foam
Of perilous seas, in faery lands forlorn.

9. What flows into the Moscow Sea?

10. "Leander, Mr. Ekenhead, and I" did what, and who am "I"?

"Water, Water, Every Where"

1. probably on the Nile. A fellah is an Arab peasant, while a felucca is a narrow boat propelled by lateen sails or oars or both.

2. Alexander Pope, in *An Essay on Criticism*. Pieria was another name for the southern face of Mount Parnassus where the Muses were believed to dwell; its waters were reputed to bestow inspiration upon those who drank of them.

3. It is the only "lake" in Scotland; all the others are called lochs.

4. Both got caught in and escaped from the Maelstrom, a whirlpool of extraordinary size off the coast of Norway.

5. That of Sindbad the Sailor, in the *Thousand and One Nights' Entertainments*.

6. The Rhine, through Lake Constance to the North Sea; the Inn, down the Engadine Valley in eastern Switzerland to the Danube and thence to the Black Sea; the Ticino, through Lake Maggiore on the Italian border to the Po and thence to the Adriatic; the Rhône through Lake Geneva (Lac Léman) to the Mediterranean.

7. In "Kubla Khan," by Samuel Taylor Coleridge:

> . . . Alph, the sacred river, ran
> Through caverns measureless to man
> Down to a sunless sea.

8. John Keats in "Ode to a Nightingale."

9. Nothing: it lies on the far side of the moon.

10. They all swam the Hellespont, now called the Dardanelles, between European and Asiatic Turkey, the "I" being Byron. Leander made the crossing nightly to visit his love, a lady named Hero, until he drowned in a storm, whereupon Hero drowned herself too. Byron and Lieutenant Ekenhead, who did it on a dare, emulated Leander, and Byron reported this matter in *Don Juan*:

> He could, perhaps, have pass'd the Hellespont,
> As once (a feat on which ourselves we prided)
> Leander, Mr. Ekenhead, and I did.

Weather

■ ■

1. Where might you encounter a simoom and a harmattan, and what is a willawaw?

2. Alexander Pope, imitating Horace, takes the dog days, those sultry weeks between mid-July and September, hard:

> Shut, shut the door, good John: fatigu'd I said
> Tie up the knocker; say I'm sick, I'm dead.
> The Dog-star rages!

Why should a star, or a dog, have these associations?

3. James Otis, an early leader of the American Revolution, came to the end that he had always prophesied for himself. What was it?

4. What meteorological condition helped Elijah depart from earth?

5. Name the author of these lines:

> The fog comes
> on little cat feet.
> It sits looking
> over the harbor and city
> on silent haunches
> and then moves on.

6. "May the wind always be at your back" is a traditional farewell among which people?

7. In the play, and later the film, *Inherit the Wind,* what principle was involved, and who were the two formidable antagonists?

8. In which production was there a haunting song titled "They Call the Wind Maria"?

9. Who, in a forecasting mood, wrote: "Tonight the crimson children are playing in the west and tomorrow it will be cloudy"?

10. During the height of the Terror in the French Revolution, Danton and Robespierre turned in early one snowy night, having decided to take a walk through Paris the next morning, but by then the snow had melted. What did Robespierre say to Danton?

Weather

1. In North Africa. Simooms and harmattans are the names of strong, hot, sand-laden winds that blow off the Sahara. A williwaw is a violent gust of cold air blowing seaward from a mountainous coast, or any sudden squall or gust of wind. (*Williwaw* is the title of Gore Vidal's first [and perhaps best] novel.)

2. The Romans believed that dog-star Sirius (the most visible star in the Greater Dog constellation), which rises with the sun from early July to mid-August, added its heat to that of the sun and therefore called the period *dies caniculares*, the small-dog, that is dogstar, days.

3. He was struck by lightning.

4. He left in a chariot of fire enveloped in a whirlwind.

5. Carl Sandburg, American poet and biographer, in "Fog" from *Chicago Poems*.

6. The Irish. The rest of an Irish farewell is "May the road rise with you, may God hold you in the hollow of His hand, and may you be in heaven a half an hour before the devil knows you are dead."

7. In 1925 William Jennings Bryan was principal attorney for the prosecution of a high school biology teacher, John Scopes, in a trial arranged to test the Tennessee statute forbidding any teaching of doctrines contradicting the Biblical account of the Creation. Even though his counsel, Clarence Darrow, had exposed Bryan's arguments to ridicule, Scopes, who had expounded the Darwinian theory of evolution, was convicted, but the fine was set aside on a technicality. Bryan died a few days later. (In the film *Inherit the Wind*, the parts of Bryan and Darrow are superbly portrayed by Frederic March and Spencer Tracy respectively.)

8. *Paint Your Wagon*, by Alan Jay Lerner and Frederick Loewe.

9. Emily Dickinson, in a letter to a friend.

10. "*Mais où sont les neiges, Danton?*" (But where are the snows, Danton?) This is a play on François Villon's famous line "*Mais où sont les neiges d'antan?*" (But where are the snows of yesteryear?)

Weights and Measures

■ ■

1. How did an English king establish the length of a yard?

2. What is the nautical significance of 252 English gallons?

3. Why, in measuring nuclear cross sections, is the unit of area equal to 10^{-24} of a square centimeter called a barn?

4. From which city is the "troy" in troy ounce derived?

5. A mile is theoretically a thousand paces of a Roman legionary, or eight furlongs; but it also theoretically is 320 what?

6. Why is an "r.c.h." the ultimate measure of fineness among practical mechanics?

7. An ordinary paper clip is handy for measuring what units of length?

8. Who said, in which work, "I have measured out my life with coffee spoons"?

9. A kilogram is a unit of weight, not distance; but how is it related to the distance from the North Pole to the equator?

10. What do Brunei, Burma, Liberia, South Yemen, and the United States have in common?

Weights and Measures

1. Henry I is reputed to have done this by extending his arm and measuring from his nose to his thumb.

2. The measure of 252 old English gallons was originally used for wine, shipped in casks called tuns, from southwest France in the Middle Ages when it was preferred to water. From this the various units of weight called tons derive.

3. Because, by the standards of nuclear physics, it is "as big as a barn."

4. The city of Troyes in France, about 100 miles southeast of Paris. It was an important trading center in the Middle Ages.

5. Anglo-Saxon ox-goads, or prodders, reckoned as being 16½ feet long.

6. It stands for "red cunt hair," said to have been the standard in bombsight calibration during World War II.

7. The diameter of a paper-clip wire measures one millimeter, while its broadest width is one centimeter.

8. T. S. Eliot, in "The Love Song of J. Alfred Prufrock."

9. A kilogram was originally defined as the weight of a one-decimeter cube of water; and a decimeter is one hundred-millionth of the distance, according to the best calculation at that time, between the North Pole and the equator.

10. They are the only countries that have not committed themselves to direct use of the metric system.

Women
■■

1. How did the wife of a Florentine merchant whose name may be rendered Frank Jolly become famous?

2. Because of her forward-area quartermaster activity in the American War of Independence, what nickname was bestowed on Mary Ludwig Hays?

3. In Charles Dickens' *Oliver Twist*, who was the only female member of Fagin's gang of thieves?

4. James Hilton wrote the novel *Rage in Heaven*. Where did he get the title?

5. Which lady began her memoirs with a sentence which unambiguously declares her professional experiences and why they may interest us: "I shall not say why and how I became, at the age of fifteen, the mistress of the Earl of Craven."?

6. How did the following similarly occupied ladies meet a common end: Mary Ann Nicholls, Annie Chapman, Elizabeth Stride, Catherine Eddowes, and Mary Jane Kelly?

7. What corklike epithet was earned by an heiress from Denver, Colorado?

8. In which famous play is the opinion given that "certain women should be struck regularly, like gongs"?

9. What was the remarkable accomplishment of Agnes Gonxha Bojaxhin?

10. Who observed: "I am perfectly willing to concede the superiority of women, if only to discourage them from pretending to be our equals"?

Women

1. By sitting for her portrait by Leonardo da Vinci in about 1504. This painting, known as the *Mona Lisa* or *La Gioconda*—her husband's name was Francesco Giocondo—hangs in the Louvre in Paris. Considered the most valuable picture in the world, it was insured for $100 million when it was last exhibited in the United States. Of the *Mona Lisa*, the English essayist and critic Walter Pater wrote, "Hers is the head upon which 'all the ends of the world are come,' and the eyelids are a little weary."

2. Molly Pitcher (Mary Ludwig Hays), so nicknamed because she carried water for her husband and other soldiers at the Battle of Monmouth in 1778. As Laura E. Richards wrote:

> Sweet honor's roll is aye the richer
> For the bright name of Molly Pitcher.

3. Nancy, the companion of Bill Sikes, who clubbed her to death for befriending Oliver.

4. From the following lines in William Congreve's one tragedy, *The Mourning Bride*:

> Heaven has no rage, like love to hatred turn'd,
> Nor hell a fury, like a woman scorned.

5. Harriette Wilson. The efforts of her publisher Stockdale to blackmail one of her later clients, the great Duke of Wellington, into paying to suppress the relevant section of Miss Wilson's memoirs is said to have elicited Wellington's yet more trenchant line: "Publish and be damned."

6. They were all victims of Jack the Ripper, in the most gruesome and bizarre series of crimes in British history: all seem to have been prostitutes, working out of Whitechapel, one of the most noisome sections of Victorian London.

7. "The Unsinkable Molly Brown," because she survived the sinking of the R.M.S. *Titanic* in 1912 and was an inspiration to all with her in the lifeboat.

8. Noël Coward's *Private Lives*.

9. She is otherwise known as Mother Theresa, "the saint of the gutters," who won the Nobel Peace Prize in 1979 for her work with the poor in Calcutta, India.

10. Sacha Guitry, French actor and dramatist.

World Literature

■ ■

1. How did a famous cathedral-dweller get his name, and who was the gypsy he befriended?

2. In which book did an author with a uninominal pseudonym write the following: "A novel is a mirror that strolls along the highway. Now it reflects the blue of the skies, now the mud puddles underneath"?

3. Which lepidopterist of professional standing spent his last days in Montreux, Switzerland, and gained a measure of notoriety by writing about a little "sorrower"?

4. How did Mme. de Sévigné, in a single prediction, show her lack of grip on both literature and potables?

5. Whose pseudonym means "Peace be upon you!"?

6. Who wrote in a cork-lined room and is reported to have used a miniature guillotine to behead rats?

7. Who is the odd man out: John Galsworthy, André Gide, Winston S. Churchill, Leo Tolstoy, Thomas Mann, Salvatore Quasimodo?

8. What happened to Marguerite Gautier in translation, and which opera was based on her story?

9. What did Marguerite Yourcenar, author of *Memoirs of Hadrian* and *Coup de Grâce*, achieve that Madame de Staël, George Sand, or Colette did not?

10. In her essay, "The Little Hours," what reason did Dorothy Parker give for not reading the French poet Paul Verlaine?

World Literature

1. In Victor Hugo's *Notre-Dame de Paris* the grotesque hunchback bell ringer Quasimodo is named from the opening words of the Introit—one of the changeable parts of the Mass—for Low Sunday: "*Quasi modo geniti infantes . . .*" (After the fashion of newborn babes . . .)—because he was found abandoned outside Notre Dame on that Sunday, which follows Easter. He conceals Esmeralda, unjustly accused of murder, in the cathedral's belfry.

2. Stendhal, the pseudonym of the French writer Henri Beyle, in *Le Rouge et le Noir* (The Red and the Black).

3. Vladimir Nabokov, the Russian-American novelist, whose most famous work was *Lolita* (the diminutive of Dolores—sorrows), about a middle-aged European intellectual's infatuation with a twelve-year-old American "nymphet"—a word Nabokov did not invent, but revived from rather elevated classic poetry. Nabokov claimed that the book was an account of his love affair with the English language.

4. She said, "Racine will go out of style, like coffee."

5. Sholom Aleichem (Shalom or Shlomo Rabinowitz), a Russian-born author best known for his humorous tales of life among the poverty-ridden and oppressed Russian Jews of the late 19th and early 20th centuries. His *Tevye's Daughters* formed the basis for *Fiddler on the Roof*.

6. Marcel Proust, the author of one of the century's greatest novels, *A la recherche du temps perdu* (Remembrance of Things Past).

7. Leo Tolstoy. All the others received the Nobel Prize for Literature.

8. The name of Marguerite Gautier, the courtesan heroine of *La Dame aux camélias* by Alexandre Dumas *fils*, was changed in translation to Camille, as was the book's title. The opera *La Traviata* by Verdi was based on the Dumas novel and play.

9. In 1981 she became the first woman to take her seat with the Immortals, the forty self-selecting members of the *Académie Français*, which was made the official arbiter of the French language by Louis XIII's minister Richelieu in the 1630s. Curiously enough, Marguerite Yourcenar became a U.S. citizen in 1945 and lives on an island off the Maine coast.

10. ". . . he was always chasing Rimbauds."

World War II

■ ■

1. On which occasion was *Tora Tora Tora* the go-ahead signal, and what does *tora* mean?

2. Which general took more territory with less loss of life than any military commander since Darius the Great, and what distinction did he share with his father?

3. Name the only officer simultaneously to serve temporarily as Vice-Admiral, Air Marshal, and Lieutenant-General. Why was he given these ranks?

4. What was the first great naval engagement where the opposing surface fleets never sighted each other, the action falling wholly to naval aircraft, antiaircraft guns, and land-based bombers?

5. Churchill complained of which operation: "I had hoped that we were hurling a wildcat on the shore, but all we had got was a stranded whale"?

6. Describe the strange military role of Meyrick E. Clifton James, H. M. Pay Corps.

7. In reply to whose message did Churchill send these lines from Arthur Hugh Clough's poem, "Say Not the Struggle Naught Availeth"?

> For while the tired waves, vainly breaking,
>   Seem here no painful inch to gain,
> Far back through creeks and inlets making
>   Comes silent, flooding in, the main.
>
> And not by eastern windows only,
>   When daylight comes, comes in the light,
> In front the sun climbs slow, how slowly,
>   But westward, look, the land is bright.

8. How did General Dwight D. Eisenhower encapsulate his service under General Douglas MacArthur?

9. Which major operations had the following code names: a) Dynamo, b) Torch, c) Dragoon, d) Market Garden, e) Sea Lion?

10. Which flamboyant commander exhorted his troops in the following fashion: "No bastard ever won a war by dying for his country. He won it by making the other poor dumb bastard die for his country . . . When you put your hand into a pile of goo that was your best friend's face, you'll know what to do . . . As for the Nazi, we're going to go through him like crap through a goose"?

World War II

1. The Japanese attack on Pearl Harbor. (*Tora* means Tiger.)

2. General of the Army Douglas MacArthur, whose "heroic conduct" during the Japanese invasion of the Philippines gained him the nation's highest decoration, the Medal of Honor, which his father, the future General Arthur MacArthur, had won by his charge up Missionary Ridge in 1863. (Although the Medal of Honor is presented "in the name of the Congress of the United States," it is incorrect to refer to it as the Congressional Medal of Honor.)

3. Lord Louis Mountbatten, later 1st Earl Mountbatten of Burma, when he was Chief of Combined Operations, so that he could easily deal with senior officers in other services.

4. The Battle of the Coral Sea in May 1942. Although the Japanese won a tactical victory, their thrust at Port Moresby, New Guinea—the jumping-off place for Australia—failed, ending the threat of invasion. In August 1942, MacArthur landed successfully on New Guinea.

5. The Anzio landing in January 1944, where the Allied troops, after an unopposed landing, failed to secure the high ground and were pinned down on the beachhead for several months by the Germans under Field Marshal Kesselring.

6. As the "double" for Field Marshal Montgomery before D-Day, he traveled throughout the Middle East to confuse German intelligence. After the war he played himself in the film *I Was Monty's Double*, starring John Mills and Cecil Parker.

7. Roosevelt's enclosing a verse from Longfellow's poem "The Building of the Ship," which included the words ". . . sail on, O Ship of State!"

8. "I studied dramatics under him for five years in Washington and four years in the Philippines."

9. a) Naval evacuation in 1940 of the British Expeditionary Force with French and Belgian troops, b) Anglo-American invasion of French North Africa in 1942, c) Allied landings in Southern France in 1944, d) the drive to relieve the airborne troops at Arnhem, e) the never-executed German invasion of Britain in 1940.

10. General George S. Patton, Jr., commander of the Third Army in 1944.

X-Rated

■ ■

1. What is the meaning of the name Xerxes?

2. What was the monogram XP used to represent?

3. Why traditionally is St. Andrew, patron saint of Scotland, associated with an X-shaped cross?

4. Which saint was one of the founders of the Society of Jesus and was known as the Apostle to the Indies?

5. The Exchequer in Britain is the governmental department charged with the collection and management of national revenue. With which game is the word associated?

6. What is the exosphere?

7. Can you explain the connection between Orson Welles and Kubla Khan?

8. What suburb of which major city has been famous for its canals lined with poplars and flowering islands?

9. Which artist painted a famous portrait titled *Madame X*, and who was she?

10. Captain Charles E. Yeager became what in the Bell X-1 in 1947?

X-Rated

1. It is the Greek form of an Old Persian word meaning literally "ruler of sprayers," a rather direct way of saying men, meaning sprayers of semen.

2. Christ or Christianity. The monogram is composed of *chi* and *rho,* the first two letters of the Greek word for Christ.

3. When the Apostle Andrew, the brother of Peter, was sentenced to be crucified, he said it would be too great an honor to be nailed to the same-shaped cross as Christ.

4. The Basque Jesuit missionary, Saint Francis Xavier, who died at sea and is buried at Goa on the western coast of India. Formerly a Portuguese colony, Goa was occupied by India in 1961: the Portuguese acknowledged this in 1974.

5. Chess. The word comes from the Old French *eschequier,* chessboard, a counting table covered with a checkered cloth as used in chess.

6. The exosphere is the outermost portion of the atmosphere, estimated to begin 300 to 600 miles above the earth.

7. In the film *Citizen Kane,* Charles Foster Kane, played by Orson Welles, built a fabulous house named Xanadu, which resembled William Randolph Hearst's "ranch" at San Simeon, California. The name is taken from Samuel Taylor Coleridge's poem "Kubla Khan" which starts:

> In Xanadu did Kubla Khan
> A stately pleasure-dome decree . . .

8. Xochimilco, an Indian name meaning "plantation of flowers," which lies just outside Mexico City and is drying up along with its metropolis.

9. John Singer Sargent. Madame X was Mme. Pierre Gautreau, who disliked the painting because of its impressionist overtones. It now hangs in the American Wing of the Metropolitan Museum of Art in New York.

10. He became the first man to exceed the speed of sound.

Lasts

■ ■

1. What is the last word of the New Testament?
2. Do you know the logical last request of the Phoenix?
3. Who followed Priam as King of Troy?
4. Name the titular characters of *The Last of the Mohicans* by James Fenimore Cooper.
5. Who was the only survivor of the Battle of the Little Bighorn in 1876, otherwise known as Custer's Last Stand?
6. Whose collaboration produced which famous Gallic last?
7. In which film, based on a novel by Dashiell Hammett and written and directed by John Huston, is this the last line: "The, er, stuff that dreams are made of"?
8. What was the last time the World Series was played in one city? Where was it and who won?
9. *"Shantih, shantih, shantih"* are the last words of which famous work, and what do they mean?
10. How did John Bunyan end *The Pilgrim's Progress?*

Lasts

1. Amen, which comes from the Hebrew word meaning "certainly" or "verily." When the early Greek and Latin scholars translated the New Testament, they simply lifted the Hebrew term to express conviction.

2. "It is my wish to be cremated."

3. No one. Priam was the last King of Troy; the Greeks razed the city.

4. Chingachgook and his son Uncas, last surviving chiefs of the Mohican (more accurately, Mohegan) Indians. Uncas bears the name of a real chieftain who had sided with the English in the Pequot War a hundred years before the time of Cooper's novel.

5. According to tradition, it was the horse Comanche. For many years after the battle he appeared in the Seventh Cavalry parades, saddled but riderless.

6. Jerome Kern and Oscar Hammerstein II, who wrote "The Last Time I Saw Paris."

7. *The Maltese Falcon*, a movie about a black enameled statuette supposedly made of gold but actually made of lead, to which Humphrey Bogart was referring.

8. The famous "Subway Series" of 1956 when the New York Yankees edged out the Brooklyn Dodgers, four games to three.

9. T. S. Eliot's *The Waste Land*. According to the author, they are the idiomatic Sanskrit equivalent of "the peace that passeth all understanding." According to some critics, the poem is "the piece that passeth all understanding."

10. ". . . meantime I bid the reader adieu."